Teaching with the Common Core Standards for English Language Arts, Grades 3–5

Also available

Teaching with the Common Core Standards
for English Language Arts, PreK–2
*Edited by Lesley Mandel Morrow,
Timothy Shanahan, and Karen K. Wixson*

Teaching with the
Common Core Standards
for English Language Arts, Grades 3–5

EDITED BY

**Lesley Mandel Morrow
Karen K. Wixson
Timothy Shanahan**

Foreword by Susan B. Neuman

THE GUILFORD PRESS
New York   London

© 2013 The Guilford Press
A Division of Guilford Publications, Inc.
72 Spring Street, New York, NY 10012
www.guilford.com

Printed in the United States of America

This book is printed on acid-free paper.

Last digit is print number: 9 8 7 6 5 4 3 2

Library of Congress Cataloging-in-Publication Data

Teaching with the common core standards for English language arts, grades 3–5 / edited
   by Lesley Mandel Morrow, Karen K. Wixson, Timothy Shanahan.
       p. cm.
     Includes bibliographical references and index.
     ISBN 978-1-4625-0791-7 (pbk.)—ISBN 978-1-4625-0793-1 (hardcover)
     1. Language arts (Elementary)—United States. 2. Education, Elementary—Curricula—
Standards—United States—States. I. Morrow, Lesley Mandel. II. Wixson, Karen K. III.
Shanahan, Timothy.
LB1576.T425 2013
372.6—dc23
                                                                    2012020687

About the Editors

Lesley Mandel Morrow, PhD, holds the rank of Professor II at the Graduate School of Education at Rutgers, The State University of New Jersey. Her research deals with early literacy development and the organization and management of language arts programs. Dr. Morrow has published more than 300 journal articles, chapters, and books. Her work has been recognized with awards including the Outstanding Teacher Educator of Reading Award and the William S. Gray Citation of Merit from the International Reading Association (IRA), and the Oscar S. Causey Award from the Literacy Research Association. Dr. Morrow is past president of the IRA and is a member of the Reading Hall of Fame.

Karen K. Wixson, PhD, is Dean of the School of Education at the University of North Carolina at Greensboro. She has published widely in the areas of literacy curriculum, instruction, and assessment. Dr. Wixson co-directed the federally funded Michigan English Language Arts Framework standards project, and served as Co-Director and Principal Investigator of the U.S. Department of Education's Center for the Improvement of Early Reading Achievement. She also served as a member of the extended work team for the Common Core English Language Arts standards. Dr. Wixson is a former board member of the National Reading Conference and the IRA.

Timothy Shanahan, PhD, is Professor of Urban Education at the University of Illinois at Chicago, where he is Director of the Center for Literacy and Chair of the Department of Curriculum and Instruction. He served on one of the expert panels that helped develop the Common Core State Standards. Dr. Shanahan's research emphasizes reading–writing relationships, reading assessment, and improving reading achievement. In 2006, he was appointed to serve on the Advisory Board of the National Institute for Literacy. Dr. Shanahan is past president of the IRA and is a member of the Reading Hall of Fame.

Contributors

Peter Afflerbach, PhD, Department of Curriculum and Instruction, University of Maryland, College Park, College Park, Maryland

James F. Baumann, PhD, Department of Learning, Teaching, and Curriculum, University of Missouri–Columbia, Columbia, Missouri

Camille L. Z. Blachowicz, PhD, Department of Reading and Language, National College of Education, National Louis University, Chicago, Illinois

Erica C. Boling, PhD, Graduate School of Education, Rutgers, The State University of New Jersey, New Brunswick, New Jersey

Jennifer Renner Del Nero, MA, Graduate School of Education, Rutgers, The State University of New Jersey, New Brunswick, New Jersey

Douglas Fisher, PhD, Department of Educational Leadership, San Diego State University, and Health Sciences High and Middle College, San Diego, California

Nancy Frey, PhD, School of Teacher Education, San Diego State University, and Health Sciences High and Middle College, San Diego, California

Linda B. Gambrell, PhD, Eugene T. Moore School of Education, Clemson University, Clemson, South Carolina

Steve Graham, EdD, Mary Lou Fulton Teachers College, Arizona State University, Tempe, Arizona

Elfrieda H. Hiebert, PhD, TextProject and University of California, Santa Cruz, Santa Cruz, California

Melanie Kuhn, PhD, Department of Curriculum and Teaching, Boston University, Boston, Massachusetts

Diane Lapp, EdD, School of Teacher Education, San Diego State University, and Health Sciences High and Middle College, San Diego, California

Jacquelynn A. Malloy, PhD, College of Education, Anderson University, Anderson, South Carolina

Lesley Mandel Morrow, PhD, Graduate School of Education, Rutgers, The State University of New Jersey, New Brunswick, New Jersey

James Nageldinger, MEd, School of Teaching, Learning, and Curriculum Studies, Kent State University, Kent, Ohio

Susan B. Neuman, EdD, Department of Educational Studies, University of Michigan, Ann Arbor, Michigan

Donna Ogle, EdD, Department of Reading and Language, National College of Education, National Louis University, Chicago, Illinois

P. David Pearson, PhD, Graduate School of Education, University of California, Berkeley, Berkeley, California

Timothy Rasinski, PhD, School of Teaching, Leadership, and Curriculum Studies, Kent State University, Kent, Ohio

Timothy Shanahan, PhD, Department of Curriculum and Instruction, University of Illinois at Chicago, Chicago, Illinois

Christina Spiezio, MEd, Graduate School of Education, Rutgers, The State University of New Jersey, New Brunswick, New Jersey

Karen K. Wixson, PhD, School of Education, University of North Carolina at Greensboro, Greensboro, North Carolina

Foreword

Susan B. Neuman

This is an exciting time for those of us in the field of reading and language arts education. Although state standards have been with us for many years, the Common Core State Standards (CCSS) in English language arts represent a landmark in the history of educational reform, a shared vision of what children should know and be able to do. The goal of the CCSS is to provide a clear and consistent framework to ensure that all students, regardless of where they may live, receive a top-notch, high-quality education, helping to prepare them for college and the workforce.

Yet as previous reforms have taught us, even the best of frameworks are dependent on the quality of their implementation. Great teaching can turn a meager curriculum into a gold mine of opportunities for students to learn; similarly, poor teaching of even the best scientifically based materials won't yield their desired results. It is the implementation of the vision that is at the heart of this reform movement. What goes on behind classroom doors will mark whether or not these standards are, at best, a great success or, at worst, one more failed initiative.

Unfortunately, we have yet to identify a science of implementation. Recent evidence, however, suggests a number of important elements. First, teachers will need a great deal of knowledge. School districts will be seriously remiss if they approach these standards as if they were a scripted curriculum. In contrast to other reforms, the CCSS require deep knowledge about text and its complexities and the scaffolds that are necessary for children to be successful readers. The CCSS are based on a theoretical approach that will be new to many teachers, both novice and midcareer. Second, we now have an accumulated evidence base that indicates that knowledge alone is insufficient. Teachers and administrators may know a great deal about instruction, but putting these reforms into practice will require a deep understanding of how to teach—the pedagogical content knowledge that enables teachers to convey these understandings to students. Third, teachers will need a strong foundation in understanding children's development and the cumulative progress of mastery, refined and applied at increasingly high levels for various purposes and in various contexts.

No doubt, it will be a challenge—for teachers and administrators who are directly responsible to our children and for evaluators and researchers who may be responsible for examining student progress. These standards are akin to "tough love" in many ways, demanding that those of us in the reading and language arts community up the ante in terms of requiring higher-level learning and higher-order thinking. They represent a pretty strong dose of knowledge and content for children, starting from the very beginning of their schooling all the way through the high school years.

From my point of view, it's about time. Reforms in education have reflected just about everything you could think of except what matters most: what we teach. When children are fed a heavy diet of nonsense—low-level curricula that reflect a little of this and a little of that—they fail to thrive. When we teach children in a way that engages their minds, involving in-depth learning that allows them to master content, we support not only greater learning but greater motivation to learn more. Furthermore, we give them the gift of information capital, the ability to traverse the knowledge economy, enabling them to direct their own future rather than have their future "directed" for them by limited job prospects.

Consequently, as a scholarly community, we should recognize that these standards represent an unparalleled opportunity for learning—for both teachers and students. Although not all will be comfortable with some of the nuts and bolts of the framework, these standards embrace the notion of equity more than any other single reform in recent decades. Essentially, they state that all students in all grades in all areas of our country must receive a rigorous, content-rich literacy program in order to be successful in the 21st century. It is a laudable goal and one worthy of our resources and strong commitment.

This book is designed to help make the CCSS a reality in classrooms. It brings together all the elements that teachers need to know: implementation strategies for use in the classroom, an understanding of child development, and how these standards may progress throughout the grades. Recognizing that early literacy begins before kindergarten, it sets out to map out the qualities of a good curriculum and its implementation in preschool. It then carefully details throughout the chapters how these standards are expressed with increasing complexity from grade to grade, providing an ongoing and cumulative progression of skills. Specialists in their fields, the contributors provide practical guidelines for implementing these standards in classrooms, along with vignettes that bring them vividly to life. Chapters provide classroom activities and questions to consider as a professional community.

As scholars, practitioners, and policymakers, we cannot afford to fail in our implementation of more rigorous standards for our students. In my experience, students are far more capable than we have traditionally given them credit for. They want to learn. They want to become expert in a domain of their interests. They want to dig deeper in content areas and read closely in order to develop knowledge and expertise. To the extent that this reform movement promotes this kind of in-depth learning, thinking, and collaborating with others in communities of practice, I applaud it and look forward to tapping children's potential in a way we have never fully done before.

Introduction

Jennifer Renner Del Nero

The Common Core State Standards (CCSS) are the first academic standards to be independently adopted by almost every state in the country. National assessments will eventually follow these standards. The purpose and intent of the Common Core standards for English language arts (ELA), as well as those for literacy in history/social studies and science education, are the focus of this book. How should these standards be put into practice for daily instruction? *Teaching with the Common Core Standards for English Language Arts, Grades 3–5* attempts to provide answers to this question. The purpose of these standards—universalizing the skills that all K–12 students in the United States will learn—is a worthwhile and necessary endeavor, yet the standards are mere words on a page unless successfully executed in the classroom. Like the children under their guidance, educators and administrators need detailed explanations and models to support them in understanding and implementing these new standards.

This volume is aimed at educators, administrators, graduate students, university professors, and others who deal with students in grades 3–5. Each of the chapters addresses one of the major ELA domains: literature, informational texts, foundational skills, writing, speaking and listening, language, technology, and assessment. They contain invaluable information, insight, and research from literacy leaders in their respective fields. These authors are fully aware of the challenges that enactment of the Common Core standards presents to educators; the chapters are written candidly and with full appreciation of the efforts it will take for educators to accomplish this goal. Their objective is twofold: to provide a theoretical background and detailed explanation of each of the CCSS/ELA standards as well as practical suggestions, classroom vignettes, models, instructional resources, and unit ideas to implement the standards. Appendix A lists all of the ELA standards for grades 3–5, organized by grade level. Appendix B, unique to this volume, contains a full thematic unit with the CCSS/ELA standards embedded throughout the daily lessons.

There are many interpretations of how the CCSS should be put into place in the classroom. There isn't one right answer. Be cautious when implementing them; think first about the instruction that works well for you right now. For example, we need to teach children in small groups and differentiate instruction using materials with which they can learn and be successful. However, in whole-class instruction, we need to use grade-level text to be sure that children are exposed to and guided through complex materials. Likewise, we need to read lots of informational text to our children, but that doesn't mean we should give up narrative text. They both are equally important. We need to focus on the language arts when we teach reading and writing, but also integrate the Common Core standards in content-area subjects. Thematic units not only help to integrate the CCSS into science and social studies, for example, but they are also motivating and relevant and they bring meaning to reading. When we pay attention to these things, reading is no longer just a skill to be learned but a skill to be used to learn other things. We need to hold on to the explicit instruction that we've learned is so important when teaching reading; but when we embed the CCSS into other content areas, children are getting reading instruction *all day* in school, not just during the language arts period. In short, we should not swing all the way toward either embracing or rejecting the new Common Core standards. Keep what you know is good in your classroom and refine it with these standards to bring more sophistication to your reading instruction.

In Chapter 1, Pearson and Hiebert orient the reader with an introduction to the Common Core standards. The authors begin with a brief history of standards in American education. They then discuss how the CCSS are necessary for successful infusion of literacy instruction throughout all the content areas. This section is followed by an explanation of how these particular standards are distinct from those of the past, including an emphasis on close critical reading and interdisciplinary connectivity. The authors provide two readings of the 10 anchor standards—one that adheres closely to the original text and another that is their personal interpretation of the content and their speculation as to its implications, including general measures that teachers can enact to meet them. Pearson and Hiebert conclude by turning a critical lens toward the standards, examining their potential complications and the further questions they pose, so that educators can successfully navigate any potential pitfalls.

Turning to the first ELA strand, reading literature, Malloy and Gambrell, in Chapter 2, discuss the importance of embedding literature into all facets of instruction in meaningful and motivational ways to promote 21st-century learning. The authors begin by making the point that the Common Core standards for reading literature aim at promoting sophisticated comprehension of texts. They then provide a definition of what "literature" is and describe the skills and understandings that teachers can help students develop through literature. Malloy and Gambrell consider reading literature within the context of the four CCSS domains—key ideas and details, craft and structure, integration of knowledge and ideas, and range of reading and level of text complexity—and unpack each with a brief theoretical background and a discussion of relevant literature in support of each domain. Following this are detailed explanations and illustrative classroom vignettes that can serve as models for teachers to use to meet these goals. Malloy and Gambrell then consider how teachers can successfully address these standards in the language arts block as well as throughout the school day. The authors conclude the chapter with additional activities and questions for reader reflection.

In Chapter 3, Ogle takes up the discussion of the second strand—reading informational texts—and maintains that the new standards call for greater attention to informational texts than in the past. She documents numerous sources that assert the importance of exposing students to high-quality print and digital informational texts in order to help them develop the skills necessary to comprehend successfully the nonfiction texts that make up the majority of content-area instruction. This section is followed by a discussion of the four subareas of reading informational texts and provides detailed explanations, classroom examples, and lesson plan ideas for teachers. Ogle then presents a vignette demonstrating the successful incorporation of informational texts throughout an entire day of instruction. The chapter ends with teacher and student resources as well as additional activity suggestions.

Rasinski, Kuhn, and Nageldinger, in Chapter 4, discuss how foundational literacy skills are necessary for successful reading comprehension. The authors unpack each of the four domains in this strand—print concepts, phonological awareness, word recognition, and fluency—and offer explanations as well as classroom vignettes that showcase particular strategies teachers can use for successful instruction in foundational skills. The authors emphasize how the key to success lies in contextualizing the skills through meaningful instructional integration throughout the school day. The chapter ends with additional instructional activities.

The Common Core standards call for additional instruction and time allotted in the school day for student composition. In Chapter 5, Graham discusses the writing standards and the four domains of this strand: text types and purposes, production and distribution of writing, research to build and present knowledge, and range of writing. Graham explains that the new standards issue a welcome call for additional emphasis on writing, but he also exposes the limitations of the writing standards in their current form. He details each component through the use of classroom vignettes and emphasizes how nurturing writing environments that support the writing process must be established in elementary classrooms. Included at the end of the chapter are lesson activities and reflection questions.

In Chapter 6, Fisher, Frey, and Lapp consider the speaking and listening standards. They begin by defining these terms and remarking how little attention has been paid to either of these areas until the advent of the CCSS. The authors provide an overview of the two domains in this strand—comprehension and collaboration and the presentation of knowledge and ideas—and offer strategies for putting these standards into daily classroom practice, with particular emphasis on "accountable talk," or partner conversation and whole-class discussion. Additional activities are included that teachers can use to successfully infuse the speaking and listening standards throughout daily instruction.

Blachowicz and Baumann, in Chapter 7, explore the language strand, focusing on vocabulary instruction and how it can be utilized for successful text comprehension. They review the theory and research that support the standards and address how teachers can bring meaningful vocabulary instruction into the daily routine through the use of classroom models. The authors then discuss strategies for incorporating vocabulary instruction in language arts, social studies, and science lessons, and offer suggestions for assessing student knowledge. The chapter ends with supplementary text resources and activities.

The importance of multimodal literacy is the focus of Chapter 8, in which Boling and Spiezio consider the issue of technology and the Common Core standards. They remark on how the new standards attempt to close the gap between the breadth of technology available and the limited exposure many students have in classrooms. The authors emphasize that technology is integrated throughout all the literacy standards, and they illustrate how it can be successfully infused in literacy instruction and in various content areas through classroom vignettes, where lessons rely on the use of specific digital media. The chapter concludes with a list of additional digital resources.

The topic of assessment in relation to the Common Core standards is taken up by Afflerbach in Chapter 9. He acknowledges that the new standards represent a series of challenges and opportunities to educators and details how new approaches to literacy assessment can help teachers meet evolving demands. Afflerbach also emphasizes the connection between formative and summative assessment and the need for a balance between the two. Assessments can form the foundation for literacy success. Moreover, well-devised assessments can serve as a tool for teachers to help students in raising the bar of academic achievement that the standards mandate.

In Chapter 10, Wixson brings together the various voices within this volume. She notes the overriding message of the previous chapters: The new standards call for integrating literacy throughout all aspects of daily instruction. Wixson takes a critical approach, considering both the benefits and limitations of thematic-based instruction, which is championed by the CCSS. She stresses that educators must maintain a balance between content and process in curriculum and instruction, including an emphasis on thoughtful theme selection and appropriate assessment. She insists that successful execution of the new standards will hinge on continuous professional development, where educators receive the support necessary to meet these high demands.

Understandably, educators have grown tired of "upsetting the apple cart" by constantly putting in the effort to revamp student instruction based on what could turn out to be only the latest educational fad—unequivocally praised at first, adopted without question or introspection, implemented without necessary supports or opportunity for collegiate conversations, executed without confidence or understanding of the original purpose or intent, and ultimately rejected and replaced by a new trend—and so the never-ending, exhausting cycle continues. However, as the writers in this volume suggest, the Common Core standards, despite their limitations, hold the promise of a positive new direction in America's literacy instruction—if they are approached thoughtfully and executed in meaningful ways that align with the intent and goals that set these standards apart from those of the past.

This book, with its critical approach, honest guidance, and abundance of examples and resources, will help educators and administrators embark on the journey to successful and lasting incorporation of the standards throughout all facets of instruction in classrooms across the nation. *Teaching with the Common Core Standards for English Language Arts, Grades 3–5*, marks the beginning of a roadmap for understanding and applying these standards in the classroom to foster meaningful literacy learning for all students and for inspiring teachers across the country to build upon this initial collection of interpretations and examples for the shared benefit of all. Let the conversation continue.

Contents

Teaching with the Common Core Standards for English Language Arts, Grades 3–5

CHAPTER 1

Understanding the Common Core State Standards

P. David Pearson
Elfrieda H. Hiebert

Standards have become a staple of the American school and curriculum since they first entered the reform scene in the early 1990s. They were conceived in the wake of the highly influential National Governors Association Conference of 1989, and have been endorsed by conservatives, liberals, and radicals alike (albeit for vastly different reasons) and reformulated many times since their inception. Schools, teachers, and students find their academic lives shaped by whatever standards hold court in their educational corner of the world. After the completely voluntary effort to produce national standards by the math community, the first major wave of standards was sponsored by federal and quasi-federal agencies, including the Office of Educational Research and Innovation and the National Academy of Sciences, with the goal of encouraging disciplinary professions (e.g., history, English language arts, and science) in the early 1990s to develop a clear statement of what students should know and be able to do at various developmental levels. The idea was that, with broad agreement on these curricular outlines of the typical progression of student performance, assessments and curricular schemes could be developed and implemented that would guarantee students would meet the benchmark performance standards along the journey to successful achievement and, eventually, participation in the world of work and higher education. Students would go on to college and into the workplace armed with the knowledge, skills, and dispositions needed to be successful in their postsecondary lives. That was the dream, the hope, and the expectation we began with in 1989. And it was still the dream in the late 1990s, when the Clinton administration undertook a valiant effort to ensure, via Title I (Improving America's Schools Act [IASA]), that all states had developed content standards and tests to measure their acquisition.

The Common Core State Standards (CCSS; National Governors Association [NGA] Center for Best Practices and Council of Chief State School Officers [CCSSO], 2010) represent the latest, and in many ways the most ambitious, version of that same vision of what standards could do for schools, teachers, and students. What is most significant about the CCSS is that, unlike the state action in response to IASA or No Child Left Behind (NCLB), the CCSS effort was driven by the states, not a federal agency or even a federally sponsored initiative. Initiated under the auspices of the NGA and the CCSSO, the CCSS are a bold attempt to ensure that at the end of the K–12 curricular journey students are prepared to enter either college or the workforce and take their place as knowledgeable, contributing members of the American economy, society, and polity. As a state-led initiative, the CCSS are intentionally designed to improve upon the current standards of individual states by creating clear, consistent, and rigorous standards to which all American students will be held, irrespective of the particular location of their residence. In short, opportunity to learn would not be an accident of a student's ZIP code.

There are many reasons for developing a common set of standards across American states, but the driving force is the potential for inequity created by the tremendous variability observed from state to state in policies and procedures related to curriculum, instruction, and assessment. Studies have shown considerable variability across states in the content and quality of state standards, state assessments used to measure student achievement, and the criteria used to gauge success on standards (Bandeira de Mello, 2011; Polikoff, Porter, & Smithson, 2011).

The CCSS were established by looking closely at standards and curriculum in sites where achievement is high. The designers of the CCSS looked carefully at standards of other countries (particularly those with high scores on international assessments) to ensure that all American students are prepared to succeed in a global economy and society. They have also been designed to reflect the knowledge and skills required to participate as workers and citizens in a digital–global world. The standard development process began with those goals required by high school graduates, proficiencies that would guarantee that students possessed college and career readiness (CCR). K–12 standards were developed to ensure learning progressions that would lead students to achieve CCR standards at the end of their K–12 school careers.

The title of the standards—*Common Core State Standards for English Language Arts & Literacy in History/Social Studies, Science, and Technical Subjects*—highlights the need for developing literacy and language proficiencies in the context of disciplinary knowledge—knowledge that extends to content-area courses rather than exclusively English language arts (ELA) courses. The CCSS aim for an integrated view of the components within the ELA at K–5: reading, writing, listening, and speaking, although there are separate (but highly similar) standards for literature and informational text. The grade 6–12 standards are first organized by discipline: ELA and then subject areas to distinguish which standards are the responsibility of the ELA curriculum (and teachers) and which are to be addressed by subject-area curricula and teachers. However, within ELA, history, or science and technology, the expectation is that reading, writing, speaking, and listening will be highly coordinated, if not fully integrated.

It is also worth noting that the CCSS are not intended to define all that can or should be taught; the standards are not intended to be a curriculum, as described within the standards: "By emphasizing required achievements, the *Standards* leave room for teachers, curriculum developers, and states to determine how those goals should be reached and what additional topics should be addressed" (NGA and CCSSO, 2010, p. 4). The intention of the standards is to provide guidance on core content of *any* curriculum, with the explicit expectation that districts, schools, and teachers will add specification and differentiation to their enactment of the core goals. Finally, they do not define the full range of support for English language learners and students with special needs. In short, the CCSS provide a core set of expectations and intentionally leave much to districts, schools, and teachers to figure out for themselves—to, if you will, put a local signature on their implementation of the core.

WHAT'S NEW AND DIFFERENT ABOUT THE CCSS?

In this section, we examine four aspects of the standards that set them apart from earlier iterations of state and/or national standards: close and critical reading, integration of language processes and disciplinary content, media/research literacy, and text complexity. We review these four in the order listed, as a way of acknowledging their progressive dissimilarity from earlier efforts. However poorly they have been implemented, neither close, critical reading nor integrated literacy is a new goal. Both have been around, in one form or another, at least since the days of John Dewey and progressive education and perhaps even earlier, in either Horace Mann's Common School Movement or Francis Parker's Quincy System (Cavanaugh, 1994). Then we move to two around which there has been considerable rhetoric but little action: disciplinary literacy and digital media as a new form of literacy. We end with the aspect that is as old as it is new and as controversial as it is commonplace: text complexity. Teachers and curriculum designers have been dealing with text complexity at least since the advent of the first readability formula (Lively & Pressey, 1923) and perhaps since the first "graded" reading series (McGuffey, 1836). However, text complexity is very new to standards documents, and this is the first set of standards that outlines specific expectations for increasing the level of challenge expected by students at each grade level.

We address each of the topics from two lenses: (1) a description of the topic that stays close to the text provided in the CCSS and (2) our "reading" of the implications for implementation inside classrooms and schools, with a special emphasis on implications that represent new rather than tried-and-true issues and practices. In the final section of the chapter, we address the dilemmas and conundrums that these standards, despite all of their advantages, bring to literacy education.

Close and Critical Reading

If there is a "first amongst equals" among the principles of the Common Core, it is surely close reading. Early on, the CCSS (2010) framers declare their commitment to this principle:

> Students who meet the Standards readily undertake the close, attentive reading that is at the heart of understanding and enjoying complex works of literature. They habitually perform the critical reading necessary to pick carefully through the staggering amount of information available today in print and digitally. They actively seek the wide, deep, and thoughtful engagement with high-quality literary and informational texts that builds knowledge, enlarges experience, and broadens worldviews. (p. 3)

The Perspective

The phrase "close reading" is used in the standards in much the way it entered the field of literary interpretation during the era of I. A. Richards and New Criticism in the mid-20th century (Richards, 1929/2008). In its canonical version, it can entail the explication and implication of every element (section, sentence, clause, phrase, word) in the text (although more often than not close readers "sample" sections of text for this sort of careful exegesis).

Appreciation of the structure of the text and the craft of the author are not the major outcomes of close reading; knowledge is. Students who read in a way that meets the standards gain strong disciplinary knowledge for their efforts, as they engage with texts in the disciplines of literature, history, science, and technical subjects. They know that different disciplines call for different types of evidence (e.g., documentary evidence in history, experimental evidence in science, textual clues in literature) and ways of formulating arguments to support claims about how the world works. Above all, students value evidence as the basic currency of academic discourse, and they are able to evaluate the claims made by the authors of texts and those that they make themselves in crafting arguments about the ideas they encounter in these texts.

One might anticipate that such a commitment to acquiring knowledge and constructing precise arguments achieves those goals at a cost; and the most likely candidate is an erosion of commitment to multicultural contributions and perspectives in literature, art, history, and science. Not so. The standards express clear commitments to cultural diversity. Early in the document, the standards announce this commitment clearly: "Students actively seek to understand other perspectives and cultures through reading and listening, and they are able to communicate effectively with people of varied backgrounds" (NGA and CCSSO, 2010, p. 4). Commitment to diversity does not imply unexamined acceptance of the ideas in the diverse array of texts students encounter. To the contrary, the same analytic and critical lenses that enable readers to critique and construct arguments are brought to bear on all texts they encounter. They evaluate other points of view critically and constructively.

Close reading is meant to occur both within and across texts, reflecting the general disposition of the standards that students are always trying to connect the ideas they encounter in a given text with other ideas from a range of sources, including previously read texts, their prior experiences, and other media (e.g., digital content).

Implications for Implementation

In our discussion of implications for close reading, one might expect us to focus on the first cluster (Standards 1–3) of Key Ideas and Details. After all, isn't a clear exposition of what the text *says* the natural result of close reading? While this might be true in a very narrow sense of what it means to read closely, this perspective misses the point of close reading. We read closely to acquire knowledge, but we cannot acquire that knowledge except in relation to what we already know; hence the significance of the third cluster of standards: Integration of Knowledge and Ideas (Standards 7–9). We also read closely to critique and evaluate the validity of the claims made by authors or the tools they use to engage and persuade readers; hence critique—the stuff of Standard 7 entails close reading in a very direct way. We are not suggesting that the other two clusters of standards—Key Ideas and Details (Standards 1–3) and Craft and Structure (Standards 4–6)—are not fundamental to integrating and using knowledge. The integration of knowledge depends on understanding the generation of key ideas and details and, when appropriate, analyses of how aspects of craft and structure influence the presentation and positioning of those key ideas and details. However, the ultimate goal of reading is (1) the integration of knowledge and ideas from text; (2) the delineation, evaluation, and critique of arguments and specific claims in a text; and (3) the analysis of ideas encountered across multiple texts and experiences to build knowledge. Put differently, close reading entails all of the standards. We privilege the last cluster because we fear that if we begin our instructional journey with the first cluster, we may become mired there and never get to the knowledge building and integration facets of the reading curriculum that is the core goal of the standards.

In order to keep students' eyes on the prize of gaining knowledge and insight from reading, we would emphasize two particular curricular and pedagogical moves:

- Teachers should give students—better yet, help students set—purposes for reading as well as promote connections to previously read texts and experiences. Such scaffolding of content does not require vast amounts of time. A simple reference to memorials or to the loss of life that results from wars may be sufficient to place Lincoln's Gettysburg Address or Winston Churchill's *Blood, Toil, Sweat, and Tears* into perspective for students.
- Students benefit from opportunities to review key ideas and themes from literature and also disciplinary areas. If knowledge is viewed to be cumulative, opportunities to review and revisit are essential. This means helping students extract common themes, topics, insights, and problems from sets of texts. The essential questions are, what's new in the text we just read, and how does it jive with what we already know about this issue?

Helping students watch their knowledge grow, change, and deepen is the ultimate goal of close reading. That is a principle not to be forgotten when one encounters a heavy dose of low-level literal comprehension questions in a well-meaning but misguided teachers' manual.

Integration of Language Processes and Disciplinary Content

The essence of reading is text complexity and the growth of comprehension. For writing, it is text types, responding to reading, and research. For speaking and listening: flexible communication and collaboration, and for language: conventions, effective use, and vocabulary. . . . By reading texts in history/social studies, science, and other disciplines, students build foundation of knowledge in these fields that will also give them the background to be better readers in all content areas. Students can only gain this foundation when the curriculum is intentionally and coherently structured to develop rich content knowledge within and across grades. (NGA and CCSSO, 2010, pp. 8, 10)

The Perspective

Integration is implicated in two assumptions about learning and content that underlie the CCSS/ELA: (1) Receptive (reading and listening) and productive (writing and speaking) language processes are integrated in learning and (2) content is viewed as the source and site of language use. That is, content acquisition requires, rationalizes, and enhances language use. The integrated view within the language arts and of the language arts with disciplinary knowledge presented by the CCSS contrasts sharply with the heavy emphasis that has been placed on reading as an encapsulated, independent subject in the years of NCLB.

In previous scholarship, the integration among the language arts and the integration of language processes and disciplinary content have often been treated separately (or not at all). In a summary of the research on integration, Gavelek, Raphael, Biondo, and Wang (2000) identified two perspectives on the integration of language arts: process driven and text driven. In the former, text selection tends to be incidental, and what matters is staying true to the processes and activities; subject-matter texts, a single literary text, or a text set related by theme or topic serve equally well in the service of language process development. In the text-driven approach, processes are taken up to the degree that they promote a clear exposition of the ideas and themes in a given text, but content acquisition trumps the practice of any given language process.

Integration of language processes around literature makes good sense, but when disciplinary content is added to the mix, the nature of instruction takes quite a different form. A disciplinary view of literacy recognizes that literacy is an essential part of any disciplinary practice and that different skills, knowledge, and reasoning processes hold sway as one moves from one discipline to the next (Heller & Greenleaf, 2007; Shanahan & Shanahan, 2008).

One of the most obvious ways in which literacy demands differ across disciplines is in the nature of the text (van den Broek, 2010). Texts that students encounter in history are quite different from those they encounter in chemistry. An obvious difference is in vocabulary, but syntax is also different, as evident in a mathematical equation and a historical document (e.g., Bill of Rights). Disciplines also vary in the uses of language and the relationships between texts and ways of developing knowledge (Moje, 2008). Shanahan and Shanahan (2008) found that the experts in different disciplinary areas approached texts in unique ways. These differences, Shanahan and Shanahan suggested, reflect variation in the values, norms, and methods of scholarship within disciplines. Historians, for example, read to ascertain the author's perspective since the heavy reliance within historical scholarship on retrospective analyses of source documents can mean selective analysis and biased interpretation.

Examples of how literacy processes can be developed with disciplinary content, even in the early elementary years, are most readily available for science instruction. The works of Cervetti and Barber (2008), Magnusson and Palincsar (2005), and Varelas, Pappas, Barry, and O'Neill (2001) provide clear examples of the attempt to embed literacy practices within a science learning framework with younger learners. In the work of Cervetti and Barber (2008), students read to deepen their knowledge for science inquiry activities. For example, a text might give detailed information of a real-world example of a scientific phenomenon (e.g., an oil spill) or a text might depict and describe different kinds of specimens that might not be available for students to examine firsthand (e.g., a close-up of sand particles depicting their size, shape, and color). Discussions and writing/documentation activities are also a prominent part of the science inquiry process in these efforts. In comparison to more "encapsulated" instruction, students from grades 2 through 5 have shown consistent advantages in their growth in science content, vocabulary, and writing (Cervetti, Barber, Dorph, Pearson, & Goldschmidt, 2009; Wang & Herman, 2005) but less consistent growth in reading comprehension.

The Reading Apprenticeship program (Greenleaf et al., 2011) provides frames for high school teachers to use in integrating disciplinary literacy practices into high school science teaching. (They also provide examples in history but science is the most carefully examined discipline.) Teachers are guided in engaging in conversations with their students in which they model and discuss how to read science texts, why people read science texts in these ways, and how to unearth, come to terms with, and summarize the content of the texts. The students use complex science texts as they engage in the intellectual work of science inquiry. High school students in Reading Apprenticeship classrooms have been found to make greater gains on standardized tests in reading and biology than students in control classrooms (Greenleaf et al., 2011).

The conceptual foundation for disciplinary knowledge as a context for supporting language learning is equally as strong within social studies as it is in science, although the real-world implementations in classrooms are much rarer; even rarer is research evaluating the impact of integrating literacy activities directly into social studies content. This discrepancy reflects the disparity in federal funding in social studies versus science; some argue that as a nation we avoid research about social studies content because of fears that it will lead to instruction and inculcation of humanistic values (Evans, 2004).

Several small-scale projects at the elementary-school level illustrate the manner in which literacy processes can be developed through and used in the service of content in social studies. Williams and colleagues (2007) describe a project in which low-income second-grade students were placed in one of three instruction conditions: (1) typical social studies content but with a comprehension treatment (instruction in text structure as well as an emphasis on questioning and graphic organizers), (2) a social studies content-only program, or (3) no instruction. The students who received the comprehension plus content treatment performed as well on the social studies as those in the content-only treatment with the additional benefits of increased performances in reading comprehension.

More projects have been conducted at the high school level, such as the instruction of historical reasoning strategies for 11th graders by De La Paz and Felton (2010), with the aim of supporting students' writing of argumentative texts on historical topics. One strategy, for example, was described as "Consider the Author," with questions such as "How does the author's viewpoint have an effect on his argument?" Students who participated in this instruction produced better elaborated and more persuasive historical arguments than comparison students.

The humanities tell a somewhat different tale, largely through the literature curriculum. The central themes of literature have been identified within philosophy, literary theory, and even psychology, but typically the themes of core reading programs are scattershot, some dealing with genres (e.g., puzzles and mysteries, fables) and others with potentially powerful themes of literature (e.g., survival, turning points) that often crumble through surface-level, almost trivial, treatment in commercial programs. The content of literature is more than a simple topic, however. Literature is the context in which writers and readers explore the human experience (Probst, 1986). Some text may not have the most profound themes, especially the texts of beginning reading. True literature, even in picture books, grapples with the great themes of human experience—for example, the relationship of the individual to family, community, and even morality. Despite its emphasis on disciplinary knowledge, the CCSS have not necessarily done a better job of identifying the content of literature than previous standards documents or, for that matter, literature anthologies available in the marketplace. In emphasizing disciplinary knowledge, however, the CCSS open the way for educators to attend to the critical content that is part of the disciplines, including the humanities.

Implications for Implementation

For true integration of disciplinary and language processes, actions need to occur outside the classroom: in state departments, in district offices, and at departmental and school levels. Granted, there are things that teachers can do on their own and even in local sites, but the critical point is that collective teacher action is required to move this agenda forward. For example:

- Educational units are going to need to achieve clarity on major curricular themes. There is some guidance on how educators can go about identifying these themes (Lipson, Valencia, Wixson, & Peters, 1993; Valencia & Lipson, 1998) and convincing peers to adopt them over more conventional approaches to curriculum.

- In literature (as in other disciplines), teachers need to make selections of texts and tasks with a clear view of the larger themes and understandings of human experience that these texts and tasks could promote. Themes are big ideas or enduring questions that have relevance for the people of a diverse society in many aspects of their lives, both in and out of school and that possess enough gravitas to sustain inquiry over time (e.g., "Culture and life experience influence how people respond to challenges they face"). This is quite different from a statement such as "Friends must learn to get along." Getting serious about the knowledge dimensions of literature teaching is essential; otherwise, literary themes may be easily trivialized into fluff that fails to build knowledge and insight.

- Science is a good place to start, not only because there is more work on the science–literacy integration agenda but also because the emerging national science standards (National Research Council, 2012) take on literacy and language as an essential part of learning science. Learning the oral and written discourses of science is as prominent in these new standards as is the acquisition of content and engagement of inquiry processes.

Research and Media

> Students cite specific evidence when offering an oral or written interpretation of a text. They use relevant evidence when supporting their own points in writing and speaking, making their reasoning clear to the reader or listener, and they constructively evaluate others' use of evidence. (NGA and CCSSO, 2010, p. 7)

The Perspective

No book, no library, no learning environment in human history has had the capacity to make available to students the volume of information, the variety of forms of information, and the connections within and across information sources that digital environments allow (Cavanaugh & Blomeyer, 2007). The digital–global age makes knowledge available in ways not experienced by previous generations. To be ready for college, the workforce, and life in this digital–global world, students need the ability to gather, comprehend, evaluate, synthesize, and report on information and ideas from an extensive volume and range of print and nonprint media. They also need to be able to evaluate, create, and contribute to information on topics and, in doing so, use the full range of media. Students' ability to use and contribute to knowledge using a range of media is embedded throughout other standards in the CCSS.

Educators, community members, and legislators all agree with the essential role of students' acquisition of high levels of proficiency in using technologies to gain, organize, critique, and share knowledge. How to reach this goal with large numbers of students in a world where new technologies and new stores of knowledge proliferate by the hour is the challenge. The research and media goal of the CCSS is known as informational literacy among the professional group that has traditionally been responsible for archiving and organizing knowledge: librarians (Rader, 2002). From the perspective of informational literacy, a distinction needs to be made between using multiple resources for acquiring knowledge and for organizing and sharing knowledge. A variety of skills and strategies are involved in using resources on the Internet to research a question or to solve a problem. As Labbo and Reinking (1999) have described it, individuals need to become their own librarians, adept at locating and evaluating sources of information. When the task involves sharing information that has been gained from research, regardless of whether it is first- or secondhand, individuals need to be able to organize their information in ways that communicate to others. To do this requires skill at selecting the appropriate media for communicating and, within any given medium, the appropriate ways to organize information.

A distinction between knowledge acquisition and knowledge communication is not articulated within the CCSS. Nor will educators find a wealth of information on how knowledge acquisition and knowledge communication with digital environments can be developed. In particular, we know of no large-scale projects, over the K–12 span, that illustrate how teachers can guide students in either the gaining knowledge or the organizing/sharing knowledge dimension. Writers from the field of information literacy frequently recommend the use of projects to develop both knowledge acquisition and knowledge communication proficiencies. Project-based learning has a long history (Darling-Hammond et al., 2008), dating back at least to Dewey within American education, and is most evident in several decades of work in science education, such as the examples described earlier.

For most teachers, project-based learning will be a challenging venture. When coupled with the demands for integration of various technologies, its widespread use, at least in the immediate future, is dim. Keeler and Langhorst (2008) have suggested that teachers be supported in ways of moving from simple integration of technology (e.g., using a particular kind of software) to more complex forms (e.g., students' contributions to a book blog) in a series of small steps. However, this progression does not address developmental issues. Developmental issues can be viewed from both the perspective of children of different ages and in terms of the cultivation of particular proficiencies in students of any age. In terms of the first concern, two critical questions must be addressed: At what age should children become involved with a variety of technologies, and how much time should be devoted? For example, how much time should kindergartners be spending with digital devices? With regard to the second face of developmental progression, the manner in which the "critical reading" of resources available on digital devices progresses has yet to be documented. The manner in which graphics, animation, and gaming components influence students' critical stance, in particular, requires examination.

There is a substantial amount of work left to be done regarding the acquisition of knowledge and the sharing/organization of knowledge by students that might ultimately guide any large-scale effort to infuse this digital perspective into American classrooms. Even a short tour of websites indicates that there is considerable teacher activity and many powerful reports on how students' acquisition of knowledge and their communication of knowledge are enhanced through technology. The movement in this domain is so rapid that documentation and evaluation lag far behind the implementations in real classrooms. The knowledge resources in a variety of media are many. The work to understand how students can be supported in powerfully using the technological resources currently available—both to acquire knowledge and communicate their own knowledge—requires documentation, evaluation, and substantial collaboration among teachers, industry, and researchers.

Implications for Implementation

Ways to support media and research proficiencies include:

- Teachers should support students, even in the primary grades, to use a variety of resources to find answers to compelling questions.
- Teachers should support students, beginning in the primary grades, to organize information that has been learned and to develop means for sharing that information.

Text Complexity

> The Reading standards place equal emphasis on the sophistication of what students read and the skill with which they read. Standard 10 defines a grade-by-grade "staircase" of increasing text complexity that rises from beginning reading to the college and career readiness level. (NGA and CCSSO, 2010, p. 31)

The Perspective

The 10th and final reading standard of the CCSS calls for students to have the capacity to read, compared with their grade-level counterparts from earlier eras, more complex texts for their own grade level. The hope, and expectation, is that by upping the ante at every grade level beginning in grade 2, within 5 or 6 years high school graduates will actually be able to read the complex texts expected of them in college and the workplace. This focus on text complexity derives from concerns that today's high school graduates are not prepared to read the materials of college or the workplace (ACT, 2006). The CCSS is the first standards document, either at the state or national level, to include a standard devoted solely to students' capacity to read increasingly complex text over the grades. In previous standards documents, student reading proficiencies were described in relation to "grade-level text," but grade-level text was assumed rather than defined.

The CCSS writers provided two sources of guidance for educators (and test makers) to determine the progression in text complexity: (1) a tripartite model of text complexity and (2) exemplars for steps along the grade-by-grade staircase. The dimensions of the tripartite model are *qualitative* (i.e., levels of meaning or purpose, structure, language conventionality and clarity, and knowledge demands), *reader and task dimensions* (i.e., elements of instruction that teachers address in assignments, lesson planning, and moment by moment scaffolding); and *quantitative* (e.g., readability formulas that address word familiarity/frequency and syntactic complexity as well as newer measures that report on referential or deep cohesion).

In Appendix A of the CCSS document, the writers indicated that further guidance on qualitative dimensions would be forthcoming, but within the standards document only one quantitative system was presented: the Lexile Framework (MetaMetrics, 2000). Lexiles for grade-level bands, starting with grades 2–3, were recalibrated to ensure that the final point on the staircase—grade 11 CCR—would match the Lexiles of college and career texts. A second form of guidance is in Appendix B, which provides text exemplars that illustrate the nature of complex and high-quality texts at different grade bands.

The specification of a grade-by-grade staircase with quantitative levels and the provision of exemplar texts for different grade bands are the features that distinguish this standards document from its predecessors. A standard that addresses the complexity of the text makes eminent sense (one can only wonder why this standard has been overlooked in previous documents). However, the underlying theory and research on text complexity that would support creation of state and district curricula and programs are in short supply.

Evidence for particular assumptions regarding text complexity within the CCSS is sparse and, in some cases, nonexistent. Two telling examples of assumptions lacking a substantive evidence base are (1) the ramp-up trajectory and (2) expectations about struggling readers. There is no basis, at least that we can determine, for beginning the ramp-up process in grade 2 to ensure that high school students are at CCR levels (Hiebert, 2012); one could make an even more plausible argument for beginning the ramp-up at, say, grade 6. Regarding the plight of struggling readers, what makes us think that the current population of struggling readers, for whom the goal of grade-level texts is elusive, will suddenly master texts that far outstrip their reading level (Hiebert & Van Sluys, in press) just because we have asked them to try harder? We do not see how we can begin to enact higher standards for increased text complexity unless we also up the ante on the availability of strategies for scaffolding students' attempts to cope with texts that far exceed their reading current capacities. And we do not see how that can happen without a dramatic increase in teachers' knowledge about text and pedagogy.

One other concern centers on complete disregard for two key ideas that have been part of the rhetoric of individualized instruction for decades: (1) that there exists an optimal trajectory of difficulty for each child and (2) that students make the most progress in mastering increasingly difficult text when they are working squarely in their "zone of comfort"—not too easy but not too hard. There is no room for between-student accommodations of this sort when the ramp-up is in play.

Our concerns aside, amidst many unanswered questions, educators in states and districts need to press on to identify texts that align with the standards. In the next section, we identify how educators can respond in responsible ways. We do underscore the need for answers to questions about text complexity from the research community. We have yet to develop the research base that could help teachers and administrators stand up to this challenge.

Implications for Implementation

We offer guidelines to three groups of educators: leaders at district and state levels, leaders at school sites (principals, literacy coaches), and classroom teachers.

At the State or District Level. In many contexts, teachers do not have the prerogative of choosing the primary texts of instruction. Often these choices are determined on a district level or by state committees (e.g., California, Texas, Florida). Decisions at these levels will likely be highly influential in the interpretation of the CCSS text complexity standard. We offer the following implementation suggestions for those involved in text selection:

• Educators need to make qualitative criteria clear for the selection of texts selected for use in states and/or districts. The four qualitative dimensions (derived from ACT,

2006) identified by the CCSS writers (levels of meaning, structure, language convention-ality and clarity, and knowledge demands) have already been presented. One instantia-tion of this system that is currently popular describes each of these dimensions on a scale of "little" to "much" and an overall score is given to a text, irrespective of differences on the four dimensions (Copeland, Lakin, & Shaw, 2012). Two questions need to the answered: (1) whether these four dimensions capture the critical traits that matter in comprehension and (2) whether different traits would not be expected to have different manifestations or different effects at particular developmental points. That is, a number that summarizes the qualitative features fails to capture the very elements of texts that should be the growing edge for students.

At the School Level. The CCSS provided exemplars of complex texts at different levels but failed to describe what made these texts complex for students at particular grade bands (they also neglected to ensure that texts fit the Lexile parameters set for grade bands). What the CCSS writers failed to do is what teachers in schools (and in pro-fessional development venues) need to do to understand how text features influence their students' understanding of texts.

• Teachers within and across grade levels need to select texts that are anchors for different points for a grade or grade band. In the case of the primary levels, where growth in reading is substantial, benchmark texts should be identified for different periods in the school year (e.g., trimesters or semesters). The texts are not the ones that are taught but, rather, provide a "North Star" for reading instruction and evaluation.

At the Classroom Level. Even when teachers are required to use to the particular texts assigned to them, their instruction can either facilitate or hinder their students' growth in learning from complex texts. Positive actions include:

• Helping students understand and appreciate the differences in vocabulary of nar-ratives and informational texts. The unique words of narratives are typically synonyms or nuanced meanings for concepts that, at their core, students know (*timid/full of fear*). The unique words of informational texts, by contrast, often represent concepts that stu-dents do not know *and* are core to understanding the content (e.g., *photosynthesis, con-vection, nonrenewable resource, inflation rate*). A reader may be able to slide by *timid* but not *photosynthesis*.

• Giving students opportunities to pursue topics of personal interest. In interna-tional comparisons, American students have adequate reading performance but their interest in reading is among the lowest in the world (Mullis, Martin, Gonzalez, & Ken-nedy, 2003). Until American students are invited to explore their interests with text, they are unlikely to read extensively unless "they have to." Even the chance to select from among two or three texts can increase students' engagement as readers (Guthrie et al., 2006). The real benefit of offering students choice is increased engagement with reading more text for longer periods of time, thus building both knowledge and stamina for read-ing on their own.

• Ensuring that students read sufficient amounts of text (*volume*) and also read increasingly longer selections (*stamina*). The amounts of time devoted to reading in class-rooms and the amount of text that students are expected to read and use in tasks appear to be less than optimal in many American classrooms (Brenner, Hiebert, & Tompkins,

2009; Hiebert, Wilson, & Trainin, 2010). If students are to be prepared for the complex texts and tasks of college and careers, increasing the amount of text they are given and the size of chunks that draw on this knowledge needs to be a priority at the elementary-school level. Opportunity, volume, and stamina should be the goals for these personal reading programs.

CONUNDRUMS, DILEMMAS, AND UNANSWERED QUESTIONS

As well intentioned as standards seem (who can oppose the goal of high achievement on rigorous standards for all students irrespective of demographic circumstances?), they have a checkered history in closing the achievement gap between educational haves and have-nots. In this section, we address what might be construed as the potential dark side of the CCSS. Unsurprisingly, most of our concerns are future oriented because they depend largely on how the standards will be implemented. The validity and efficacy of the CCSS, as with all previous standards efforts, will depend not so much on the goals they promote but on the degree to which they are implemented in a way that *supports* and *defines* excellence, so that they actually *do* promote more equitable achievement rather than just provide another opportunity for us to demonstrate to ourselves what we have known for all too long: that we, as a profession and a nation, are much better at advancing the achievement of those students least in need of our help. (See Lagana-Riordan & Aguilar, 2009, for an account of how the last decade has seen children of the wealthiest Americans make the greatest gains in achievement.) In this section, we address several of these potential unintended consequences, with the goal of maximizing the likelihood that we do not fall victim to them as these promising standards are translated into curriculum, pedagogy, and assessment in schools.

Our experience in working with the standards since their adoption in June 2010 in a variety of settings has brought several of these troubling possibilities to the surface. We share them here not so much to discourage educators from adopting and adapting the standards as to ensure that educators use them with a complete awareness of their constraints and affordances.

Upping the Ante on Text Complexity

An explicit goal of the CCSS is to increase the challenge level of the texts that students read in grades 3–12. The stated purpose of this move is to close, or at least narrow, the gap in text complexity of approximately 200 Lexiles (roughly two grade levels) that exists between the average grade 12 text and the average college freshman text. The expectation is that if the profession can gradually increase text challenge over the grades, in a few years students will leave high school ready to meet the challenge of college freshman-level texts. The further hope is that this process will eventually reduce our reliance on remedial courses—about 40% of entering freshman take them—in community colleges and universities.

This is a noble goal, but it is not at all clear how it can be achieved. Merely raising the bar on the complexity of texts that students are required to read at any grade level will not make it happen. Right now, educators struggle to help students meet the challenge of the texts that fall short of the mark for college readiness at the high school level. What makes us think that by raising the expectations and exhorting teachers and students to try harder we will all meet the challenge? It reminds us of the early days of

the first standards movement in the 1990s, when the theory of action was that by raising the bar all the players in the system—administrators, teachers, and students—would
be motivated to try harder to meet higher expectations. That is, standards/assessment/
accountability would lead to clear expectations and motivation, leading to higher levels
of performance. It didn't work! By the mid-1990s, reformers had learned that they had
to add professional development and teacher knowledge and practices to their theories of
action as mediating variables to help meet the challenge.

Without infusing major changes in professional development for teachers and curriculum designers (so that those who design and deliver challenging texts understand the
critical features of texts), increasing text complexity will be little more than a cruel hoax
visited upon teachers and students. Increased text challenge will not lead to increased
capacity for students to deal with complexity without increased teacher scaffolding and
knowledge of the nature of text and language (see Fillmore & Snow, 2000) and how to
scaffold conversations around text (see Murphy, Wilkinson, Soter, Hennessey, & Alexander, 2009) in order to manage complexity. It is not at all clear to us how anything short of
a major investment in the development of teacher knowledge about text at all levels and
in all disciplines will allow that to happen.

Keeping Our Word on Models of Complexity

The standards document promises to assess text complexity in the three ways described
earlier: quantitatively, qualitatively, and by matching reader to text and task. Our fear is
that both the qualitative and reader–text dimensions will either drop out when the standards are implemented at the state level or, equally as problematic, they will be given only
token lip service. In short, states and districts will monitor the quantitative indices, leaving the other two categories to "fend for themselves." Thus, when all is said and done,
only the quantitative indices will have any "teeth" and bear any consequences in shaping
curricular expectations. It this happens, it will be a great loss to the teaching profession
because teachers have much to learn about the nature of text complexity and ways of
responding to it in collaborative examinations of a particular text and how to manage its
tough patches when attempting to make it accessible to their students.

Some educators, ourselves included, were expecting the CCSS sponsors to create
resources, such as a share website, where teachers can contribute their plans or successful
accounts of how they had engaged their students in reading and responding to particular
texts. Imagine what a resource that might be—where any teacher could find 5, 10, 20, 50,
or even 100 accounts of how other teachers in specific settings with particular groups of
students had negotiated their way through commonly used texts. The teachers' editions
of basals and literature anthologies would pale in comparison to such highly contextual-
ized stories of classroom implementation.

Our skeptical nature compels us to predict that the qualitative and reader–text
dimensions will never see the light of day as the standards are implemented. Nothing
would please us more than to be chided a decade from now for having been so pessimistic
now.

We Already Do That!

In any organization, a major strategy for dealing with the novelty of change is to assimi-
late it by asserting prior ownership, expressed in the often-heard response, "That's

nothing new! I've been doing that for years!" The implication is that if we are already doing it, then there is no reason to change what we are doing. So business as usual prevails! Reform accommodated! Next?

The degree to which this sort of assimilation of the CCSS is possible depends entirely on the "grain size" at which the match between past and future practice is made. If a state committee lines up the CCSS with their current ELA standards and asks, "Where in our current standards do we have language that maps onto the CCSS?", then they will be able to easily dismiss the CCSS as "same old, same old." However, if they take a more careful, deliberate approach to examining the CCSS ELA—where they examine the entire "logic" of the standards, complete with the appendices that define tasks, exemplars, and common texts that might be used—then there will be little overlap between the old and the new. For starters, few, if any, state standards we know of ground the standards within genre and disciplinary contexts in the same way and at the same level of detail of the CCSS. Likewise, few state standards documents invite an integrated view of the ELA *and* support an analysis of the synergies between ELA and disciplinary learning in the way the CCSS do. In short, only a shallow reading and mapping will support pigeonholing the CCSS as nothing new; dipping even slightly below the surface of both existing and new standards demands a call to action for a new way of thinking about the relationship between ELA and disciplinary learning.

Bait and Switch

We chose this highly pejorative metaphor of bait and switch intentionally as the title for this section not because we believe that the designers of the standards and its implementation documents had any malevolent intentions in mind when they shaped this effort, but because that's what things look like from the perspective of the consumers of the standards—the educators at the local level who will have to live with the consequences of their implementation. If we only had to deal with the standards, this might never have become a concern. However, the recent publication of "Publishers' Criteria" (Coleman & Pimentel, 2011) on the Common Core standards website alarms us greatly and leads us to wonder whether the letter and spirit of the standards document have been sacrificed at the altar of shaping published programs and materials. We will unpack passages from the publishers' guidelines and compare them with statements from the original standards documents to allow readers to decide for themselves whether the bait and switch label is appropriate.

Language from the Standards

Earlier, we suggested that the standards are noteworthy (and a refreshing change from the "mandate" frenzy of NCLB) for the degrees of freedom that they cede to the local level, even classroom teachers, with our citation from the introduction (p. 2) that the standards "leave room for teachers, curriculum developers, and states to determine how those goals should be reached and what additional topics should be addressed."

This statements sounds similar to the logic of standards in the first wave (early 1990s): Standards specify the goals of instruction, leaving the means of achieving them to teachers, schools, and districts. For the first several years of the standards movement, this logic prevailed. Then NCLB came along and mandated schools to use curricula that were based on "scientifically-based reading research" (SBRR), which was interpreted to be whatever was in the National Reading Panel (National Institute of Child Health and Human Development, 2000) report. Once this was done, both the ends (the standards) and the means (the set of curriculum programs that met the SBRR standard) of reading curriculum were set, leaving no room for teacher prerogative or local signature. Could something like this happen with the CCSS?

We provide a sequence of verbatim passages from the "Publishers' Criteria" (Coleman & Pimentel, 2011) to illustrate how they undermine the promise of teacher choice in the standards themselves:

Regarding the Nature of Texts

A significant percentage of tasks and questions are text dependent. . . . Rigorous text-dependent questions require students to demonstrate that they not only can follow the details of what is explicitly stated but also are able to make valid claims that square with all the evidence in the text. Text-dependent questions do not require information or evidence from outside the text or texts; they establish what follows and what does not follow from the text itself. (p. 6)

Regarding Questions and Tasks

The Common Core State Standards call for students to demonstrate a careful understanding of what they read before engaging their opinions, appraisals, or interpretations. Aligned materials should therefore require students to demonstrate that they have followed the details and logic of an author's argument before they are asked to evaluate the thesis or compare the thesis to others. (p. 9)

Staying Close to the Text

Materials make the text the focus of instruction by avoiding features that distract from the text. Teachers' guides or students' editions of curriculum materials should highlight the reading selections. . . . Given the focus of the Common Core State Standards, publishers should be extremely sparing in offering activities that are not text based. (p. 10)

These directives to publishers directly contradict the commitment to teacher prerogative promised in the standards (setting aside for another essay the fact that they reveal a professionally suspect and long-abandoned text-centric perspective on the topic of close reading). The biblical reference "The Lord giveth, the Lord hath taketh away" seems apt here: Promise teachers some professional choice in the standards and then direct publishers to write teacher guides with scripts that remove all the choice! Bait and switch? You decide.

Assessment

It comes as a surprise to absolutely no one who has lived through the last 20 years of educational reform that the assessments developed to measure progress in meeting curriculum standards matter more than the standards themselves (National Research Council, 1999; Pearson, 2007; Shepard, Hannaway, & Baker, 2009). The very logic of accountability systems demands that assessments play this lynchpin role. And the tighter we make the link between standards and assessment, and the finer the grain size at which we measure progress (e.g., a subtest for every letter sound rather than a subtest for letter sounds as a group), the greater the likelihood that assessments will drive instructional activities in the classroom (Paris, 2005; Pearson, 2007). If this practice is followed to its logical conclusion, then the assessment system becomes the default curriculum, shaping virtually all aspects of instruction as schools "teach to the test" through test preparation activities that can last for weeks, even months, in anticipation of the state standards test.

This puts a great burden on the tests we use to monitor progress—for individual students, teachers, and schools. What if the tests are not up to the task? What if they do not really measure the knowledge or the process they are designed to measure? Then students will have practiced, and teachers will have taught, material or skills that do not actually lead to increases in what is supposed to be measured. Haladyna, Nolen, and Hass (1991) have aptly labeled this shortcoming "test score pollution," which refers to an increase or decrease in a score on a test without an accompanying increase or decrease in the construct being measured. In short, students might get better (or worse) reading test scores without reading any better (or worse) than before.

Pollution is a concern for all assessments. Complex performance assessments and even portfolio systems can fall victim to the malady just as easily as multiple-choice standardized tests. When the stakes attached to an assessment are high, the temptation to seek higher scores without greater learning is always there, and it must be monitored with vigilance. Surely we want students to achieve higher scores on assessments, but because they learned more about the content or practice assessed and not because they practiced the test format and content more assiduously and more often. In the early 1990s, when the first standards movement was born, there was a widespread call for complex performance tasks to replace what most scholars regarded as the more easily corruptible standardized tests. To paraphrase Resnick and Resnick (1992) and Wiggins (1999), if schools are going to teach to the test, then let's have tests worth teaching to—a noble goal that is still quite elusive in our educational system. Why? We believe that it is the stakes that are attached to a test, not its content or format, that propel the counterproductive teaching-to-the-test syndrome that we all complain about but continue to enact annually in our schools.

As Pearson (2007) has pointed out, this situation makes a mockery of the age-old tradition of transfer as the gold standard for assessing learning. If what is "on the test" is highly consequential, what well-meaning teacher would encourage students to eschew what is right in front of them and instead study and apply what they are learning to novel (and risky, in terms of test scores) tasks and formats? Practicing what is on the test is an age-old tradition, spawning the phrase "the tradition of past exams" as a way of characterizing what students did (and do) to prepare for tests of consequence for either themselves or their schools. It doesn't seem to matter whether it is a low-level high school exit exam or an advanced placement exam (or a bar exam for that matter): Teaching to the test is a pervasive practice, one that discourages extending one's knowledge or skill far beyond the boundaries of the anticipated test.

Stakes aside, we believe that more complex assessment tasks—tasks that require the orchestration of many skills, strategies, and concepts—stand a much better chance of promoting productive, engaging pedagogy than do multiple-choice assessments of componential skills, particularly in reading and writing assessments—and so apparently do the developers in the two large consortia that have been funded to build world-class assessments of the Common Core standards. Both Partnership Assessment for Readiness for College and Careers (PARCC; 2011) and Smarter Balanced Assessment Consortium (SBAC; 2012) are developing hybrid assessments that balance the use of multiple-choice tests to maximize coverage of lower-level skills and concepts with extended constructed response (short essays of 100–300 words) and genuine performance tasks (activities that might take 2 or 3 hours to complete over more than 1 day) to measure deeper learning or transfer of skills and knowledge to new scenarios.

It remains to be seen whether these consortia will be successful in building exams that rely on complex performance for task completion and employ human judgment in scoring. The major question is whether these assessments will pass the tests of feasibility, affordability, and psychometric rigor when they are put to use in wide-scale assessment systems across the entire grade span. We recall the burst of enthusiasm that accompanied the performance assessment efforts of the early 1990s (Pearson, Spalding, & Myers, 1998; Valencia, Hiebert, & Afflerbach, 1994), as well as the bitter disappointment that ensued when these assessments did not stand up to the financial (who can afford to score them?), political ("Don't be evaluating my kid's values and thoughts—just whether he mastered the facts of the curriculum"), and psychometric (the assessments cannot demonstrate intertask generalizability—the scores of individuals might well be an accident of the particular task they were asked to complete). And it wasn't that there were no success stories. There were. For example, the assessments in states like Maryland, Kentucky, Vermont, and Washington survived for years with some combination of performance tasks and portfolios. Eventually, by the time NCLB was in place, however, all but a few pockets of these traditions had been replaced with conventional multiple-choice assessments. As we look toward the future, we wonder: In schools where financial resources are scarce, where political will is weak, and where stakes for individuals are high, can this new batch of constructed response and performance tasks meet the daunting challenge that lies ahead of them?

In one sense, there is no choice. The challenge must be met, primarily because mastery of the CCSS for the ELA cannot be measured easily (if at all) with simple, skill-by-skill multiple-choice tests. Perhaps some of the standards in Cluster 1, Key Ideas and Details, could be measured with simpler tests, and maybe even some of the structural aspects of text invited by Cluster 2—Craft and Structure. But few if any of the standards in Cluster 3—Integration of Knowledge and Ideas—lend themselves to anything less than constructed responses and, even more appropriately, performance examinations. So the challenge is there. The assessment players in PARCC and SBAC seem to be prepared to try to develop these sorts of measures and make them work, even as a part of large-scale assessment. It remains to be seen whether we, as a profession, will succeed in meeting a challenge that our predecessors have consistently failed to meet.

CODA

Our goal in this opening chapter is modest: to emphasize what the standards are really about, to discern what is new and different about them (and their implications when trying to implement them), and to heighten awareness of some of the vexing issues that require resolution as we move toward implementation (or decide what's worth implementing and what isn't).

In truth, our modest introduction is little more than a prelude to the remainder of this volume. In the chapters that follow, you will reencounter the themes and issues of which we have only scratched the surface here, plus many more that space did not permit us to touch upon. With greater awareness of these issues, readers will develop a clearer sense of how to manage local efforts to implement, accept, and/or reject the CCSS—what to emphasize, what to downplay, what to tackle first, what later, what never. We wish you well in the process and on the journey. It certainly won't be boring. And with a little luck it will be both interesting and worthwhile.

REFERENCES

ACT. (2006). *Reading between the lines: What the ACT reveals about college readiness in reading.* Iowa City, IA: Author.

Bandeira de Mello, V. (2011). *Mapping state proficiency standards onto the NAEP scales: Variation and change in state standards for reading and mathematics, 2005–2009* (NCES 2011-458). Washington, DC: U.S. Government Printing Office.

Brenner, D., Hiebert, E. H., & Tompkins, R. (2009). How much and what are third graders reading?: Reading in core programs. In E. H. Hiebert (Ed.), *Reading more, reading better* (pp. 118–140). New York: Guilford Press.

Cavanaugh, C., & Blomeyer, R. (Eds.). (2007). *What works in K–12 online learning.* Washington, DC: International Society for Technology in Education.

Cavanaugh, M. P. (1994). *A history of holistic literacy: Five major educators.* Westport, CT: Praeger.

Cervetti, G. N., & Barber, J. (2008). Text in hands-on science. In E. H. Hiebert & M. Sailors (Eds.), *Finding the right texts: What works for beginning and struggling readers* (pp. 89–108). New York: Guilford Press.

Cervetti, G. N., Barber, J., Dorph, R., Pearson, P. D., & Goldschmidt, P. G. (2009, April). *Integrating science and literacy: A value proposition?* Symposium paper presented at the annual meeting of the American Educational Research Association, San Diego, CA.

Coleman, D., & Pimentel, S. (2011). *Publishers' criteria for the Common Core State Standards in English language arts and literacy, grades 3–12.* Washington, DC: Council of the Chief State School Officers and National Association of State Boards of Education.

Copeland, M., Lakin, J., & Shaw, K. (2012, January 26). Text complexity and the Kansas Common Core standards for English language arts and literacy in history/social studies, science, and technical subjects. Retrieved from *www.ccsso.org/Resources/Digital_Resources/The_Common_Core_State_Standards_Supporting_Districts_and_Teachers_with_Text_Complexity.html.*

Darling-Hammond, L., Barron, B., Pearson, P. D., Schoenfeld, A. S., Stage, E., Zimmerman, T. D., et al. (2008). *Powerful learning: What we know about teaching for understanding.* San Francisco: Jossey-Bass.

De La Paz, S., & Felton, M. K. (2010). Reading and writing from multiple source documents in history: Effects of strategy instruction with low to average high school writers. *Contemporary Educational Psychology, 35,* 174–192.

Evans, R. W. (2004). *The social studies wars: What should we teach the children?* New York: Teachers College Press.

Fillmore, L. W., & Snow, C. E. (2000). *What teachers need to know about language.* Washington, DC: Center for Applied Linguistics.

Gavelek, J. R., Raphael, T.E ., Biondo, S. M., & Wang, D. (2000). Integrated literacy instruction. In M. L. Kamil, P. B. Mosenthal, P. D. Pearson, & R. Barr (Eds.), *Handbook of reading research* (Vol. III, pp. 587–607). Mahwah, NJ: Erlbaum.

Greenleaf, C. L., Litman, C., Handon, T. L., Rosen, R., Boscardin, C. K., Herman, J., et al. (2011). Integrating literacy and science in biology: Teaching and learning impacts of Reading Apprenticeship professional development. *American Educational Research Journal, 48,* 647–717.

Guthrie, J. T., Wigfield, A., Humenick, N. M., Perencevich, K. C., Taboada, A., & Barbosa, P.

(2006). Influences of stimulating tasks on reading motivation and comprehension. *Journal of Educational Research, 99,* 232–245.

Haladyna, T. M., Nolen, S. B., & Haas, N. S. (1991). Raising standardized achievement test scores and the origins of test score pollution. *Educational Researcher, 20*(5), 2–7.

Heller, R., & Greenleaf, C. L. (2007). *Literacy instruction in the content areas: Getting to the core of middle and high school improvement.* Washington, DC: Alliance for Excellent Education.

Hiebert, E. H. (2012). The Common Core's staircase of text complexity: Getting the size of the first step right. *Reading Today, 29*(3), 26–27.

Hiebert, E. H., & Van Sluys, K. (in press). Standard 10 of the Common Core State Standards: Examining three assumptions about text complexity. In K. Goodman & R. C. Calfee (Eds.), *Using knowledge from the past to create the future: Perspectives from the Reading Hall of Fame.* Washington, DC: Council of Chief State School Officers.

Hiebert, E. H., Wilson, K. M., & Trainin, G. (2010). Are students really reading in independent reading contexts? An examination of comprehension-based silent reading rate. In E. H. Hiebert & D. R. Reutzel (Eds.), *Revisiting silent reading: New directions for teachers and researchers* (pp. 151–167). Newark, DE: International Reading Association.

Keeler, C. G., & Langhorst, E. (2008). From PowerPoint to podcasts: Integrating technology into the social studies. *Social Studies Research and Practice, 3*(1), 164–175.

Labbo, L. D., & Reinking, D. (1999). Negotiating the multiple realities of technology in literacy research and instruction. *Reading Research Quarterly, 34,* 478–492.

Lagana-Riordan, C., & Aguilar, J. (2009). What's missing from No Child Left Behind? *Children and Schools, 31*(3), 135–142.

Lipson, M. Y., Valencia, S. W., Wixson, K. K., & Peters, C. W. (1993). Integration and thematic teaching: Integration to improve teaching and learning. *Language Arts, 70,* 252–262.

Lively, B. A., & Pressey, S. L. (1923). A method for measuring the vocabulary burden of textbooks. *Educational Administration and Supervision, 9,* 389–398.

Magnusson, S. J., & Palincsar, A. S. (2005). Teaching to promote the development of scientific knowledge and reasoning about light at the elementary school level. In M. S. Donovan & J. D. Bransford (Eds.), *How students learn: Science in the classroom* (pp. 421–474). Washington, DC: National Academies Press.

McGuffey, W. H. (1836). McGuffey's first eclectic reader. Cincinnati, OH: Truman & Smith. Retrieved March 14, 2011, from *www.gutenberg.org/files/14640/14640-pdf.pdf.*

MetaMetrics. (2000). *The Lexile framework for reading.* Durham, NC: Author.

Moje, E. B. (2008). Foregrounding the disciplines in secondary literacy teaching and learning: A call for change. *Journal of Adolescent and Adult Literacy, 52*(2), 96–107.

Mullis, I. V. S., Martin, M. O., Gonzalez, E. J., & Kennedy, A. M. (2003). *PIRLS 2001 international report: IEA's study of reading literacy achievement in primary school in 35 countries.* Chestnut Hill, MA: International Study Center, Boston College.

Murphy, P. K., Wilkinson, I. A. G., Soter, A. O., Hennessey, M. N., & Alexander, J. F. (2009). Examining the effects of classroom discussion on students' high-level comprehension of text: A meta-analysis. *Journal of Educational Psychology, 101,* 740–764.

National Governors Association Center for Best Practices and Council of the Chief State School Officers. (2010). *Common Core State Standards for English language arts & literacy in history/social studies, science, and technical subjects.* Washington, DC: Author.

National Institute of Child Health and Human Development. (2000). *Report of the National Reading Panel. Teaching children to read: An evidence-based assessment of the scientific research literature on reading and its implications for reading instruction* (NIH Publication No. 00-4769). Washington, DC: U.S. Government Printing Office.

National Research Council. (1999). *Testing, teaching, and learning: A guide for states and school districts.* Washington, DC: National Academies Press.

National Research Council. (2012). *A framework for K–12 science education: Practices, crosscutting concepts, and core ideas.* Washington, DC: National Academies Press.

Paris, S. G. (2005). Reinterpreting the development of reading skills. *Reading Research Quarterly*, *40*(2), 184–202.

Partnership for Assessment of Readiness for College and Careers. (2011, November). PARCC model content frameworks: English language arts/literacy (Grades 3–11). Retrieved March 18, 2012, from *www.parcconline.org/sites/parcc/files/PARCC%20MCF%20for%20 ELA%20Literacy_Fall%202011%20Release%20(rev)pdf.*

Pearson, P. D. (2007). An endangered species act for literacy education. *Journal of Literacy Research*, *39*(2), 145–162.

Pearson, P. D., Spalding, E., & Myers, M. (1998). Literacy assessment in the New Standards Project. In M. Coles & R. Jenkins (Eds.), *Assessing reading 2: Changing practice in classrooms* (pp. 54–97). London: Routledge.

Polikoff, M. S., Porter, A. C., & Smithson, J. (2011). How well aligned are state assessments of student achievement with state content standards? *American Educational Research Journal*, *48*(4), 965–995.

Probst, R. E. (1986). Three relationships in the teaching of literature. *English Journal*, *75*(1), 60–68.

Rader, H. B. (2002). Information literacy 1973–2002: A selected literature review. *Library Trends*, *51*, 242–259.

Resnick, L. B., & Resnick, D. (1992). Assessing the thinking curriculum: New tools for educational reform. In B. R. Gifford & M. C. O'Connor (Eds.), *Changing assessments: Alternative views of aptitude, achievement and instruction* (pp. 37–75). Boston: Kluwer.

Richards, I. A. (2008). *Practical criticism: A study of literary judgment.* Warrington, UK: Myers Press. (Original work published 1929)

Shanahan, T., & Shanahan, C. (2008). Teaching disciplinary literacy to adolescents: Rethinking content-area literacy. *Harvard Educational Review*, *78*, 40–59.

Shepard, L., Hannaway, J., & Baker, E. (2009). *Standards, assessment and accountability.* Washington, DC: National Academy of Education.

Smarter Balance Assessment Consortium. (2012, January 6). Content specifications for the summative assessment of the Common Core State Standards for English language arts and literacy in history/social studies, and technical subjects. Retrieved March 18, 2012, from *www. smarterbalanced.org/wordpress/wp-content/uploads/2011/12/ELA-Literacy-Content-Specifications_010612.pdf.*

Valencia, S. W., Hiebert, E. H., & Afflerbach, P. (Eds.). (1994). *Authentic reading assessment: Practices and possibilities* (pp. 218–227). Newark DE: International Reading Association.

Valencia, S. W., & Lipson, M. Y. (1998). Thematic instruction: A quest for challenging ideas and meaningful learning. In T. E. Raphael & K. H. Au (Eds.), *Literature-based instruction: Reshaping the curriculum* (pp. 95–123). Norwood, MA: Christopher Gordon.

van den Broek, P. (2010). Using texts in science education: Cognitive processes and knowledge representation. *Science*, *328*, 453–456.

Varelas, M., Pappas, C., Barry, A., & O'Neill, A. (2001). Examining language to capture scientific understandings: The case of the water cycle. *Science and Children*, *38*(7), 26–29.

Wang, J., & Herman, J. (2005). *Evaluation of Seeds of Science/Roots of Reading Project: Shoreline science and terrarium investigations.* Los Angeles: CRESST/University of California, Los Angeles.

Wiggins, G. P. (1999). *Assessing student performance: Exploring the purpose and limits of testing.* San Francisco: Jossey-Bass.

Williams, J. P., Nubla-Kung, A. M., Pollini, S., Stafford, K. B., Garcia, A., & Snyder, A. E. (2007). Teaching cause–effect text structure through social studies content to at-risk second graders. *Journal of Learning Disabilities*, *40*(2), 111–120.

CHAPTER 2

Reading Standards for Literature

Jacquelynn A. Malloy
Linda B. Gambrell

The Common Core State Standards (CCSS) for the reading of literature emphasize the sophistication of what students read and the skill with which they read it. It is expected that students will demonstrate steady growth with respect to comprehending more from text and making more inter- and intratext connections. Students deserve instruction using the very best literature because good stories challenge their intellect, inspire their imagination, help them make sense of the world, and nurture their desire to read (Fisher, Flood, & Lapp, 1999; Morrow, Freitag, & Gambrell, 2009). In this chapter, we focus on the reading of literature in grades 3 through 5. Although the reading of informational text is equally important, as discussed further in Chapter 3 (this volume), high-quality literature can be used to promote deep and thoughtful comprehension of increasingly complex texts, and we focus here on the standards for this strand.

Literature is most often thought of in terms of works of creative imagination, including poetry, drama, and fiction. Broadly speaking, however, the term *literature* encompasses a wide range of texts, from creative writing to scientific works, and a range of genres that includes poetry, drama, folktales, myths, fables, legends, fantasy, realistic fiction, historical fiction, autobiography, and biography (Norton & Norton, 2010). The central feature of literature is that it is intended to entertain; however, it can also inform, such as when works are based on history, art, culture, science, and law. The reading of literature promotes self-discovery, enhances our understanding of others, expands our understanding of issues and circumstances, models successful problem solving, and allows us to experience places, people, situations, and relationships we might not otherwise encounter.

Reading well transforms the lives of individuals and increases the likelihood of academic and economic success. If students are to succeed in academics and in life, they must learn to read well, and the key to reading well is comprehension. Reading and comprehending literature involve both "extracting" and "constructing" meaning from written text, with text being defined as a range of material, from traditional books to digital files. Students read and comprehend text by acquiring meaning, confirming meaning, and creating meaning. Thus, reading comprehension can be defined as the process of meaning making (Gambrell, Block, & Pressley, 2002).

The Common Core State Standards for English Language Arts and Literacy in History/Social Studies, Science, and Technical Subjects were designed to support a determined and creditable future perspective: that of preparing students from kindergarten forward with the skills they will need to participate meaningfully and successfully in a global society where critical expertise in an ever-changing communication landscape is vital. With particular regard to the reading of literature, the standards are based on the deep and critical construction of meaning that will afford them the following 21st-century skills:

- The close attentive reading that is the heart of understanding and enjoying complex works of literature;
- The wide, deep, and thoughtful engagement with high-quality literary and informational texts that builds knowledge, enlarges experience, and broadens world views;
- The cogent reasoning and use of evidence that is essential to both private deliberation and responsible citizenship in a democratic republic (National Governors Association [NGA] Center for Best Practices and Council of Chief State School Officers [CCSSO], 2010, p. 3).

These skills are essential for the types of literacy that will be required of learners when they enter the adult world, and underlie the grade-level standards from kindergarten to grade 12. These college and career readiness anchor standards are as follows:

Key Ideas and Details
1. Read closely to determine what the text says explicitly and to make logical inferences from it; cite specific textual evidence when writing or speaking to support conclusions drawn from the text.
2. Determine central ideas or themes of a text and analyze their development; summarize the key supporting details and ideas.
3. Analyze how and why individuals, events, and ideas develop and interact over the course of a text.

Craft and Structure
4. Interpret words and phrases as they are used in a text, including determining technical, connotative, and figurative meanings, and analyze how specific word choices shape meaning or tone.
5. Analyze the structure of texts, including how specific sentences, paragraphs, and larger portions of the text (e.g., a section, chapter, scene, or stanza) relate to each other and the whole.
6. Assess how point of view or purpose shapes the content and style of a text.

"Great! What is your brain ready to do while I read?" Mrs. Cresep prompts.

"Think!" shouts the class.

"Why?"

"Because reading is thinking!" her students enthusiastically respond.

"Excellent. Then let's get to it," says Mrs. Cresep, smiling as she turns to the first page.

What Mrs. Cresep does so well with her third-grade students is to bring attention to their level of cognitive engagement when introducing a new learning task. While she does this to introduce lessons across the content areas, the instructional practice of preparing readers to read is a well-documented part of the scaffolded reading experience (SRE) introduced by Graves and Graves (2003) and supported in research by Cooke (2002) and Laing, Peterson, and Graves (2005). In short, the SRE is a framework for planning prereading, during-reading, and postreading activities that scaffold readers in engaging with text to derive meaning. This vignette of Mrs. Cresep's classroom is an example of a prereading strategy intended to prepare students to listen with a purpose, which should support them in cognitively engaging with the text. Having a question in mind as they begin to hear the story allows them to begin the activity with their brains up and running. Mrs. Cresep makes the importance of cognitive engagement instrumentally explicit in her teaching, referring to their brains as a personal tool that is at their disposal and that requires their attention in order for it to develop. In prompting students to engage in the "every person response" of pointing to their temples when they hear evidence in the story, she is giving them a purpose for listening and interacting with the text.

In the prior example, asking and answering questions is a part of the prereading strategy, but questioning continues as a useful marker of engagement during and after reading as well. In addressing these questions, teachers can guide students to discriminate between information found *in the text* that can lead to answers and what can be inferred about the story when combining what the author offers with the reader's background knowledge. As students move through the grades, teachers can guide their students in keeping their minds engaged in making meaning from the text and in supporting their conclusions with evidence from the text.

Key Ideas and Details: Standard 2

The second standard in this category addresses the following CCR anchor standard: *Determine central ideas or themes of a text and analyze their development; summarize the key supporting details and ideas.* In grades 3 through 5, the standard is broken down as shown in Table 2.2.

The focus of this standard is twofold: first to recount and summarize what was read and then to determine the theme of the story, drama, or poem. In third grade, this is referred to as a central message, lesson, or moral, and is readily accessible in traditional stories such as folktales and fables. As the standard moves to the fourth-grade level, more emphasis is placed on finding support for the theme using details in the text, and at the fifth-grade level, the student is encouraged to explore how characters contribute to the development of the theme. In the following vignette, Mrs. Flemons's fifth-grade students are encouraged to search for clues to the theme of poems by first learning more about the author and his setting.

TABLE 2.2. Reading Standards for Literature: Key Ideas and Details (Standard 2)

Grade 3 students	Grade 4 students	Grade 5 students
2. Recount stories, including fables, folktales, and myths from diverse cultures; determine the central message, lesson, or moral and explain how it is conveyed through key details in the text.	2. Determine a theme of a story, drama, or poem from details in the text; summarize the text.	2. Determine a theme of a story, drama, or poem from details in the text, including how characters in a story or drama respond to challenges or how the speaker in a poem reflects upon a topic; summarize the text.

LITERATURE STANDARDS IN ACTION: KEY IDEAS AND DETAILS

"Yesterday, we explored the life and background of the poet Langston Hughes on the Internet. Roberto, could you please pull out the foam board that has our bio Post-it notes? We organized these into a time line of his life and talked briefly about the period in our history known as the Harlem Renaissance," reminds Mrs. Flemons.

After reviewing the time line and discussing some of the major events in the poet's life, Mrs. Flemons brings out a stack of folders and sets them on the small-group table. "Now that you know a little about the man and the time in which he lived, let's take a look at his poetry. Each of these folders holds copies of one of Mr. Hughes's poems—the title of the poem is on the front cover. I'd like you to look through the folders during free time today and choose one poem that looks interesting to you. You can look through as many as you like, but choose only one and put it in your homework folder. Before we dismiss today, we'll talk about what we're going to do with them."

Later that day, Mrs. Flemons asks her students to pull out the Langston Hughes poem they chose. "Tonight, I'd like you to read your poem three times. Read it the first time silently, then the second time out loud. The third time you read it, I want you to underline five words in the poem that you think are important to what the poem *means*. You know something about the author and the challenges he faced as a writer in the early part of the 1900s. So use this information to think about what he wants the reader to understand from his poem. Tomorrow, we'll set aside some time to share what you think."

The next day, students meet in small groups according to their chosen poem. "So how do your 'important words' compare?" asks Mrs. Flemons. "If you have something different than your classmates, please offer a reason for why you chose the words you did. You may have a sense about what the author is trying to say that is helpful or different. Remember, Mr. Hughes is trying to send a message to us here, and great poets always choose their words very carefully. Take about 10 minutes and see if you can figure out what the message is, and then we'll share what we've got. We'll see if it fits with who we thought Langston Hughes was from our biographical research on him. You may begin now, please."

What Mrs. Flemons is hoping to impress on her fifth graders is that poets have reasons for writing what they write, and that part of their craft is to carefully choose words and arrangements of words to get a message to the reader. As with any good mystery, unlocking the theme to a poem requires some background research on the part of the investigator. For this reason, the preliminary online research on the life of Langston

Hughes and the literary period of the Harlem Renaissance is key to preparing students to determine the themes in his poems. Assigning students to focus on the words they think are important to the meaning of the poem focuses their attention on evidence from the text to support their group discussion of the theme of the poem. In this way, Mrs. Flemons facilitates clear connections between authors and literary themes.

Key Ideas and Details: Standard 3

The final standard in this category addresses the following CCR anchor concept: *Analyze how and why individuals, events, and ideas develop and interact over the course of a text*. The standard is addressed across the grades as shown in Table 2.3.

In gleaning the key ideas and supporting details of text, Standard 3 directs students to attend to specific story elements in order to comprehend the story. In third grade, describing characters and their influence on the sequence of events in a work of literature is foundational to exploring characters, settings, and events in greater detail. In fifth grade, students should be prepared to compare and contrast story elements within a text, which is supported by a fourth-grade focus on describing singular elements well, as demonstrated in the following vignette.

LITERATURE STANDARDS IN ACTION: KEY IDEAS AND DETAILS

Mr. Sullivan gathers his fourth graders to the reading area and instructs them to bring their reading journals with them. As they find seats on ottomans, bean bags, and pillows, he projects an image of a book they read earlier in the year onto the interactive white board. "Remember *Frindle*?" he queries.

"Yeah, Nicolas is still my hero. I wish I could get away with everything he did!" chortles Maurice.

"You do," challenges Kiera, as sniggers of laughter erupt.

"Well, I'm glad you liked *Frindle* because our next read-together is a book by the same author, Andrew Clements," Mr. Sullivan redirects. "It's called *No Talking*, and it pits boys against girls in a battle of wills."

"Oooo—I'll bet I know how that will go!" a voice calls out from the back of the room.

"Well, maybe you do and maybe you don't." Mr. Sullivan smiles. "We'll just have to read and find out, eh? But let's make it interesting. Whenever there's a standoff, like there will be with the fifth-grade students and the teachers in this story, it's helpful as a reader to try to understand the character of each of the main players. What are they like and why do they do what they do?"

TABLE 2.3. Reading Standards for Literature: Key Ideas and Details (Standard 3)

Grade 3 students	Grade 4 students	Grade 5 students
3. Describe characters in a story (e.g., their traits, motivations, or feelings) and explain how their actions contribute to the sequence of events.	3. Describe in depth a character, setting, or event in a story or drama, drawing on specific details in the text (e.g., a character's thoughts, words, or actions).	3. Compare and contrast two or more characters, settings, or events in a story or drama, drawing on specific details in the text (e.g., how characters interact).

" Like profiling someone, right, Mr. Sullivan?" asks Bella.

"Yes, just like that! In fact, that's a great analogy. There are four characters in this book who will have their own reasons for taking a stand in this story: two fifth graders, Dave and Lynsey; the principal, Mrs. Hiatt; and a teacher, Mr. Burton. As we read the first chapter today, choose one of those characters and profile them—that is, take notes about what they look like, what they say, and what they do." Mr. Sullivan projects a new slide of a three-column table with the headings Look, Say, and Do.

"Make a table in your notebook that has three columns, like this," Mr. Sullivan continues, pointing to the table projected on the white board. "You can wait until the end of the first chapter to decide who you want to profile, but I want you to try to become an expert on this character. As we read through the rest of the chapters tomorrow and then all of this week, take notes on how your character looks, the types of things he or she says and does. Then you'll want to think about what this says about the characters and why they do what they do—their reasons and motivations. Try to become an expert on your character and speak for him or her when we talk about the story, got it?"

"Got it!" the class replies.

Mr. Sullivan supports his students in a during-reading activity by having students profile a character. He provides a scaffold for the activity by directing students to focus on how their chosen character is described in the text as well as by what the character does and says. During the reading of the first chapter, Mr. Sullivan pauses frequently to think aloud about these explicit details in the text, supporting students in noticing and recording both explicit details and implicit hints to a character's personality and motivations. As he progresses through the chapters, he is keen to gradually release this responsibility to the students as they become experts on their character and, ideally, begin to offer explanations for why the characters in the story behave as they do. In this way, he leads them to understand story elements in literature in a deep and personal manner.

Craft and Structure: Standard 4

In the category of Craft and Structure, Standard 4 addresses the following CCR anchor standard: *Interpret words and phrases as they are used in a text, including determining technical, connotative, and figurative meanings, and analyze how specific word choices shape meaning or tone.* The standard changes across the grade levels as shown in Table 2.4.

TABLE 2.4. Reading Standards for Literature: Craft and Structure (Standard 4)

Grade 3 students	Grade 4 students	Grade 5 students
4. Determine the meaning of words and phrases as they are used in a text, distinguishing literal from nonliteral language.	4. Determine the meaning of words and phrases as they are used in a text, including those that allude to significant characters found in mythology (e.g., *Herculean*).	4. Determine the meaning of words and phrases as they are used in a text, including figurative language such as metaphors and similes.

Standard 4 begins a focus on the author's craft in creating a work of literature and the structure or form of that work. Specifically, this standard directs the learner's attention to figurative language and words that have classical etymologies. In the third grade, an understanding of literal versus nonliteral words serves as entree to developing facility with figurative language elements, which might include *similes*, *hyperbole*, *alliteration*, *metaphors*, *personification*, *onomatopoea*, and *oxymorons* (*shampoo*). In the following vignette, however, Mrs. Dreesbach's fourth-grade class is attending to classical elements directly by reading and performing Greek myths.

LITERATURE STANDARDS IN ACTION: CRAFT AND STRUCTURE

"Move into your base groups, please," instructs Mrs. Dreesbach. "We've got a job to do and it's going to take a lot of planning and cooperation."

Her students recognize her use of the word *job* to mean that their soon-to-be announced project was going to extend beyond the classroom. Once settled, Mrs. Dreesbach continues:

"As you probably recall from last year, the third graders are learning about ancient Greece." Mumbled confirmation from students greets this statement. "So we've been asked by the third-grade teachers to share some of our expertise with their students."

"So what do they want us to do?" asks Celeste.

"They want us to come up with some dramatic interpretations of Greek myths—to tell some of the stories in an interesting way for the third graders. You can do a Reader's Theatre type of thing where you just read your parts, or a short play with props and acting—it's up to your group. But you need to make it understandable to third graders, which might be difficult because some of the words in Greek myths are not very common and may be hard to understand."

"So how do we do that?" asked Jonathan.

"Let's take a look," said Mrs. Dreesbach, passing out copies of *Greek Myth Plays* by Carol Pugliano-Martin. "We'll read through the first play together and pick out words that might be difficult for third graders to understand. Then we can think of ways to make it easier to understand."

"Maybe we could give them a cheat sheet with the confusing words on them," offered Chelsea.

"Or we could have one of us 'pause' the play and explain words?" Donovan thought aloud.

"All good ideas," agreed Mrs. Dreesbach, "And you can keep those in mind as we read through this first play together. Then you and your group choose one of the plays from the book to work on. Once you've brainstormed what *kind* of 'dramatic interpretation' you want to do, we can make a plan for getting it done."

By reading and performing Greek myths, Mrs. Dreesbach allows her class to explore the language of a classical culture and learn about characters and events that are often alluded to in literature. The activity she chooses to support this standard offers opportunities to explore vocabulary, build fluency through the repeated readings that are required to rehearse a performance, and develop background knowledge of another culture. Having a real audience and purpose for engaging in the activity delivers an element of importance and excitement that gives students a reason to do their best.

Craft and Structure: Standard 5

Standard 5, which continues the focus on craft and structure of text, addresses the following CCR anchor standard: Analyze the structure of texts, including how specific sentences, paragraphs, and larger portions of the text (e.g., a section, chapter, scene, or stanza) relate to each other and the whole. The standard is expressed across the grades as shown in Table 2.5.

In attending to the structure of literature, Standard 5 focuses on the parts-to-whole aspects of various forms of writing, such as stories, dramas, and poetry. Beginning with a familiarity of the terms used to refer to these written forms, such as *chapter*, *scene*, or *stanza*, a more evaluative and critical stance to understanding the completed structure of a piece can be understood, as exemplified in the following vignette featuring Ms. Harrison's third-grade class as they are guided through a series of units on individual forms with lessons in making comparisons and distinctions.

LITERATURE STANDARDS IN ACTION: CRAFT AND STRUCTURE

Ms. Harrison welcomes her third graders back from lunch. "I need you all on the carpet in five, so please put your things away and find a spot—and bring your individual white boards and markers, please."

As students settle in from the break, Ms. Harrison opens a program on the interactive white board. She directs their attention to the board, where a series of words in boxes are floating in a slow progression across the screen.

"We've completed a unit on stories that included chapter books, and then a unit on poems and another on plays. And we've learned a lot of words that have to do with these types of literature. Do you see some of those words here?" she asks.

"I see the word *scene* and it's a part of a play," offers Jasmine.

"Do you agree, class?" Ms. Harrison gestures for Jasmine to come to the board as students respond affirmatively. Then she touches the three icons at the bottom of the display. The words *stories*, *plays*, and *poems* each appear on one of the icons. "Jasmine, could you drag the word *scene* into the icon that looks like a script? Great. A scene is a part of a play. Can someone else tell Jasmine another word that is a part of a play?"

"The word *act*—see? It's right there close to the top of the board," directs James.

"Do you agree that an *act* is a part of a play?" Ms. Harrison queries as Jasmine slides the word to the script icon. "How is that different from a scene?"

TABLE 2.5. Reading Standards for Literature: Craft and Structure (Standard 5)

Grade 3 students	Grade 4 students	Grade 5 students
5. Refer to parts of stories, dramas, and poems when writing or speaking about a text, using terms such as *chapter*, *scene*, and *stanza*; describe how each successive part builds on earlier sections.	5. Explain major differences between poems, drama, and prose, and refer to the structural elements of poems (e.g., verse, rhythm, meter) and drama (e.g., casts of characters, settings, descriptions, dialogue, stage directions) when writing or speaking about a text.	5. Explain how a series of chapters, scenes, or stanzas fits together to provide the overall structure of a particular story, drama, or poem.

"Well, a play has acts and an act has scenes, right?" Sammy suggests.

"Does that sound right to everyone?" Ms. Harrison prompts and students nod in agreement. "So then, what do scenes have?"

"Lines!"

"And how do we know whose line is whose?"

"By the character names," the class chimes.

"They're in all caps," adds Maurice.

"Right. So Jasmine, see if you can find the word box with CHARACTER NAMES in all caps to slide into the script icon. And we'll need to drag the word lines in there as well."

Jasmine drags and drops each of the words associated with plays and dramas into the script icon. Ms. Harrison then asks her to click on the icon to open it, revealing all of the words associated with this literary format.

"Now you get to be clever. With your elbow partner, draw a diagram that shows how all of these words used to talk about parts of a script relate to each other. For example, Sammy already helped us remember that a scene is a part of an act, right? How could you draw that?"

Ms. Harrison gives the students a few moments to draw their diagrams before asking them to hold up their white boards, inviting a few pairs of students to share their ideas. She then provides instructions for center time, noting that one of the centers will be at the white board, where they can work in groups to create similar sorts and diagrams for the literary formats of chapter books and poems. "OK, does everyone know which center to go to first? Excellent! Blue Group with me at the guided reading table, please!"

Ms. Harrison supports her students in understanding the terminology related to forms of literature through the use of organizing structures, such as those that can be developed using interactive white board software. In fact, she has created several "games" for organizing these terms beyond the one just described, and students work in groups during center time to practice their familiarity with them at the white board. One of these activities invites students to mark and refer to actual stories, dramas, and poems by drawing and labeling the structure of the piece on the white board. Her expectation is that students use this terminology when discussing the texts they read together during small-group and whole-class discussions.

Craft and Structure: Standard 6

The third and final standard in the category of craft and structure supports the CCR anchor standard that further fosters critical analysis: *Assess how point of view or purpose shapes the content and style of a text*. The standard shifts its focus across the grades as shown in Table 2.6.

TABLE 2.6. Reading Standards for Literature: Craft and Structure (Standard 6)

Grade 3 students	Grade 4 students	Grade 5 students
6. Distinguish their own point of view from that of the narrator or those of the characters.	6. Compare and contrast the point of view from which different stories are narrated, including the difference between first- and third-person narrations.	6. Describe how a narrator's or speaker's point of view influences how events are described.

As students move through the grades, Standard 6 guides them in developing an awareness of the influence of point of view in order to fully understand the characters and events in a story. In order to develop an understanding of how events can differ depending on a character's viewpoint, students first learn to identify and compare or contrast these various perspectives. In the following vignette, Mr. Maneno's fifth-grade class uses this analysis as a springboard to a Writer's Workshop, where they will write from the perspective of an antagonist in a folktale or legend.

LITERATURE STANDARDS IN ACTION: CRAFT AND STRUCTURE

Mr. Maneno strolls to the assortment of legends and folktales that have accrued on the display shelf in the classroom library. Choosing one of the books, he raises the book, displaying the cover to the class, and inquires: "So, Robin Hood—good guy or bad guy?"

"Good guy," says Trevor, affirmed by several other students.

"Who says?" Mr. Maneno probes.

"Well, he stole from the rich to give to the poor, so that makes him a good guy, right?" offers Ginnella.

"Yeah, but he stole, and that's not a good thing," Marcus reasons.

"So if you were a poor person and Robin Hood stole some money from a traveling merchant and gave it to you, he'd be your hero, right?"

Students nod their agreement.

"But if you were the rich guy he stole it from, he's just a thief," Simon calls out.

"It seems that your point of view makes a difference in the telling of the story, doesn't it?" Mr. Maneno questions as he pulls a book from his briefcase. "Here is a version of the Robin Hood story you might not have heard before." Mr. Maneno, holds up the second book.

"What makes this one different?" asks Meghan.

"This!" Mr. Maneno grins, flipping the book over to reveal the back cover. "This is the story from the point of view of the sheriff of Nottingham. Do you think his telling of the Robin Hood story will be any different?"

"Oh, yeah," grins Alecia. "He's probably going to make him out to be a juvenile delinquent!"

"Well, we're going to read this new point of view of Robin Hood. This will inspire us to think about what other points of view are missing from some of our favorite legends up here." Mr. Maneno points to the other books on display. "Then, my friends, we are going to give voice to some of those characters who might have something else to say about our favorite heroes. Are you game?"

A resounding "Yeah!" from the class reveals their eagerness.

Mr. Maneno is a gifted writing instructor who makes good use of the reading of literature to both entertain and inspire his students. Each year he succeeds in developing a community of writers who read and readers who write, keeping the connections between enjoying and creating stories and other forms of communication productive and invigorating. His students have learned to read with an eye to how a piece is crafted and are guided in deconstructing what makes a good story, drama, or poem "work" before using that information to craft their own versions. This encourages a deep understanding of the author's craft as well as a wide awareness of the various structures that can be used to develop entertaining and informative writing.

Integration of Knowledge and Ideas: Standard 7

Only two of the three standards in the category of Integration of Knowledge and Ideas relate to the use of literature in the classroom. The first, Standard 7, builds on students' maturing appreciation for literature: *Integrate and evaluate content presented in diverse media and formats, including visually and quantitatively, as well as in words.* The standard is expressed across the grades as shown in Table 2.7.

Understanding the visual elements of literature, drama, and poetry in grades 3–5 requires not only an awareness of visual elements but also a sense of how these elements support and enhance the meaning of the text. Moving from an evaluation of illustrations and descriptive writing, students can come to develop a broader appreciation for the visual arts and their contribution to communicating literature. In the vignette that follows, Mrs. Starzyk's third-grade class is beginning this journey.

LITERATURE STANDARDS IN ACTION: INTEGRATION OF KNOWLEDGE AND IDEAS

Mrs. Starzyk has just completed a presentation on the history of the Caldecott Medal awards for artwork in picture books to her third-grade students. Today she carries to each table group a stack of books, one for each student. Each of the books is a Caldecott award winner.

"Today, we're going to select our own Caldecott Medal book. Each of you is going to serve as a judge, rating a book you choose from the stack and then coming up with a nomination from your group."

"Cool," says Peggy. "What are we looking for? How do we decide?"

"Good question," responds Mrs. Starzyk, placing a stack of judging forms on their desks. "The Caldecott judges have five areas that they look at, but we're going to condense it to just three. Look up here at the screen, please." A judging form, which she placed under the document camera, is projected for large-scale viewing. "Here's what the judges might think about when they look at the illustrations. First, is the art really good? That is, are you really impressed with how well the artist created the illustrations?" She uses two of her favorite book covers—one a watercolor and the other graphic art—as examples, giving her justification for why she thinks they're good examples of this criterion. "The second thing they might look for is how well the illustrations help readers to understand the story. For example, in this illustration, I can really tell that the boy is frustrated." She places another illustration under the document camera. "And here, in *The Giving Tree*, the line drawings really help us to see how the tree loves the boy, don't you think? Without these illustrations, it would be hard to imagine how the tree and the boy have this long-term relationship!"

TABLE 2.7. Reading Standards for Literature: Integration of Knowledge and Ideas (Standard 7)

Grade 3 students	Grade 4 students	Grade 5 students
7. Explain how specific aspects of a text's illustrations contribute to what is conveyed by the words in a story (e.g., create mood, emphasize aspects of a character or setting).	7. Make connections between the text of a story or drama and a visual or oral presentation of the text, identifying where each version reflects specific descriptions and directions in the text.	7. Analyze how visual and multimedia elements contribute to the meaning, tone, or beauty of a text (e.g., graphic novel, multimedia presentation of fiction, folktale, myth, poem).

Mrs. Starzyk projects yet another illustration. "And here is the last criterion we can use to judge our books. How well do the illustrations appeal to the intended audience, in this case kids your age? Do they look like something only grown-ups would like or something that is kid-friendly?"

"So do we judge our own book first?" Shannon questions.

"Yes. You'll need to read through your book and pay attention to the illustrations. Are they well done? If so, check the box on your judging form that says, 'The artwork is really good'." Mrs. Starzyk points out the first statement on the judging form. "Then give some thought to how well the illustrations help you to understand the story. Do they help you see the action or understand how a character feels? If so, check the box beside the second statement, 'The illustrations help me understand the book better.' And last, if you think the illustrations are really appealing for kids, check the box by the third statement: 'The illustrations would be interesting to children.' Got it?"

Students nod their agreement.

"Then let's get started! Choose a book from the stack and give it a read. After you've filled out the judging form, meet with your group and talk about whether your book should be nominated for the class award from your table. Only one book can be nominated from a group, so be sure to have good reasons why you think a book is a good choice or not. Try to choose a strong candidate for the class vote and be ready to give a good 'book sell' to convince the rest of the class to vote for the book you choose. We can also have some runners-up if we feel there is more than one good choice. Mrs. Walworth has offered to let us make a display in the media center of our favorite Caldecott winners. So let's get reading!"

At this level, Mrs. Starzyk's third graders are given a purpose for attending to the interactions between text and art by participating in a classwide Caldecott judging event. The judging form that students use to evaluate the books they read support them in applying a critical eye to the ways in which the illustrator contributes to the comprehension of a story and supports the reader in taking pleasure from reading it. In later grades, this awareness can be broadened across a range of visual media and graphical/textual integrations, such as graphic novels and digital presentations.

Integration of Knowledge and Ideas: Standard 9

The final standard that addresses the integration of knowledge and ideas relates to the CCR anchor standard that supports the continued development of students' analytical skills: *Analyze how two or more texts address similar themes or topics in order to build knowledge or to compare the approaches the authors take.* Across the grades, the standard is expressed as shown in Table 2.8.

In the context of integrating knowledge and ideas across texts, students in third through fifth grades begin to look at an author's body of work as well as the themes that are prevalent in different genres of literature, as illustrated in the following vignette. Mrs. Gore's fourth-grade class has just completed a unit that addressed the identification of the theme of a story, or Standard 2, as well as a unit on how geography affects the way people live. Mrs. Gore is now introducing a new unit for the English language arts that will explore traditional tales from various cultures. Let's see how she weaves Standard 9 into her lesson.

TABLE 2.8. Reading Standards for Literature: Integration of Knowledge and Ideas (Standard 9)

Grade 3 students	Grade 4 students	Grade 5 students
9. Compare and contrast the themes, settings, and plots of stories written by the same author about the same or similar characters (e.g., in books from a series).	9. Compare and contrast the treatment of similar themes and topics (e.g., opposition of good and evil) and patterns of events (e.g., the quest) in stories, myths, and traditional literature from different cultures.	9. Compare and contrast stories in the same genre (e.g., mysteries and adventure stories) on their approaches to similar themes and topics.

LITERATURE STANDARDS IN ACTION: INTEGRATION OF KNOWLEDGE AND IDEAS

Mrs. Gore opens the laptop cart and reminds students of the protocol for getting a laptop out of the cart and booting it up. As students set up their computers at their desks, she opens a browser on the interactive white board.

"OK, my friends. We're going to do some exploring today. Someone remind me what the seven continents are."

"Europe, Asia," begins Lindsay.

"North America, South America," adds Chris quickly. His response is followed by moments of quiet.

"We've got three more As left," prompts Mrs. Gore to ignite deeper thinking.

Scott catches her clue: "Australia . . . Africa . . . and Antarctica!"

"Great! Now, do all of these continents have people living on them?"

"Well, Antarctica doesn't really, unless you count the scientists," says Juan.

"For today, we're only going to consider the continents that have cultures on them, so you're right—Antarctica is out." She writes the names of the other six continents on the board. "Because today we're going to find some traditional stories from each of these six continents. Traditional stories are handed down from generation to generation, often told orally, like stories around the campfire. Long ago, people made up stories about how they think things happened, like about how the stars got in the sky."

"Like Greek myths?" asks Sheena. "One of them is about how the sun goes across the sky everyday."

"Yes, very much like that," Mrs. Gore confirms. "Today we're going to find, and then compare, traditional stories about how the world was created, or 'creation stories.' Most native cultures have one, and they might be different from continent to continent." She opens the browser and directs students to the screen.

"Let's talk through how we can find traditional stories and what key words we should use to narrow our search down to creation stories from different areas of the world." She collaborates with students in testing out theories of how to locate creation stories from different parts of the world.

"Great. Now that we know what we're looking for, let's get into groups of four. Each group can choose a continent and find a creation story—a traditional tale about how the world was created. Remember that with a traditional tale the author is unknown. The story was handed down and we don't know quite where it started. Let's get online and see what we can find!"

Mrs. Gore integrates geography and literature in the lesson by leading her class in a search for a particular type of traditional tale from the different continents. This use of literature to compare and contrast the stories handed down in various regions of the world provides an opening to discussion of how geography and culture interact to influence the development of folktales and myths. This integration of social studies and literature supports students in understanding not only the stories they read but also the cultures where they originated.

Range of Reading and Level of Text Complexity: Standard 10

The sole standard in the category of Range of Reading and Level of Text Complexity addresses the CCR anchor standard for proficiency: *Read and comprehend complex literary and informational texts independently and proficiently.* The standard is expressed across the grades as shown in Table 2.9.

Clearly, the goal as students move through grades 3 through 5 is to achieve and maintain proficiency in accessing grade-level texts with independence. Standard 10 requires vigilance on the part of the classroom teacher in assessing individual students and designing appropriate guided instruction to help all students reach grade-level proficiency and in extending these skills as they are able. Reading-level assessment should occur frequently enough that appropriate texts could be selected to support the teaching of Standards 1 through 9 through careful selection of texts, as demonstrated in the following vignette.

> ### LITERATURE STANDARDS IN ACTION: RANGE OF READING AND LEVEL OF TEXT COMPLEXITY
>
> Fourth-grade teachers Andrea and Kathy meet in the school book room during their planning period. They have been charged by their grade-level team to choose book club options that could be used in an upcoming thematic unit on the Civil War.
>
> "I'm hoping to find some good historical fiction this year. Last year, my students really seemed to get a sense of what it was like to live through the Civil War and Reconstruction Era from a kid's point of view," Kathy offers as they preview the texts on the shelves. "I think adding the book club to the unit is a great idea for this year."

TABLE 2.9. Reading Standards for Literature: Range of Reading and Level of Text Complexity (Standard 10)

Grade 3 students	Grade 4 students	Grade 5 students
10. By the end of the year, read and comprehend literature, including stories, dramas, and poetry, at the high end of the grades 2–3 text complexity band independently and proficiently.	10. By the end of the year, read and comprehend literature, including stories, dramas, and poetry, in the grades 4–5 text complexity band proficiently, with scaffolding as needed at the high end of the range.	10. By the end of the year, read and comprehend literature, including stories, dramas, and poetry, at the high end of the grades 4–5 text complexity band independently and proficiently.

"It does make it relatable," agrees Andrea. "But the trick is to find a range of choices that our kids can read on their own, and my students' reading levels are all over the place this year."

"I know," Kathy commiserates. "We have the grade-level equivalents and interest levels here," she adds, indicating the shelf labels under groups of books. "But that's not the best way to tell. Look here, for instance," she continues, pulling a novel from the shelf and leafing through it. "I used this one as a read-aloud last year, and even though it says it has a 3.5 grade equivalent, there are a lot of difficult words in here." She indicates a passage from the text. "I had to stop and do a fair amount of explaining when I read it with the class, which is fine for a read-aloud, but not so much for independent reading. If only it had a few more illustrations to back up some of these geographical references. My kids will have a hard time picturing just how close some of these battles were without them."

"I know what you mean," agrees Andrea. "I think we need to take a careful look at each one of these in order to put together a good selection for them to choose from for the book clubs. The numbers don't give the full story!"

Learning to read well, with deep and thoughtful comprehension, is a journey toward reading increasingly complex texts. One of the key elements of the CCSS for reading literature is that all students must be able to comprehend texts of steadily increasing complexity as they progress through the grades. Being able to read complex text independently and with strong comprehension is essential for high academic achievement—as well as for adult recreational reading down the line. If students do not develop the ability to read complex literature independently, they will read less in general (NGA and CCSO, 2010, Appendix 4). Research suggests that the more students read, the better readers they become (Allington & McGill-Franzen, 2003; Anderson, Wilson, & Fielding, 1988; Cunninghan & Stanovich, 1998; Taylor, Frye, & Maruyama, 1990), emphasizing the importance of developing students' ability to read increasingly complex texts. Accordingly, avoidance of "complex texts is likely to lead to a general impoverishment of knowledge, which, because knowledge is intimately linked with reading comprehension ability, will accelerate the decline in the ability to comprehend complex texts" (NGA and CCSSO, 2010, Appendix 4).

As teachers work with students to steadily increase the complexity of the literature they are able to read with concentration and stamina, they will need to develop skill at determining how easy or difficult a particular text is to read. The CCSS present a three-part model for thinking about and measuring text complexity that includes qualitative, quantitative, and reader and task dimensions. The use of these measures of text complexity will help teachers match texts to students and instructional tasks. The three-part model emphasizes the complexities of making judgments about the difficulty level of texts.

Qualitative Dimensions of Text Complexity

Teachers will need to make informed decisions about aspects of text—levels of meaning or purpose, structure, language conventions and clarity, and knowledge demands—are best measured by teachers, and they will need to make informed decisions about these aspects of text. Toward this end, the CCSS suggest that these four factors should be interpreted as a continuum of difficulty rather than discrete "stages."

1. Levels of meaning: Easier literary texts (less complex) are represented by texts with a single level of meaning, while more difficult literary texts (more complex) are represented by texts with multiple levels of meaning, such as satires, where the literal message of the author is at odds with the underlying message.
2. Structure: The structure of literary texts can range from simple and conventional (low complexity), complex, implicit, and unconventional (more complex). For example, less complex literary texts tend to relate events in chronological order, whereas more complex texts make use of time and sequence manipulations, such as flashbacks and flashforwards.
3. Language conventionality and clarity: Less complex texts have language that is literal, clear, contemporary, and conversational, whereas more complex texts use language that is figurative, ironic, ambiguous, or otherwise unfamiliar.
4. Knowledge demands: Literary texts that make few assumptions about the students' experience and cultural knowledge are generally less complex than texts that make greater assumptions.

Quantitative Dimensions of Text Complexity

The quantitative dimensions of text complexity can be measured or counted, such as word length and word frequency, sentence length, and text cohesion. These aspects are difficult, if not impossible, for a teacher to evaluate efficiently. A number of formulas and software tools are available to help teachers assess these difficult aspects of text and will become increasingly useful.

Formulas to determine text difficulty include the Flesch-Kincaid Grade Level, Dale–Chall Readability Formula, and the Fry Graph Readability Formula. Software currently available include the Lexile Framework for Reading (MetaMetrics, Inc.), ATOS (Renaissance Learning), and Coh-Metrix (University of Memphis). Each of these formulas and software tools has strengths and limitations that need to be considered when assessing text complexity.

Reader and Text Dimensions of Text Complexity

The third dimension of text complexity encompasses reader and task considerations. Accordingly, these aspects of text complexity are related to variables specific to the reader—for example, level of motivation, knowledge, and experiences—and task-specific variables such as purposes for reading and types of questions posed. Reader and task variables must be considered when determining whether a text is appropriate for a given student.

Teachers must use their professional judgment, experience, and knowledge of their students and the instructional tasks to evaluate reader and task variables. Reader variables include cognitive abilities such as attention, memory, and the ability to draw inferences, as well as motivation (interest, purpose, self-efficacy as a reader, and appreciation of the value of reading) and knowledge (vocabulary and comprehension skill). Task-related variables include purpose for reading and the type of reading being done (pleasure, to answer questions, to prepare for a discussion). It is important to note that students need opportunities to expand their reading abilities, but they also need to experience the satisfaction and pleasure of easy reading so long as there is general movement toward texts of higher levels of complexity across the school year.

Clearly, professional educators face a multifaceted task in guiding their students through increasingly complex texts in pursuit of meeting the grade-level standards in grades 3 through 5. Choosing texts that match both readers and standards is a balancing act that requires vigilance and attention to current best practices in pedagogy. In the following section, we discuss the elements of the language arts block that can support this endeavor as well as the teaching practices that are best supported by the research literature.

USING THE STANDARDS THROUGHOUT THE SCHOOL DAY

The previous section provided a look into the classrooms of some exemplary teachers and their implementation of CCSS. These teachers embrace the integration of content-area reading with literature instruction that incorporates technology as classroom tools for learning. While the vignettes highlighted serve as inspiration for the teaching of the CCSS, they need to be viewed within the overarching structure of the language arts block.

Structuring the Language Arts Block

The language arts block is often allotted a generous portion of the school day in most districts. The teaching of literature is well supported by assembling a classroom library that includes a variety of genres with a wide range of reading levels and text complexity. Effective educators are also proficient in creating text sets that include both narrative and expository texts on a topic or author groupings that suit the CCSS and interest levels of the students. Establishing a productive working relationship with the media center faculty can buttress the classroom offerings by rotating selected choices through the classroom library on an interim basis.

The language arts block can be configured in many ways, but should include attention to several specific elements in particular:

1. *Teacher read-aloud.* The teacher read-aloud should play a primary role in presenting reading strategies and new skills to students. The beauty of the read-aloud is that it is supported by teacher modeling and thinking aloud, which permits exposure to literature at a challenging level for the students. The strategic read-aloud should include a repeatable definition of the strategy presented as well as a relevancy statement that supports student engagement. For example: "Prediction is a guess about what might happen next in the story. We make our predictions based on what we already know. This helps us to keep our brains switched on while we read, because we want to see if our guess is right."

2. *Guided instruction.* Small-group, skill-based reading instruction is a crucial element of the language arts block if we are interested in helping students of varying levels achieve the standards on grade level and beyond (see Fountas & Pinnell, 2001). This requires attention to formatively assessing students during the presentation of the skill or strategy through practices such as the "every person response" or through follow-up individual and group activities. Noticing the students who are with you, those who are

lost, and those who are well beyond the targeted learning outcome is essential to forming fluid and dynamic groups for guided instruction. The guided instruction itself requires careful attention to the text–reader match to support students in accessing the learning outcome at an effectively instructional level.

3. *Word study.* As students move across the grades, explicit instruction in decoding strategies and vocabulary can be addressed through targeted mini-lessons on increasingly complex word structures, patterns, and vocabulary that are essential to understanding the texts they read. There are well-researched and easily implementable programs, such as *Words Their Way* (Bear, Invernizzi, Templeton, & Johnson, 2011) and *Word Journeys* (Ganske, 2000), that can be used to structure mini-lessons and follow-up guided and independent center activities that move students through a developmental sequence of increasingly challenging tasks. Word study supports students in word recognition and vocabulary as well as spelling. Additional support for including these elements in the language arts block can be found in Chapters 4 and 7 of this book.

4. *Self-selected reading.* In order for students to fully appreciate the value of the skills and strategies that support the reading of literature, time should be devoted to the independent reading of self-selected texts. Support for this practice is discussed later in this section. Students can be nurtured toward developing personal reasons for reading through teacher and student book recommendations, access to a wide range of genres and reading levels, and support in choosing texts that are at a "just right" level for enjoying independently. Teachers can further support the practice of reading by conferencing with students periodically on their developing reading interests, integration of reading strategies when reading alone, and ability to share what they have read.

Supporting the Standards through Pedagogy

For many students in grades 3 through 5, good reading comprehension comes easily, while for others it is a difficult and sometimes confusing process. Students who are skilled readers use a variety of strategies, become deeply engaged in what they are reading, monitor and evaluate what they are reading, and are able to relate what they read to their own lives (Block & Parris, 2008; Pressley, 2000). According to Pressley (2000), lack of attention to any of these factors will increase the likelihood that reading comprehension development will be impeded.

What is required to improve the reading comprehension of literature for elementary students in grades 3 through 5? Among the elements of effective reading comprehension identified by Duke, Pearson, Strachan, and Billman (2011), the following two are particularly relevant for instruction designed to support students in reading literature with deep and thoughtful comprehension:

1. Provide students with a volume and range of literary texts.
2. Teaching comprehension strategies using literature.

Provide Students with a Volume and Range of Literary Texts

Classrooms where students have ample opportunities to engage in sustained reading provide the foundation that is essential for supporting the development of reading comprehension. Students who are good comprehenders read more than students who struggle with comprehension (Guthrie, 2004). Simply put, reading practice helps students become better readers. A number of studies have documented that time spent reading, or volume of reading, is associated with both reading proficiency and intrinsic motivation to read (Allington & McGill-Franzen, 1993; Foorman et al., 2006; Mizelle, 1997; Taylor et al., 1990). Given the evidence supporting volume of reading, Hiebert (2009) argues that it is surprising that the amount of time students spend in sustained reading of text during the school day has not increased substantially over the years.

In the content areas, text sets that focus on a topic under study, such as a science unit on inventors, could include a variety of genres and reading levels, thereby serving not only as a resource for learning but also as an enticement for reluctant readers. Biographies of inventors and informational books that highlight remarkable inventions could be collected alongside novels and stories on the topic. For example, *The Inventor's Times: Real-Life Stories of 30 Amazing Creations*, which presents inventions as breaking news stories, and the Tom Swift, Young Inventor series would round out a text set with something of interest for a variety of young readers.

Teaching Comprehension Strategies Using Literature

Students require independent facility with comprehension strategies in order to take on the demands of reading increasingly complex text. Block and Pressley (2002) suggest that students be taught to use well-validated comprehension strategies. There are a number of research-based comprehension strategies that, if taught, have been shown to improve reading comprehension (Duke & Pearson, 2002; Duke et al., 2011; National Institute of Child Health and Human Development, 2000; RAND Reading Study Group, 2002). While there are variations across these lists and terminology, there is general agreement that the following six strategies are beneficial: prediction, think-aloud, story structure, visual imagery, summarization, and question generation.

1. *Prediction*. Prediction involves engaging students in using their existing knowledge to make predictions and then reading to confirm—or disconfirm—these predictions. According to Duke and Pearson (2002), prediction is particularly effective in the reading of narrative text. Research indicates that engaging in prediction increases comprehension and memory of stories (Anderson, Wilkinson, Mason, & Shirey, 1987; Neuman, 1988). Several studies suggest also that prediction activities increase story comprehension only when the predictions are explicitly compared with the text, suggesting that the verification process is as important as the prediction process (Anderson et al., 1987; Fielding, Anderson, & Pearson, 1990).

As prior knowledge supports the quality of the predictions made, predicting supports content-area integration as well. For example, when studying the Civil War, a teacher read-aloud using a text such as *Diary of a Drummer Boy* assists students in using their growing understandings of the events of the war to make predictions about what might happen next in the story.

2. *Think-aloud*. This comprehension strategy involves saying what you are thinking (thinking aloud) while engaging in the reading process. Think-aloud has been shown to improve student comprehension under two different conditions: when students think-aloud while reading and when teachers routinely model think-aloud while reading to

students. According to Duke and Pearson (2002), although studies have generally examined the effect of teacher think-aloud when used as part of a package of reading comprehension strategies, the common finding of positive effects across these studies suggests that teacher think-aloud is an effective strategy (Paris, Cross, & Lipson, 1984).

The strategy of having students think aloud also has been proven effective in increasing reading comprehension. It appears that when students think aloud, it decreases impulsive reading behaviors, such as jumping to conclusions (Meichenbaum & Asnarow, 1979), and leads to more thoughtful and purposeful reading. In addition, student think-alouds have been shown to improve comprehension monitoring (Baumann, Seifert-Kessel, & Jones, 1992).

3. *Story structure.* Research supports the value of teaching students to use story structure to organize their understanding of important ideas. For narratives or stories, text is commonly organized according to character, setting, goal, plot episode, and resolution. Research has shown positive effects for explicit instruction in story structure, and the effects transfer to the subsequent reading of new texts (Fitzgerald & Spiegel, 1983; Gersten, Fuchs, Williams, & Baker, 2001; Greenewald & Rossing, 1986; Morrow, 1984; Nolte & Singer, 1985).

4. *Visual imagery.* The old adage "A picture is worth a thousand words" may explain why the strategy of visual imagery enhances reading comprehension. A robust body of literature indicates that students of all reading abilities profit from instruction on the use of visual imagery. When students are provided with instruction and are encouraged to "make pictures in your head," they have a framework for organizing and remembering text (Gambrell & Bales, 1986; Gambrell & Jawitz, 1993; Pressley, 1976). In addition, comprehension is further enhanced when literature is accompanied by text-relevant illustrations, and students are encouraged to use the illustrations in the text to create a "movie in their head" about what is happening in the story (Gambrell & Jawitz, 1993).

As demonstrated in the vignette featuring Mrs. Dreesbach's classroom, supporting Standard 4: Craft and Structure, visualizing can help students to imagine a culture with which they may not be familiar. Developing the lesson, Ms. Dreesbach may choose to have students collaborate on creating scenes, with the assistance of the art teacher, and designing costumes for a presentation to the third graders.

5. *Summarization.* The ability to summarize requires students to read large units of text, determine and differentiate important from unimportant ideas, and then synthesize those ideas in order to create a new coherent text summary that represents the ideas of the original (Dole, Duffy, Roehler, & Pearson, 1991). Research suggests that instruction in summarizing improves not only the ability to summarize text, but also overall text comprehension. There are a number of approaches to the teaching of summarization. The work of McNeil and Donant (1982) focused on a rule-governed approach, teaching students to engage in the following process:

- Delete unnecessary material.
- Delete redundant material.
- Compose a word to replace a list of items.
- Compose a word to replace individual parts of an action.
- Select a topic sentence.
- Invent a topic sentence if one is not available.

Other approaches to summarizing text are more holistic, such as the GIST procedure where students *Generate Interactions between Schemata and Text* (Cunningham, 1982). In this procedure, students create summaries of 15 or fewer words for increasingly larger amounts of text.

6. *Question generation.* Teaching students to generate their own questions while reading literature has been shown to improve reading comprehension. Perhaps the most widely used strategy is Question-Answer-Relationships (QAR), developed by Raphael and colleagues (Raphael & Pearson, 1985; Raphael & Wonnacott, 1985). This procedure engages students in the process of differentiating three types of questions about text: Right There (the answer is explicitly stated), Think and Search (the answer requires searching the text and identifying inferential text connections), and On My Own (the answer must be generated from the students' prior knowledge). Research on QAR and extensions of this procedure (i.e., QAR Plus) reveal that teaching students to ask questions about text improved their ability to generate questions. According to Duke and Pearson (2002), the most compelling evidence for teaching students to generate their own questions comes from the research on teaching routines that include question generation, such as reciprocal teaching and (Palincsar & Brown, 1984) and transactional strategies instruction (Pressley, 2000).

Reading comprehension instruction should be taught using the gradual release of responsibility model, which transfers responsibility for the use of the strategy from the teacher to the student in the following five stages (Duke et al., 2011):

Stage 1: The teacher provides an explicit description of the strategy and when and how it should be used.
Stage 2: The teacher and/or students model the strategy in action.
Stage 3: Teacher–student collaborative use of the strategy in action.
Stage 4: Teacher guides the students in using the strategy, gradually releasing responsibility to the students.
Stage 5: Students independently use the strategy.

Instruction using the gradual release of responsibility model is inherently recursive; the teacher cycles back through the model as students meet increasingly complex texts. As Duke and colleagues (2011) point out, the gradual release of responsibility instructional model represents a "virtuous cycle." Each time students encounter a new topic or a text that is more complex, such as with intricate language or excessively obscure words, they will need a little scaffolding to "get their sea legs" in those new textual waters. The gradual release of responsibility is in keeping with the CCSS in recognizing that instructional scaffolding is necessary and desirable, and that "instruction must move generally toward *decreasing scaffolding* and *increasing independence*, with the goal of students reading independently" (NGA and CCSSO, Appendix A, p. 9).

CONCLUSION

Deep and thoughtful comprehension of literature is the goal of the ELA Common Core standards related to reading for grades 3–5. Key points in the reading standards include the following:

- The standards across grades 3–5 present a "staircase" of increasing complexity in the texts students must be able to read in order to be ready for the demands of college- and career-level reading.
- The standards require the progressive development of reading comprehension so that as students progress through grades 3–5, they are able to gain more from whatever they read.
- Students in grades 3–5 are expected to build knowledge, gain insights, explore possibilities, and broaden their perspective through reading a diverse array of classic and contemporary literature.
- The standards across grades 3–5 mandate certain critical types of content for all students, including classic myths and stories from around the world.

Teachers can support their students in accessing literature across the grade levels by designing a language arts block that provides explicit instruction in targeted skills, strategies, and word study as well as opportunities to respond to literature through discussion and collaborative endeavors. The vignettes provided in this chapter were selected to highlight the use of literature in integrated and thematic instruction and reading/writing connections and to showcase the integration of technology in teaching the CCSS. By carefully choosing texts that match the CCSS and the reading levels of students and providing effective reading instruction, teachers can create a context for developing deep, rich comprehension of literature that supports students in acquiring the literary skills needed to participate fully in a 21st-century world.

BOOKS FOR TEACHING
THE READING LITERATURE STANDARDS IN GRADES 3–5

Title	Author	Publisher
Pushing Up the Sky: Seven Native Plays for Children	Joseph Bruchac	Dial Books
The Ink Garden of Brother Theophane	C. M. Millenq	Charlesbridge
Where the Sidewalk Ends	Shel Silverstein	Harper & Row
Moon over Manifest	Claire Vanderpool	Delacorte Press
Amazing Grace	Mary Hoffman	Penguin
The Invention of Hugo Cabret	Brian Selznick	Scholastic
Math Curse	Jon Scieszka	Viking
Sideways Stories for Wayside School	Louis Sachar	HarperCollins
John Henry	Julius Lester	Penguin Group
Mr. Poppers Penguins	Richard and Florence Atwater	Little, Brown

ACTIVITIES AND QUESTIONS

Activities

1. *Reading Literature Anchor Standards 1–10, Literature Integration.* In grade-level teams, create a matrix of state-level content standards in the column headings (i.e., Civil War, Inventors, Ecology) and the grade-level CCSS for reading literature in the row headings. Using this matrix as a guide, collaborate on choosing texts that are on, below, and above grade level that would be suitable for integrating literature in the teaching of content-area topics. Use this information to create text sets that can be shared among the grade-level team.

2. *Reading Literature Anchor Standard 5, Reading/Writing Interactions.* Looking across the CCSS for writing, choose grade-level literature that exemplifies a style of writing. Develop a checklist of structural elements that can be extracted from the text and then used by students when learning to write an original piece during Writer's Workshop. The checklist can be a valuable tool when peer or self-editing the piece.

3. *Reading Literature Anchor Standard 7, Technology Integration.* Work in teams to create an interactive white board program that includes practice games for various CCSS learning targets, such as was highlighted in the vignette for Standard 5. These programs, once created, can be used for instruction as well as for follow-up center activities.

4. *Reading Literature Anchor Standard 10, Structuring the Language Arts Block.* Given a set period of time for the language arts block, such as 90 minutes or 120 minutes, create a weekly schedule that includes attention to the important elements for addressing the reading of literature during the language arts block, as outlined in the Using the Standards throughout the School Day section. Consider too that literacy instruction can extend beyond the literacy block through the use of integrated units that incorporate the content areas.

5. *Reading Literature Anchor Standard 10, Evaluating Texts.* Choose three to five literary texts that are currently used on a regular basis in the teaching of language arts. Using the three-part model outlined for Standard 10 in the Putting the Standards into Practice section, determine the complexity of each text; in particular, consider the ability range of students who could access each text meaningfully. This activity should guide the teacher in developing a procedure for evaluating texts to include in whole-class, group, and individual reading instruction.

Questions

1. What does the term *text complexity* mean? Discuss what teachers can do to support students in developing the skills and strategies they need to become independent readers who can read increasingly complex text.

2. This chapter contains a list of recommended research-based comprehension strategies. Compare and contrast this list with your classroom practice.

3. What literature genres should students in grades 3–5 be reading? Brainstorm teaching strategies and techniques that are particularly appropriate for various genres that will support students in meeting grade-level CCSS.

REFERENCES

Allington, R. L., & McGill-Franzen, A. (2003). The impact of summer loss on the reading achievement gap. *Phi Delta Kappan*, *85*(6), 68–75.

Anderson, R. C., Wilkinson, I. A. G., Mason, J. M., & Shirey, L. (1987, December). Prediction versus word-level questions. In R. C. Anderson (Chair), *Experimental investigations of prediction in small-group reading lessons*. Symposium conducted at the 37th annual meeting of the National Reading Conference, St. Petersburg, FL.

Anderson, R. C., Wilson, P. R., & Fielding, L. G. (1988). Growth in reading and how children spend their time outside of school. *Reading Research Quarterly*, *23*, 285–303.

Baumann, J. F., Seifert-Kessel, N., & Jones, L. A. (1992). Effect of think-aloud instruction on elementary students' comprehension monitoring abilities. *Journal of Reading Behavior*, *24*, 143–172.

Bear, D. B., Invernizzi, M., Templeton, S., & Johnston, F.. (2011). *Words their way: Word study for phonics, vocabulary, and spelling instruction* (5th ed.). Boston: Allyn & Bacon.

Block, C. C., & Parris, S. R. (2008). *Comprehension instruction: Research-based best practices* (2nd ed.). New York: Guilford Press.

Block, C. C., & Pressley, M. (2002). *Comprehension instruction: Research-based best practices*. New York: Guilford Press.

Cooke, C. L. (2002). *The effects of scaffolding multicultural short stories on students' comprehension, response, and attitudes*. Unpublished doctoral dissertation, University of Minnesota.

Cunningham, A. E., & Stanovich, K. E. (1998, Spring/Summer). What reading does for the mind. *American Educator*, *22*, 8–15.

Cunningham, J. W. (1982). Generating interactions between schemata and text. In J. A. Niles & L. A. Harris (Eds.), *New inquiries in reading research and instruction* (pp. 42–47). Rochester, NY: National Reading Conference.

Dole, J. A., Duffy, G. G., Roehler, L. R., & Pearson, P. D. (1991). Moving from the old to the new: Research on reading comprehension instruction. *Review of Educational Research*, *61*, 239–264.

Duke, N. K., & Pearson, P. D. (2002). Effective practices for developing reading comprehension. In A. E. Farstrup & S. J. Samuels (Eds.), *What research has to say about reading instruction* (3rd ed., pp. 205–242). Newark, DE: International Reading Association.

Duke, N. K., Pearson, P. D., Strachan, S. L., & Billman, A. K. (2011). Essential elements of fostering and teaching reading comprehension. In S. J. Samuels & A. E. Farstrup (Eds.), *What research has to say about reading instruction* (4th ed., pp. 51–93). Newark, DE: International Reading Association.

Fielding, L. G., Anderson, R. C., & Pearson, P. D. (1990). *How discussion questions influence children's story understanding* (Technical Report No. 490). Urbana: University of Illinois, Center for the Study of Reading.

Fisher, D., Flood, J., & Lapp, D. (1999). The role of literature in literacy development. In L. B. Gambrell, L. M. Morrow, S. B. Neuman, & M. Pressley (Eds.), *Best practices in literacy instruction* (pp. 119–135). New York: Guilford Press.

Fitzgerald, J., & Spiegel, D. L. (1983). Enhancing children's reading comprehension through instruction in narrative structure. *Journal of Reading Behavior*, *15*, 1–17.

Foorman, B. R., Schatschneider, C., Eakin, M. N., Fletcher, J. M., Moats, L. C., & Francis, D.

J. (2006). The impact of instructional practices in grades 1 and 2 on reading and spelling achievement in high poverty schools. *Contemporary Educational Psychology, 31*, 1–29.

Fountas, I. C., & Pinnell, G. S. (2001). *Guiding readers and writers, grades 3–6: Teaching comprehension, genre, and content literacy.* Portsmouth, NH: Heinemann.

Gambrell, L. B., & Bales, R. J. (1986). Mental imagery and the comprehension monitoring performance of fourth and fifth grade poor readers. *Reading Research Quarterly, 21*, 454–464.

Gambrell, L. B., Block, C.C., & Pressley, M. (2002). Improving comprehension instruction: An urgent priority. In C. C. Block, L. B. Gambrell, & M. Pressley (Eds.), *Improving comprehension instruction* (pp. 3– 16). San Francisco: Jossey-Bass.

Gambrell, L. B., & Jawitz, P. (1993). Mental imagery, text illustrations and young children's reading comprehension. *Reading Research Quarterly, 28*, 264–276.

Ganske, K. (2000). *Word journeys: Assessment—guided phonics, spelling, and vocabulary instruction.* New York: Guilford Press.

Gersten, R., Fuchs, L. S., Williams, J. P., & Baker, S. (2001). Teaching reading comprehension strategies to students with learning disabilities: A review of research. *Review of Educational Research, 71*(2), 279–320.

Graves, M. F., & Graves, B. B. (2003). *Scaffolding reading experiences: Designs for student success* (2nd ed.). Norwood, MA: Christopher-Gordon.

Greenewald, M. J., & Rossing, R. L. (1986). Short-term and long-term effects of story grammar and self-monitoring training on children's story comprehension. In J. A. Niles & R. V. Lalik (Eds.), *Solving problems in literacy: Learners, teachers, and researchers—35th yearbook of the National Reading Conference* (pp. 210–213). Rochester, NY: National Reading Conference.

Guthrie, J. T. (2004). Teaching for literacy engagement. *Journal of Literacy Research, 36*(1), 1–29.

Hiebert, E. H. (Ed.). (2009). *Reading more, reading better.* New York: Guilford Press.

Laing, L. A., Peterson, C., & Graves, M. F. (2005). Investigating two approaches to fostering children's comprehension of literature. *Reading Psychology, 26*, 387–400.

McNeil, J., & Donant, L. (1982). Summarization strategy for improving reading comprehension. In J. A. Niles & L. A. Harris (Eds.), *New inquiries in reading research and instruction* (pp. 215–219). Rochester, NY: National Reading Conference.

Meichenbaum, D., & Asnarow, J. (1979). Cognitive behavior modification and metacognitive development: Implications for the classroom. In P. Kendall & S. Hollon (Eds.), *Cognitive behavioral interventions: Theory, research and procedures* (pp. 11–35). New York: Academic Press.

Mizelle, N. B. (1997). Enhancing young adolescents' motivation for literacy learning. *Middle School Journal, 24*(2), 5–14.

Morrow, L. M. (1984). Effects of story retelling on young children's comprehension and sense of story structure. In J. A. Niles & L. A. Harris (Eds.), *Changing perspectives on research in reading language processing and instruction—33rd yearbook of the National Reading Conference* (pp. 95–100). Rochester, NY: National Reading Conference.

Morrow, L. M., Freitag, E., & Gambrell, L. B. (2009). *Using children's literature in preschool to develop comprehension.* Newark, DE: International Reading Association.

National Governors Association Center for Best Practices and Council of Chief State School Officers. (2010). *Common Core State Standards for English language arts & literacy, history/ social studies, science, and technical subjects.* Washington, DC: Author.

National Institute of Child Health and Human Development. (2000). *Teaching children to read. An evidence-based assessment of the scientific research literature on reading and its implications for reading instruction* (NIH Publication No. 00-4769). Washington, DC: U.S. Government Printing Office.

Neuman, S. (1988). Enhancing children's comprehension through previewing. In J. Readence & R. S. Baldwin (Eds.), *Dialogues in literacy research—37th yearbook of the National Reading Conference* (pp. 219–224). Chicago: National Reading Conference.

Nolte, R., & Singer, H. (1985). Active comprehension: Teaching a process of reading comprehension and its effects on achievement. *The Reading Teacher, 39*, 24–31.

Norton, D. E., & Norton, S. E. (2010). *Through the eyes of a child: An introduction to children's literature.* Upper Saddle River, NJ: Merrill.

Palincsar, A. S., & Brown, A. L. (1984). Reciprocal teaching of comprehension fostering and monitoring activities. *Cognition and Instruction, 1*, 117–175.

Paris, S. G., Cross, D. R., & Lipson, M. Y. (1984). Informed strategies for learning: A program to improve children's reading awareness and comprehension. *Journal of Educational Psychology, 76*, 1239–1252.

Pressley, M. (1976). Mental imagery helps eight-year-olds remember what they read. *Journal of Educational Psychology, 68*, 355–359.

Pressley, M. (2000). What should comprehension instruction be the instruction of? In M. Kamil, P. Mosenthal, P. D. Pearson, & R. Barr (Eds.), *Handbook of reading research* (Vol. 3, pp. 545–562). Hillsdale, NJ: Erlbaum.

RAND Reading Study Group. (2002). *Reading for understanding: Toward an R & D program in reading comprehension.* Santa Monica, CA: Science and Technology Policy Institute, RAND Education.

Raphael, T. E., & Pearson, P. D. (1985). Increasing students' awareness of sources of information for answering questions. *American Educational Research Journal, 22*, 217–236.

Raphael, T. E., & Wonnacott, C. A. (1985). Heightening fourth-grade students' sensitivity to sources of information for answering comprehension questions. *Reading Research Quarterly, 20*, 282–296.

Taylor, B. M., Frye, B. J., & Maruyama, G. M. (1990). Time spent reading and reading growth. *American Educational Research Journal, 27*(2), 351–362.

CHILDREN'S BOOKS CITED

Appleton, V. *Tom Swift: Young inventor* series. New York: Simon & Schuster/Aladdin.

Brill, M. T. (1998). *Diary of a drummer boy.* Minneapolis, MN: Millbrook Press.

Clements, A. (1996). *Frindle* (B. Selznick, illustrator). New York: Simon & Schuster.

Clements, A. (2009). *No talking* (M. Elliott, illustrator). New York: Simon & Schuster.

Driscol, D., & Zigarelli, J. (2003). *The inventor's times: Real-life stories of 30 amazing creations* (B. Ashburn & C. Sheller, illustrators). New York: Scholastic.

Granowsky, A. (1993). *Robin Hood/The sheriff speaks* (D. Griffin & G. Fitzhugh, illustrators). Boston: Steck-Vaughn.

Pugliano-Martin, C. (2008). *Greek myth plays: 10 Readers Theater scripts based on favorite Greek myths.* New York: Scholastic.

Stewart, S. (1997). *The gardener* (D. Small, illustrator). New York: Farrar Straus Giroux.

CHAPTER 3

Reading Standards
for Informational Text

Donna Ogle

One of the greatest changes for elementary teachers in the implementation of the Common Core State Standards (CCSS) is the expectation that the reading of informational texts will receive equal attention in the classroom as the reading of literature. Many teachers and school districts have built their reading instruction with fiction as the center, giving informational reading short shrift. In addition, social studies and science, natural places to build students' competence in reading informational texts, are often barely taught in many parts of the country (Dorph et al., 2007; Mathis & Boyd, 2009). The CCSS make clear that in classrooms where there has been little attention to informational reading major changes are in order; for students to be college and career ready, they need to be able to navigate a full range of text types, from literary fiction and nonfiction to informational and procedural texts of a variety of types, including electronic sources, articles, and visual displays. Students need to be immersed daily in reading from a full range of materials that are both challenging and richly engaging.

There are strong arguments for a shift in focus to informational reading: The analysis of reading demands of colleges and career preparation programs by those charged with developing the CCSS spotlighted the gap between the complexity of reading materials needed in those programs and the levels of reading achieved by U.S. high school students. In fact, there is approximately a 200-Lexile difference between the texts that graduating high school students can read competently and the average level of first-year college and career texts (Stenner, Koons, & Swartz, in press; see CCSS Appendix A). This finding led to the conclusion that students need to read more challenging texts (at higher levels of complexity) from the elementary grades onward if they are to be able to comprehend the texts they will need to read beyond secondary school (Achieve, 2007; National Governors Association [NGA] Center for Best Practices and Council of Chief State School Officers [CCSSO], 2010).

College faculty have also confirmed that a shift to more reading of informational texts is needed because of the literacy demands beyond high school. Instructors of 1,897 courses across a variety of disciplines at 944 2- and 4-year colleges across the country completed a survey regarding the utility and applicability of the CCSS (Gewertz, 2011). The results from faculty affirmed the importance of the standards in English language arts. According to Gewertz (2011),

> In English/language arts, the speaking and listening skills were the ones seen as the most highly applicable by instructors across the disciplines. Standards in literary reading got somewhat lower applicability ratings. But those focusing on informational reading were seen as highly relevant. Instructors from non-English/language arts courses, in particular, saw the standards for reading in specific disciplines, such as science and social studies, as applicable to their courses. (p. 1)

Support for balancing informational reading and fiction in elementary classrooms comes from many sources. Both the initial analysis of the needs for college and career reading abilities and the response from college faculty underscore the importance of informational reading. The National Assessment of Educational Progress (NAEP) has already incorporated this recognition of the importance of informational reading in the elementary grades and beyond: At the fourth-grade level, the NAEP assessment includes an equal number of literary and informational passages; by 10th grade 70% of the passages are informational and 30% are literary.

Research studies conducted to learn how readers process informational texts and those that have tested particular instructional approaches both point to the reality that informational texts are more challenging and, therefore, deserve more attention, and that such instruction positively impacts students' comprehension (Afflerbach, Pearson, & Paris, 2008; Heller & Greenleaf, 2007; Pressley et al., 1992). The National Reading Panel (2000) provides a good summary of empirical research studies and highlights the value of instruction in summarizing, asking and answering questions, using text structure, metacognitive development, and participating in small-group discussion. It also identifies as efficacious transactional strategy instruction (Pressley et al., 1992), in which teachers introduce, model, and support the use of a variety of strategies as needed, including among others the use of prior knowledge, visualization, summarization, and prediction. This research program involved longitudinal classroom studies conducted with first-, second-, and fourth-grade students.

The more attention elementary teachers give to developing students' familiarity with informational texts and building their strategic approaches to reading, learning with, and critically analyzing such texts, the more likely it is that students will be successful in using more complex texts at earlier grades than is now the case. This is the challenge posed by the CCSS!

A LOOK AT THE READING STANDARDS FOR INFORMATIONAL TEXT

The standards for informational text reading in grades 3–5 are organized into four groups: Key Ideas and Details, Craft and Structure, Integration of Knowledge and Ideas, and Range of Reading and Level of Text Complexity. (It is worthwhile to have this list of standards available as you read the rest of this chapter; see Appendix A, this volume.)

The key to these standards is that students need to regularly develop their ability to read and comprehend increasingly difficult texts so that by the end of each grade level they can comprehend a variety of informational texts at the high end of the text complexity band "independently and proficiently" (CCSS, p. 14); this is the last and key standard, identifying the range of reading and level of text complexity expected of students.

Successful reading is conceptualized in specific standards and is very text based in the CCSS. Comprehension does not prioritize text-to-self or text-to-world connections, for example. Most of the focus is on ensuring that readers develop a deep understanding of each text read, able to use specific examples and details in a text in explaining what a text says or means by identifying key ideas and details (Standards 2–4). Fourth graders are expected to be able to explain sequences of events, procedures, or concepts; by fifth grade, students should be able to explain "relationships or interactions" between people or events, ideas, or concepts in a text.

The standards for understanding craft and structure (Standards 4–6) are very important, especially because they are often overlooked in grades 3–5. In comparison to fiction, where there is one general story structure, informational texts are structured in a variety of ways, and these are critical to students developing an understanding of the texts themselves and to understanding the authors' purposes and perspectives. In third grade, students are to use text features and search tools to locate information within a text; by fourth grade, they are to describe the overall internal structure of the text and by fifth grade to compare and contrast two or more texts.

Within this group of standards, there is one (Standard 4) on determining the meaning of academic and domain-specific vocabulary within a text. (This standard is amplified in the language standards for vocabulary acquisition and use in Standards 4–6.) Attention to vocabulary is important because so much of the content students need to learn is carried in the concept terms. As Marzano (2004) demonstrated, depth of content vocabulary is directly related to students' knowledge; when one has vocabulary and can identify particular ideas, one has resources for thinking.

The third standard in the Craft and Structure section (Standard 6) deals with the identification of one's own point of view and being able to distinguish it from the perspective of the author of the text. By fourth grade, students compare and contrast first- and secondhand accounts; in fifth grade, they analyze multiple accounts of the same event or topic.

The third group of standards relates to the integration of knowledge and ideas (Standards 7–9) both within a single text and across two (third and fourth grades) or more (by fifth grade) texts. Important in these standards is that students learn to integrate various forms of information—visual, oral, and digital—including animations or interactive elements on Web pages. They also need to analyze the ways authors structure their ideas and use evidence. Finally, even in third grade, students compare and contrast key ideas in two texts on the same topic; by fourth grade, they integrate information to write or speak about a topic; and in fifth grade, the standard expands to integration of information from several texts in order to write or speak knowledgeably. These standards can easily be linked to the writing standards, where students should be engaged in several small research projects during each year (see Standards 7–9 for writing).

Comprehension of informational texts requires specific foci and orientation on the part of the reader. To meet the last and summative standard (10)—that students read and comprehend informational texts, including history/social studies, science, and technical texts at the high end of the grade-level complexity band—students need ample opportunities to read a variety of texts on the same topic, just as they have been doing with fiction, so they can build a reservoir of examples of what authors can do in presenting information to readers. The more teachers use exemplar texts and connect them as models for students' writing, the more likely it is that children will be willing to explore the depths of informational text construction and authors' options in presenting their own information and ideas. It is important to note that the standards give little attention to students' personal connections to the content being read. However, research makes clear that comprehension requires background knowledge of the topic, so teachers need to develop instructional frames that help students build on what they know, challenge their ideas, and expand their knowledge and understanding.

PUTTING THE CCSS INTO PRACTICE

In this section, both instructional priorities for teaching informational reading in grades 3–5 and suggestions for organization are discussed. Examples are included from teachers who are already incorporating much of what the standards ask.

A good starting place in thinking of your own classroom or grade level is to assess your students' knowledge of and interest in informational texts and your own program supports. Identify how much informational reading students engage in each day, and make a list of the types of texts they will become accustomed to reading during the school year. Also chart the amount of informational texts you, the teacher, read orally to students during your read-aloud times. To know more about your students' interests, it is helpful to use an informal interest inventory to identify materials you can suggest when students select independent reading materials (Ogle, 2011).

Early in the year you also want to informally assess students' knowledge of the features of informational texts they read (e.g., table of contents, chapter titles, headings, captions, visual displays, glossary, index, bold and italicized items). Several activities and short tests developed by Mackin (Ogle, 2011, pp. 186–188) illustrate how easily teachers can learn what their students already know about text features. In addition, by informally asking students to interpret particular visual displays you will learn important information about their ability to interpret information contained in these formats. With all these data, you can plan a more targeted instructional program.

In schools where there has been a good guidance in developing students' reading of informational texts, third graders may be confident using these features of informational texts, features that are not generally even included in fiction. If students are not familiar with using these features, it is important to start by introducing these and guiding students to use text features when reading both articles and books or textbooks (Blachowicz & Ogle, 2008).

Following are four key guidelines that can help in designing the instruction needed to create secure and competent readers of informational materials.

First, whenever possible, always use more than a single text with students. Even when doing read-alouds, try to present more than one author's perspective. If you use textbooks as core materials, enhance the selections with other resource materials so students begin to think of authors as writers who need to make choices, and select particular perspectives in what they write. When comparing a few texts, students can develop an understanding that major tasks of writers include knowing which information to include and which to exclude and establishing their stance in relation to the material.

TABLE 3.1. Reading Standards for Informational Text: Craft and Structure (Standard 5)

Grade 3 students	Grade 4 students	Grade 5 students
5. Use text features and search tools (e.g., key words, sidebars, hyperlinks) to locate information relevant to a given topic efficiently.	5. Describe the overall structure (e.g., chronology, comparison, cause/effect, problem/solution) of events, ideas, concepts, or information in a text or part of a text.	5. Describe the overall structure (e.g., chronology, comparison, cause/effect, problem/solution) of events, ideas, concepts, or information in a text or part of a text.

As you begin a read-aloud from an informational article or book, identify the author and share some information about him or her. You might ask, "Why do you think the author wrote this?" after reading a section of the text. If there is any content that seems unclear, this can be a good time to suggest that students might rephrase or recast the content. Involving students in thinking like authors can create a much more engaged group of listeners. Once the first text is completed, follow it up with a second and possibly a third, explaining to students they can become more expert in the content and analyze how another writer handled the same or a similar topic. This kind of read-aloud leads nicely into small-group reading, where discussions of interesting aspects of texts and authors can be nurtured.

Second, early in the year, especially in third grade, help students identify some of the most commonly used text organizational patterns in informational materials, often identified as description, chronology, compare–contrast, cause–effect, and problem–solution. Using graphic organizers may provide support for students who are less familiar with these patterns. At a more sophisticated level, asking students to write two to three drafts of a report using a different organizational pattern for each deepens their understanding of ways ideas can be organized.

Some effective teachers introduce these structures as students study a particular topic; they share the tables of contents of several books and help students identify different patterns of organization. As they do this, they are implementing the informational text reading Standard 5. Table 3.1 above provides the descriptions of this standard for each grade level.

The example in the vignette that follows is taken from a third-grade teacher's lesson that focused students' attention on the various ways authors can organize and present information on the topic of butterflies.

INFORMATIONAL TEXT STANDARDS IN ACTION: CRAFT AND STRUCTURE

"We have just read parts of three books on butterflies," says Mrs. Briger. "I want you now to look at the tables of contents for these books." (She displays these on a Smart Board.) "What do you notice about how the author organized the information in the first book?"

Carter responds, "It follows the life cycle from larvae to caterpillar to pupae to butterfly."

"Yes," says Mrs. Briger, "and at the end of the book, did you notice the diagram of the stages of the life cycle so we have a quick summary in visual form? It is interesting to follow the stages of the butterfly's life." (The teacher has her students look at the circle diagram showing the life stages, a good way to visualize this organizational pattern.) "Now, let's look at the second book, *Butterflies and Moths*. Did this author follow the life cycle, or use another way of presenting information?"

Katelynn answers, "This author compared moths and butterflies. The chapters look at different parts of the insects—habitat, descriptions, life stages (that's like the cycle!), connections to humans, and enemies."

"Why do you think this author chose this comparison for his writing?" Mrs. Briger asks.

Ryan thinks aloud, "Maybe so we can think about how different moths are from butterflies. Even though they look a lot alike, they are really, really different!"

Jack adds, "I didn't know there were differences until we read this book, so it helped me a lot. Now I can look at them and see differences."

Mrs. Briger follows up: "So this book helped you understand different things about butterflies and their relatives. Good! We call that using a compare–contrast organization."

Introducing a new book, Mrs. Briger says, "Now, here is the table of contents of the third book, *Great Migrations: Butterflies*—the mystery of the migrating monarchs. What can you tell about this author's interests and way of organizing the book?"

Jack eagerly answers, "Well, I like this book best because it gives us a real understanding of what happens when butterflies migrate—and raises good scientific questions. It's much more than the basic life cycle, but doesn't even mention moths so it stays focused."

"Good thinking again!" the teacher says. "The book follows the time line, or chronology, of the journey of monarchs from North America to Mexico. It also shows where they go, so seeing the map helps readers follow their travels. When we read books with this structure, we can find words like *first, next, on the trip*, and *finally*. Now, I want to share with you yet another way an author has organized a book on butterflies. Here is Kjel's book. Let me show you a few pages and you tell your partner how the author has been able to include information in a different format." (Kjel's is an alphabet book with an in-depth paragraph on each butterfly.) "Let's look at a few more books and see if you can tell how the authors have organized what they want to explain about butterflies and other animals."

Because looking at books and articles from the perspective of their overall structure is often new to students, it requires regular encouragement on the part of the teacher to help them use these organizational structures as they read. These structures are very important to students when they summarize articles and short books they have read. It may help if teachers diagram or map the underlying structures and supply key words that help students move from one main idea to the next until they become confident in knowing how to structure summaries.

Third, students need to take an active role in thinking about the text ideas as they read. A major goal of the CCSS (Standards 1 and 2; see Table 3.2) is that students learn to ask and answer questions to demonstrate that they understand a text; to do so, they also need to be able to summarize or explain the main idea using specific information from the text. This means that teachers need to provide regular opportunities for students to think deeply about the texts they read—both asking and answering questions about the texts and demonstrating their comprehension. One way to build this focus on the text as a whole and to help students think deeply about the relationships among ideas and details is to have them engage in structured forms of comprehending and interrogating texts.

Partner Reading and Content, Too (PRC2) is one such routine that develops deep informational reading (Ogle, 2011). Teachers create text sets of short, informational

TABLE 3.2. Reading Standards for Informational Text: Key Ideas and Details (Standards 1–2)

Grade 3 students	Grade 4 students	Grade 5 students
1. Ask and answer questions to demonstrate understanding of a text, referring explicitly to the text as the basis for the answers.	1. Refer to details and examples in a text when explaining what the text says explicitly and when drawing inferences from the text.	1. Quote accurately from a text when explaining what the text says explicitly and when drawing inferences from the text.
2. Determine the main idea of a text; recount the key details and explain how they support the main idea.	2. Determine the main idea of a text and explain how it is supported by key details; summarize the text.	2. Determine two or more main ideas of a text and explain how they are supported by key details; summarize the text.

books (e.g., Rigby, National Geographic, Heinemann) on major topics in their social studies and science curricula that reflect the range of reading levels of their students. Periodically, throughout the school year, they use PRC2 with the appropriate text set as part of the content units to help students improve their informational reading. When using PRC2, teachers generally have students read with their partners two to three times a week for 20 minutes or more each session. Initially, teachers partner students using test data and fluency snapshots, so both students have nearly equal reading ability and can engage fully. Teachers model how to preview and then read through the book with a partner sitting side by side. In the process, students:

- Preview the whole book, looking at the organization, illustrations, and special features.
- Read the first two pages silently.
- Reread their own page (student on the right reads the right side, student on the left reads the page on the left side of the book) and write a good question for discussion on a sticky note or worksheet.
- Read their page orally and engage the partner in discussion of their question, and then reverse roles and move on to the next two pages.
- Share one of the most important or interesting things learned with the whole class at the conclusion of the PRC2 reading session.

In this process, students learn to attend to the text by focusing on two pages at a time, receiving the author's ideas and questioning and discussing as they read, and in the process become more aware of the vocabulary and discourse style of the author. Students learn that their questions should be meaty—fat, not thin, permitting ping-ponging of ideas between partners—and should be ones the questioner is interested in discussing. Because some groups of students have difficulty constructing their own questions, teachers developed a scaffold to help them get started. On the question guide sheet are four questions:

- What was most important on this page and why?
- What was most interesting and why?
- What was confusing and why?
- How could the author have made this clearer?

For many students, these questions help them better understand ways to think about the texts they read and to gain confidence in their ability to ask questions about the content. Students transfer this active engagement to independent reading by learning to mark texts or write on sticky notes. This partner reading also draws students' attention to the visual displays on the pages, and partner conversations about their meaning are often clarifying and useful. Many students simply have skipped over these forms of information previously, but the more careful reading of the texts helps them expand their focus to all the information.

The following vignette comes from a two-partner discussion as they read a book on science and health as part of their science unit. The two-page spread they are discussing is about the importance of a correct diet for health.

INFORMATIONAL TEXT STANDARDS IN ACTION: KEY IDEAS AND DETAILS

Having just finished reading her page orally to Maria, Alma says, "My question is, What do you think is most important in what I just read to you?"

Maria responds, "There is much that is important in what you read. I think the most important was the effects of obesity. I didn't realize how bad it can be; even diabetes can be caused by bad eating. Do you agree that this is the most important idea?"

Alma says, "Well, I agree that it is important, but I think just as important is what the author says about preventative measures. If you know you can avoid diabetes or heart disease with a good diet and physical activity, you have an opportunity to live a good, long life."

"That makes sense," agrees Maria. "But the author doesn't say what happens if an obese person begins to lose weight with a good diet, and also begins physical activity an hour a day. Will they be able to have a better chance to improve their health?"

"I don't know" responds Alma. "But if someone doesn't do anything, it seems like they will die prematurely. We have to do all we can to help our families learn how important it is to follow a good diet and get exercise. Thank you for helping me think more about what the author wrote."

Experiences using PRC2 have reinforced the importance of providing scaffolds for students to read, ask text-based questions, and be able to answer questions using text-based information. When teachers use PRC2 for several units across the year, they see substantial improvement in students' learning and their ability to read and discuss challenging texts (Ogle, 2011; Ogle & Correa-Kovtun, 2010).

This example illustrates how opportunities to read deeply and discuss informational texts with partners can enhance students' engagement with text ideas and vocabulary. As Alma and Maria showed, they were aware of the "author" of the text they were reading. This is an important component of the CCSS, and is the particular focus of another routine that develops students' careful reading of informational texts: Question the Author (Beck, McKeown, Hamilton, & Kucan, 1997). In this routine, the focus is on developing students' awareness of their own and the author's perspectives by asking questions of the author, in a sense critically analyzing the success of the author for them as readers. This small-group approach to reading and analyzing informational texts is very useful in helping students meet Standard 6 in the Craft and Structure domain. (See Table 3.3.)

TABLE 3.3. Reading Standards for Informational Text: Craft and Structure (Standard 6)

Grade 3 students	Grade 4 students	Grade 5 students
6. Distinguish their own point of view from that of the author of a text.	6. Compare and contrast a firsthand and secondhand account of the same event or topic; describe the differences in focus and the information provided.	6. Analyze multiple accounts of the same event or topic, noting important similarities and differences in the point of view they represent.

Question the Author is a teacher-led discussion that is generally used with small groups as they read content materials. Students are guided by the teacher to interrogate the text they are reading, pausing periodically to think deeply by focusing on what the author has accomplished by writing the text. The teacher models questions like:

What do you think the author was trying to say here?
What is the purpose of this illustration?
What was the author's purpose in including this information?
What did the author leave out?
What else could the author have said to make this clearer?

By learning to ask questions like these, students assume a new role in relation to the texts they read. No longer are they just to absorb and retell what they read; instead, they learn to think about the intent and success of authors. This can be very empowering as it lightens the heavy load of dense content learning by making the readers equal partners with the authors in constructing meaning.

INFORMATIONAL TEXT STANDARDS IN ACTION: CRAFT AND STRUCTURE

Mrs. Haskell leads her class in an author discussion. "Now that we have read these two paragraphs about California before the Gold Rush, let's think about what we learned and how clear the author was in giving us this background. Who wants to tell us what they think the author's main point is?"

Selena responds, "I think the author is trying to make us think there were lots of folks in California even when the Mexicans controlled it. Mexico didn't want North Americans to get the land."

"Good, Selena. How did the author convince you of that idea?"

Selena further adds, "The author said that there were about 150,000 Native Americans and 6,000 Californios—people of Spanish or Mexican descent. That's a lot of detail. However, I wonder how they knew that. Then they give the example of how John Sutter, a Swiss person, did get land."

Thomas contributes, "That may be a good example, but the author also made it seem that Sutter was an unusual man. It says he was a charming man—and he must have been brave or he wouldn't have come to California in early 1800s, would he?"

Lauren follows up: "I think the author should have given more examples of how Mexico kept Americans out of California. All we know is that Sutter got land."

Emily adds, "I also think the authors should have been more clear about Mexico owning California. How did they get it? How could they keep Americans out?"

The snippet above from a small-group discussion among strong fifth-grade readers is shared to indicate how the Question the Author routine shifts the focus of discussion from what the students understand to how well the author has presented the ideas in the text and what might be missing.

Fourth, when reading informational texts, remember that these are authored just as pieces of fiction are, and attention to the author and the quality of the written text can help students understand the role of authorship and writing across genres. Remember that the major changes in the CCSS reflect the importance of immersing students in quality texts that deepen their knowledge and expand their interests and abilities to both read and write for 21st-century demands (see Table 3.4).

In using texts of all kinds in the classroom, ask students to attend to the author of each piece they read, look for other pieces they have read by the same author, and in some cases do some research on the writers of the materials you and they use. Look for information about the authors on the Web and show videos of authors when possible. There are some very interesting writers of informational materials, and some can be highlighted each year. Even when students read textbooks, they can be introduced to the author/team and position themselves in relation to actual authors.

It is important that students read quality texts and supplemental materials by well-known authors. There are many good sources for locating these, among them the National Science Teachers Association and the National Council of Social Studies, which publish their recommendations of outstanding new trade books annually. In addition, the International Reading Association and the National Council of Teachers of English give annual awards to the best informational books, and these lists are published in their respective journals as a resource for teachers. Likewise, librarian groups—such as the American Library Association, Association for Library Services to Children, and International Board of Books for Young Children—have their own award selection lists. Taken together, these provide a wealth of quality books for teachers to use. In addition, guidelines for selecting good books and suggested quality student materials are readily available (see Knoell, 2010; Moss & Loh, 2010; Olness, 2007). The CCSS guidelines for

TABLE 3.4. Reading Standards for Informational Text: Range of Reading and Level of Text Complexity (Standard 10)

Grade 3 students	Grade 4 students	Grade 5 students
10. By the end of the year, read and comprehend informational texts, including history/social studies, science, and technical texts, at the high end of the grades 2–3 text complexity band independently and proficiently.	10. By the end of year, read and comprehend informational texts, including history/social studies, science, and technical texts, in the grades 4–5 text complexity band proficiently, with scaffolding as needed at the high end of the range.	10. By the end of the year, read and comprehend informational texts, including history/social studies, science, and technical texts, at the high end of the grades 4–5 text complexity band independently and proficiently.

determining text complexity (Appendix A) are a good tool for thinking about the range of materials needed in a classroom to suit the variety of purposes and student characteristics.

Most of the books listed in the final section of this chapter were recommended by the children's librarian at National Louis University, Toby Rajput, formerly a librarian for the Chicago Public Schools. Librarians are great partners in selecting the array of reading materials teachers need to stimulate and sustain students' exploration of the world and their particular interests. They should not be overlooked; you can get help from librarians online even if they are not readily available in your community.

USING THE CCSS THROUGHOUT THE SCHOOL DAY

Teachers who have developed integrated units of study using themes from science and social studies will have an easier time adjusting their classroom activities to the new standards. In fact, there are several groups that provide model units criteria and frameworks for such instruction (see *http://engageny.org*; Pearson, Cervetti, & Tilson, 2008). Children need to be motivated and engaged if they are going to read deeply from informational texts; they also need to read several articles and books on the same general topic in order to build their background knowledge so they can be both critical readers and use what they learn in their writing. Teachers can maximize their instructional time and build students' interest and motivation to learn by integrating content instruction with the standards for informational reading.

One example comes from a third-grade teacher, Ms. Scalin, who uses integrated units designed around major social studies and science topics as a framework for building both content knowledge and literacy skills among her very diverse student population (comprising many whose native language is Spanish or another language). One of her first units in the fall is a rich integrated unit on insects. She begins by creating a large K-W-L ("what we know, what we want to know, what we learned") chart that stays on the classroom wall throughout the unit so students can continue to add questions and share information they learn. Early in the unit Ms. Scalin does an in-depth study of butterflies and then helps students select their own insect to research, which forms the basis of a report to be shared with the class. She has developed a large classroom library of books and magazine articles about different types of insects written at the range of reading levels of her students and uses media programs and Internet resources to bring these to life for her students.

Each day part of her reading and writing is taught through the science content; one of her first mentor lessons is helping students identify the different ways informational books on the same topic can be structured (see vignette on pp. 54–55 of this chapter). She uses her fluency snapshot data to partner students at the same reading and language level so they can read science books and discuss the content, using discipline-based vocabulary comfortably. Sometimes she uses the PRC2 framework, in which students learn to read, ask questions of each other, and discuss each page of text. Ms. Scalin also builds her writing instruction into her integrated units. In this unit, the students keep science journals and learn to make observational notes. Their final projects involve writing a report on their selected insect.

By taking advantage of the district's science program, Ms. Scalin can have live insects in the classroom, and each day students chart the changes in the insect (e.g., when

STUDENT TEXTS FOR UNIT ON BUTTERFLIES

Arnosky, J. (1996). *Crinkleroot's guide to knowing butterflies and moths.* New York: Simon & Schuster.

Boring, M. (1999). *Caterpillars, bugs and butterflies* (take-along guide). London: Cooper Square.

Lasky, K. (1993). *Monarchs.* New York: Harcourt Brace.

Marsh, L. (2010). *Butterflies* (Great Migrations series). New York: National Geographic Children's Books.

Opler, P. A., & Peterson, R. T. (1998). *Butterflies and moths* (Peterson First Guides series). Boston: Houghton Mifflin.

Sandved, K. B. (1996). *The butterfly alphabet.* New York: Scholastic.

Wright, A. B. (1993). *Caterpillars of North America* (Peterson First Guides series). New York: Houghton Mifflin.

Web-Based Resources for Unit on Butterflies

www.wingsofhopebutterflygardens.org

www.learner.org/north/monarch

www.readwritethink.org/classroom-resources/calendar-activities/monarch-butterflies-begin-their-20279.html

http://scientificamerican.com/observationblog/KatherineHarmon.11-23-2011
    Monarch butterfly genome gives clues to a slew of migration mysteries.

www.technewsworld.com/story/71681.html
    Butterfly wings offer guiding light for nanotech innovations.

studying the life cycle of a butterfly, students monitored the stages and development—from caterpillar to chrysalis to butterfly. Students, as budding scientists, are engaged in observational research, keeping "field notes" and learning to summarize what they see. They combine these firsthand experiences with what they learn from the print resources and the Web as they build their knowledge.

In the last few years, Ms. Scalin has also found ways to expand her students' awareness of the variety of ways that scientific information is communicated. She introduces her students to two websites about insects and guides them in exploring the resources therein. This last year she found the website *www.wingsofhopebutterflygardens.org* very useful. She was able to show students how scientists chart data using the link to a British article, "The Hot and Cold of Butterfly Dancing," and then contrasted that presentation with one from University of Massachusetts Medical School: "Well-Equipped Travelers: Monarch Butterflies and Their Sun Compass Machinery." Another title ("Butterfly Wings Offer Guiding Light for Nanotech Innovation") provoked a discussion about the meaning of *nanotech* and peaked several students' curiosity about how wings can be that interesting and about the meaning and other uses of nanotechnology, which a few students had heard of elsewhere. With the teacher's guidance, the class looked online for the meaning of the term and compared three different sites. In this investigation, they learned that *nano* is a measurement equal to one-billionth. The class also was able to evaluate the usefulness of the information in the three sites and decided that the nanotechnology for kids section at *www.explainthatstuff.com* was most helpful. Students explained their choice as follows: It gave the specific meaning of "nano," provided a chart with the comparisons of measurements in nanos and meters, and had examples of how nanotechnology is being used. The teacher then asked the class to predict what the article about butterfly wings and nanotech innovations might be about. This whole activity led the students to a broader understanding of how their interest in insects could evolve into very sophisticated science.

CONCLUSION

A major shift for many schools and districts is the CCSS focus on informational reading. The standards elaborate the expectations for students in grades 3–5, starting with the ability to ask and answer questions that reveal their understanding of the texts. This immediately makes clear that students must have an active role in their reading experiences; it is not enough simply to be able to answer questions posed by teachers or to be able to read fluently and rapidly.

Teachers need to invite children into the world of informational materials by creating interesting inquiries and reasons to use the great resources available. Using a variety of text materials helps students identify the differences in the text organization and external features of informational writing compared with fiction. Because informational texts rely heavily on varied graphic layouts of information (e.g., photographs, charts, maps, tables, maps, cartoons), teachers have a real responsibility to show students how to understand these components of texts. As part of the practice of reading regularly from varied forms of information—magazine articles, news stories, books, and online resources—teachers can highlight these important features.

Within this chapter, several activities that put students in the center of their reading and responding to informational texts have been described. These include helping students compare and contrast different authors' presentations of information on the same topic, identifying the text structure used in particular texts and using them in summarizing what has been learned, focusing on the authors of quality texts, and reading closely and discussing texts with partners or engaging in reflection of an author's success as part of small-group experiences.

The more teachers integrate instruction in science and social studies with reading and language arts, the more depth of understanding students will develop. These deeper study units also facilitate students' expansion of academic vocabulary and familiarity with varied forms of discourse. For students who are initially less familiar with the materials and content, engaging them in sustained meaningful and activity-focused units will help them succeed as learners. Providing a rich supply of books and other print materials that students can read independently will also increase their willingness to read more challenging texts and expand their reading capacity. The more students know about the content, the deeper their interests become, and their focus helps them develop the vocabulary central to what they are learning. All of this prepares students for challenging reading.

SUGGESTED RECENT INFORMATIONAL TEXTS
FOR CLASSROOM USE IN GRADES 3–5

Third Grade

Adoff, A. (2011). *Roots and blues: A celebration.* New York: Clarion Books.
Baher, J. (2010). *Mirror.* Somerville, MA: Candlewick Press.
Hill, L. C. (2010). *Dave the potter: Artist, poet, slave.* Boston: Little, Brown.
Martin, J. B. (2010). *The chiru of High Tibet: A true story.* New York: Houghton Mifflin.

Science

Guiberson, B. Z. (2010). *Earth: Feeling the heat.* New York: Henry Holt.
Cole, J., & Degan, B. (2011). *The magic school bus and the climate change.* New York: Scholastic.
Campbell, S. C. (2010). *Growing patterns: fibonnacci numbers in nature.* Honesdale, PA: Boyds Mill Press.
Simon, G. (2010). *Global warming.* New York: Smithsonian/Collins.

Fourth Grade

Capaldi, G. (2008). *A boy named Beckoning: The true story of Dr. Carlos Montezuma, Native American hero.* Minneapolis, MN: Carolrhoda Books.
Nelson, S. D. (2011). *Black Elk's vision: A Lakota story.* New York: Abrams.
Myers, W. D. (2008). *Ida B. Wells: Let the truth be told.* New York: Amistad.
Milway, K. S. (2010). *The good garden: How one family went from hunger to having enough.* Tonawanda, NY: Kids Can Press.

Science

Chin, J. (2009). *Redwoods.* New York: Macmillan.
Montgomery, S. (2011). *Kakapoo rescue: Saving the world's strangest parrot.* New York: Houghton Mifflin Harcourt.
O'Donnell, L. (2007). *The world of food chains with Max Axiom, super scientist.* North Mankato, MN: Capstone Press.
Skerry, B. (2011). *Face to face with manatees.* New York: National Geographic.

Fifth Grade

Freedman, R. (2008). *Lafayette and the American revolution.* New York: Holiday House.
Murphy, J. (2010). *Crossing: How George Washington saved the revolution.* New York: Scholastic.
Sheinkin, S. (2010). *The notorious Benedict Arnold: A true story of adventure, heroism & treachery.* New York: Roaring Brook Press.
Van Rynbach, I. (2010). *The taxing of the cows: A true story about suffrage.* New York: Clarion Books.

(cont.)

Science

Deem, J. M. (2008). *Bodies from the ice: Melting glaciers and the recovery of the past.* New York: Houghton Mifflin Harcourt.

Johnson, R. L. (2011). *Journey into the deep: Discovering new ocean creatures.* New York: Millbrook.

Robbins, K. (2010). *For good measure: The ways we say how much, how far, how heavy, how big, how old.* New York: Roaring Brook Press.

Mortensen, L. (2010). *Come see the earth turn: The story of Léon Foucault.* Berkeley, CA: Tricycle Press.

Sis, P. (2002). *Tree of life: A book depicting the life of Charles Darwin, naturalist, geologist and thinker.* New York: Farrar Straus Giroux.

ACTIVITIES AND QUESTIONS

Questions

1. What are the strongest arguments for balancing fiction and informational texts in grades 3–5?

2. What are the greatest challenges in doing so?

3. What are your best sources for locating high-quality informational texts and magazines? What Web-based resources can you use to enhance your teaching?

Activities

1. Elementary-grade teachers seldom have opportunities to read either high school or college-level texts. Working with a few others, if possible, collect some examples of both of these upper-level reading requirements. List what you see as challenges, and discuss how you are preparing students for these. If you are still preservice, you are more familiar with college-level text requirements; try to identify which skills are appropriate for each level of public schooling.

   To guide your reflection, the following questions can help you identify differences in the reading demands of these texts and those that students read in the early grades.

   • How dense are the ideas, and are connections made to what students already know?

   • How much information is presented visually/graphically?

   • How many vocabulary terms are introduced that need to be known and used?

   • How apparent are the authors, their backgrounds, and their biases in these materials?

2. Adults often have difficulty predicting what students will find challenging as they read informational texts. Select a passage from a social studies or science text used by students with whom you have contact. Make a photocopy of a page

and highlight the sections or components (perhaps a chart) that you think will be most challenging. Then ask a student to read and discuss with you that same section using the original text. Compare and contrast your expectations with the student's understanding. You might also make a second copy of the text passage and ask the student to underline those ideas that are most important on a second reading of the text and even ask the student to summarize what he or she read. By focusing on just one reader, it is often possible to understand more about how he or she constructs interpretation of this text—and probably other texts also.

3. The reading standards for informational text in the CCSS seem well suited to integrated curriculum units. If you are already using integrated units of instruction, take one unit that you may have some questions about and list all the reading materials that you have available for students to use. Identify their lexile levels or use whatever system of marking text difficulty you know and analyze the range of materials students can read. Are there some levels that need more texts? Do you have some challenging texts and others that you use for reading aloud? Are there some materials that will be easier entry texts for less secure students? Do the materials represent a good array of text formats and perspectives? If you need more, go online and find what other teachers are using with the same content; or go to one of the library websites, where librarians can assist you in finding more materials.

If you are not using integrated units, then think of a part of your curriculum that you would like to experiment with and create a map of some possible ideas and ways you could combine teaching content with literacy.

REFERENCES

Achieve. (2007). *Closing the expectations gap 2007: An annual 50 state progress report on the alignment of high school policies with the demands of college and work*. Washington, DC: Author.

Afflerbach, P., Pearson, P. D., & Paris, S. G. (2008). Clarifying differences between reading skills and reading strategies. *The Reading Teacher, 61*, 364–373.

Beck, I. L., McKeown, M. G., Hamilton, R. L., & Kucan, L. (1997). *Questioning the author: An approach for enhancing student engagement with text*. Newark, DE: International Reading Association.

Blachowicz, C., & Ogle, D. (2008). *Reading comprehension: Strategies for independent learners* (2nd ed.). New York: Guilford Press.

Dorph, R., Goldstein, D., Lee, S., Lepori, K., Schneider, S., & Venbateson, S. (2007). *The status of science education in the Bay Area: Research brief*. Unpublished manuscript, University of California, Berkeley, Lawrence Hall of Science.

Gewertz, C. (2011, August 31). Academics find common standards fit for college but academics maintain some skills are missing. *Education Week*, pp. 1, 13–14.

Heller, R., & Greenleaf, C. (2007). *Literacy instruction in the content areas: Getting to the core of middle and high school improvement*. Washington, DC: Alliance for Excellent Education.

Knoell, D. L. (2010). Selecting and using nonfiction in grades K–12 social studies and science. In K. Ganske & D. Fisher (Eds.), *Comprehension across the curriculum: Perspectives and practices K–12* (pp. 246–275). New York: Guilford Press.

Marzano, R. J. (2004). *Building background knowledge for academic achievement: Research on what works in schools*. Alexandria, VA: Association of Supervision and Curriculum Development.

Mathis, P. B., & Boyd, N. C. (2009). Who is teaching social studies? Pre-service teachers' reactions. *Research and Practice in Social Science, 4*(3), 76–85.

Moss, B., & Loh, V. S. (2010). *35 strategies for guiding readers through informational texts*. New York: Guilford Press.

Moss, B., & Newton, E. (2002). An examination of the informational text genre in basal readers. *Reading Psychology, 23*(1), 1–13.

National Governors Association Center for Best Practices and Council of Chief State School Officers. (2010). *Common Core State Standards for English language arts & literacy in history/social studies, science and technical subjects*. Washington, DC: Author.

National Reading Panel. (2000). *Report of the National Reading Panel: "Teaching Children to Read" summary*. Washington, DC: U.S. Government Printing Office.

Ogle, D. (2011). *Partnering for content literacy: PRC2 in action. Developing academic language for all learners*. Boston: Pearson.

Ogle, D., & Correa-Kovtun, A. (2010). Supporting English-language learners and struggling readers in content literacy with the partner reading and content, too routine. *The Reading Teacher, 63*, 532–542.

Olness, R. (2007). *Using literature to enhance content area instruction: A guide for K–5 teachers*. Newark, DE: International Reading Association.

Pearson, P. D. (2009). The roots of reading comprehension instruction. In S. E. Israel & G. G. Duffy (Eds.), *Handbook of research on reading comprehension* (pp. 3–31). New York: Routledge.

Pearson, P. D., Cervetti, G. N., & Tilson, J. L. (2008). Reading for understanding. In L. Darling-Hammond & B. Barron, P. D. Pearson, A. H. Schoenfeld, E. K. Stage, T. D. Zimmerman, et al. (Eds.), *Powerful learning: What we know about teaching* (pp. 71–112). San Francisco: Jossey-Bass.

Pressley, M., El Dinary, P. B., Gaskins, I. W., Schuder, T., Bergman, J., Almasi, J., et al. (1992). Beyond direct explanation: Transactional instruction of reading comprehension strategies. *Elementary School Journal, 92*, 513–555.

Stenner, A. J., Koons, H., & Swartz, C. W. (in press). *Text complexity and developing expertise in reading*. Chapel Hill, NC: MetaMetrics.

CHAPTER 4

Reading Standards
Foundational Skills

Timothy Rasinski
Melanie Kuhn
James Nageldinger

The essential goal of reading instruction is to develop in students the ability to comprehend the various texts that they may encounter in life. In order to comprehend or construct meaning from texts, students are taught to employ various comprehension strategies. Certain comprehension strategies have been shown through research to facilitate readers' textual understanding (see Chapters 2 and 3, this volume). However, in order for these strategies to be employed optimally, students must acquire some degree of proficiency in certain foundational reading skills (Willingham, 2007). The Common Core State Standards for the English language arts (CCSS; National Governors Association [NGA] Center for Best Practices and Council of Chief State School Officers [CCSSO], 2010) has identified specific foundational skills that are essential to reading comprehension in grades K–5: print concepts, phonological awareness, phonics and word recognition, and fluency (see Table 4.1). We illustrate in Figure 4.1 how these skills form the foundation for successful reading comprehension. Reading comprehension requires readers to read text with a minimal level of fluency; fluency depends on readers' ability to decode or recognize the words in the text; and word recognition requires students to have mastered basic print concepts and phonological or speech sound awareness.

Print concepts refers to the ability of readers to recognize and understand basic features or conventions of written texts. These include left-to-right, top-to-bottom, and page-by-page progression of print; recognition of all upper- and lowercase letters of the alphabet; and the understanding that spoken words are represented in print by specific letter sequences and that individual words are separated by spaces in print. Phonological awareness refers to the ability of readers to recognize individual words, syllables, and sounds (phonemes) in spoken language. Print concepts and phonological awareness skills should be mastered by the end of grade 1. (A thorough discussion of these foundational skills for PreK–grade 2 is presented in the first volume of this series.)

TABLE 4.1. Reading Standards: Foundational Skills

Grade 3 students	Grade 4 students	Grade 5 students
Phonics and Wortd Recognition		
Know and apply grade-level phonics and word analysis skills in decoding words.	Know and apply grade-level phonics and word analysis skills in decoding words.	Know and apply grade-level phonics and word analysis skills in decoding words.
a. Identify and know the meaning of the most common prefixes and derivational suffixes. b. Decode words with common Latin suffixes. c. Decode multisyllable words. d. Read grade-appropriate irregularly spelled words.	a. Use combined knowledge of all letter–sound correspondences, syllabication patterns, and morphology (e.g., roots and affixes) to read accurately unfamiliar multisyllabic words in context and out of context.	a. Use combined knowledge of all letter–sound correspondences, syllabication patterns, and morphology (e.g., roots and affixes) to read accurately unfamiliar multisyllabic words in context and out of context.
Fluency		
Read with sufficient accuracy and fluency to support comprehension.	Read with sufficient accuracy and fluency to support comprehension.	Read with sufficient accuracy and fluency to support comprehension.
a. Read on-level text with purpose and understanding. b. Read on-level prose and poetry orally with accuracy, appropriate rate, and expression on successive readings. c. Use context to confirm or self-correct word recognition and understanding, rereading as necessary.	a. Read on-level text with purpose and understanding. b. Read on-level prose and poetry orally with accuracy, appropriate rate, and expression on successive readings. c. Use context to confirm or self-correct word recognition and understanding, rereading as necessary.	a. Read on-level text with purpose and understanding. b. Read on-level prose and poetry orally with accuracy, appropriate rate, and expression on successive readings. c. Use context to confirm or self-correct word recognition and understanding, rereading as necessary.

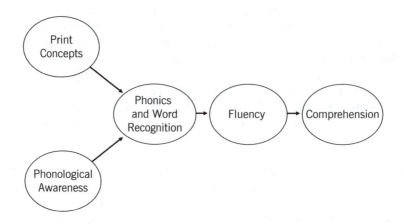

FIGURE 4.1. Foundational reading skills' contribution to comprehension.

Along with print concepts and phonological awareness, phonics and word recognition (henceforth described as word recognition) and reading fluency are also key foundational skills. Word recognition refers essentially to the ability of readers to apply phonics and other word analysis skills in translating the printed version of words into their oral equivalents. Because students are initially exposed to simple and relatively short words in kindergarten through grade 2, word recognition begins at these grades. However, because the words that students encounter in texts are increasingly complex, word recognition instruction continues to be called for in grades 3 through 5 (and generally beyond grade 5).

Clearly, one of the essential differences between reading and listening is that reading requires readers to translate written words into their oral representations. A long history of scholarly writing has advocated word recognition instruction as an essential element in reading programs (Adams, 1990; Chall, 1967; Moats, 2000; National Reading Panel, 2000; Stahl, Duffy-Hester, & Stahl, 1998). Successful reading requires proficiency in word recognition; unsuccessful reading is often marked by difficulties in this essential foundational skill. Juel (1994), for example, found that of 24 students who were poor readers in the first through fourth grades, 22 experienced significant difficulty in word recognition. By fourth grade these students' word recognition proficiency had yet to achieve a level expected of second-grade students. Similarly, Valencia and Buly (2004) reported that 41% of fourth-grade students who failed a state reading proficiency test (a silent reading comprehension assessment) manifested difficulty in word recognition.

Reading fluency refers to the ability to read words in text with sufficient accuracy, automaticity, and expression (prosody) to support comprehension (Rasinski, 2010; Rasinski, Reutzel, Chard, & Linan-Thompson, 2011). As with word recognition, fluency instruction begins at the kindergarten level. However, because texts become increasingly complex with every successive grade, reading fluency instruction needs to continue for most students through grade 5 (and beyond).

Scholarly recognition of the importance of fluency in reading is more recent than word recognition (Allington, 1983; Chomsky, 1976; National Reading Panel, 2000; Samuels, 1979; Schreiber, 1980). Three competencies are normally associated with reading fluency. The first, accuracy in word recognition, has been discussed earlier in this chapter. Word recognition automaticity refers to the ability to read the words in text not only accurately but also automatically or effortlessly. When readers are able to devote a minimal amount of their limited cognitive resources to word recognition, they are able, then, to maximize the resources they can apply to reading comprehension (LaBerge & Samuels, 1974; Rasinski, Reutzel, et al., 2011). Automaticity is normally measured by the number of words a reader can read correctly on grade-level passages. Research has demonstrated a remarkably strong relationship between measures of word recognition and automaticity even beyond grade 5 (Rasinski et al., 2005).

Prosody or expression in reading refers to the ability of readers to read orally with expression that reflects the meaning conveyed by the author (Rasinski, Reutzel, et al., 2011). Prosody is most commonly measured in the classroom environments simply by listening to readers read grade-level material orally and rating students' expression using a rubric that describes various levels of expressive reading. Like automaticity, research has demonstrated strong relationships between measures of oral reading prosody and silent reading comprehension for students beyond the primary grades (Daane, Campbell, Grigg, Goodman, & Oranje, 2005; Pinnell et al., 1995; Rasinski, Rikli, & Johnston, 2009).

Interestingly, despite the recognition of word recognition and fluency as important proficiencies for reading success, recent surveys of experts in the field reflect an increasing attitude that both word recognition and fluency are not and should not be important topics for reading instruction (Cassidy, Ortlieb, & Shettel, 2011). We believe that this diminution of word recognition and reading fluency is largely due to the ways in which they are often presented—for example, through scripted instructional programs, which present them as an outcome in and of themselves and divorced from the goal of reading, which is comprehension.

In the following section, we present instructional strategies for teaching the anchor foundational standards of word recognition and fluency in grades 3 through 5. Examination of the six word recognition and fluency anchor standards for grades 3 through 5 (Table 4.1) demonstrates a spiral of increasingly complex and flexible levels of competency required for each of the standards. Thus, the same basic principles for teaching each of the foundational anchor standards applies for each grade level; the words and texts used for instruction at each grade level, however, should be incrementally more complex and challenging.

PUTTING THE CCSS FOUNDATIONAL READING SKILLS INTO PRACTICE

In this section, we present instructional strategies for teaching the word recognition and fluency standards, along with selected vignettes that describe how these strategies might be applied in grades 3–5. Again, we ask readers to keep in mind the spiraling nature of both the word recognition and fluency standards. Students are essentially expected to continue to develop the same basic competency but with increasingly complex and challenging materials; this may mean that the materials used are taken from content-area texts, such as science and social studies units, or fictional texts that can be paired with content-area subjects (e.g., *Johnny Tremain* [Forbes, 1943] could be paired with discussion of the American Revolution). The strategies that we describe can be applied at each of the grade levels covered in this chapter. The essential difference between the instructional strategies used at each grade level is the focus on increasingly complex and challenging words and texts.

Phonics and Word Recognition

3. Know and apply grade-level phonics and word analysis skills in decoding words.

   Grade 3:
   a, b, c. Identify and know the meaning of the most common prefixes and derivational suffixes; decode words with common Latin suffixes; decode multisyllable words.

   Grades 4 and 5:
   a. Use combined knowledge of all letter–sound correspondences, syllabication patterns, and morphology (e.g., roots and affixes) to read accurately unfamiliar multisyllabic words in context and out of context.

Although there is no one best way to teach word recognition to all students, there are certain instructional principles that can guide the creation of effective word recognition instruction. Two key principles are focusing on word patterns and guided word building. These principles can applied to nearly all the subtopics described in the Phonics and Word Recognition anchor standard.

Focusing on Patterns in Words

In the primary grades, one effective word recognition strategy is to help students recognize consistent letter patterns in words, often called rimes or word families. Rimes are valued because they are found in many English words and are fairly consistent in their pronunciation. For example, the *-are* rime can be used in many one-syllable English word such as *care, fare, dare, mare,* and *stare* as well as multisyllabic words such as *careful, beware, unaware, prepare,* and *warehouse.*

In a similar fashion, there are letter patterns that not only have a consistent pronunciation that also have meaning embedded in them. These patterns are often referred to as morphemic patterns and are often in the form of prefixes, suffixes, and root words that are derived from Latin and Greek (Rasinski, Padak, Newton, & Newton, 2011). Knowledge of one Latin- or Greek-based prefix, suffix, or root can help students determine the pronunciation and meaning of a multitude of words. For example, the root *tract* means to *pull, draw,* or *drag.* Knowledge of this root and its meaning can help students with words such as *tractor, traction, retraction, protractor, abstract, attract, subtraction, contract,* and *extract,* among many others.

An effective way to present morphemic patterns is to introduce students to the pattern, its pronunciation and meaning, and, last, English words that contain the pattern. These words can be displayed for students to read and use regularly in their oral and written language. A special display that is useful for morphemic analysis is a Word Spoke Chart, wherein the word root or affix is written in the center of the chart along with its meaning; then English words containing the root or affix are added to the chart on spokes that emanate from the center. For example, a Word Spoke Chart using the prefix *sub-* (meaning *below* or *under*) would have *submerge, submarine, subterranean, subway, subdue,* and *substitute* emerging from the center. The teacher would guide students in dividing the words into their parts, pronouncing the words, and discussing how the essential meaning of each word is related to *below* or *under.* The following vignette shows how a fifth-grade teacher explores word roots with students.

FOUNDATIONAL SKILLS STANDARDS IN ACTION: PHONICS AND WORD RECOGNITION

There is a crowd around two different boards in Mrs. McNaughton's fifth-grade classroom. She just listed the Latin/Greek root of the week, and the two teams are busy building words. This is something she started doing the first week of school, when she explained to her students that 90% of all the words in the English language that have two or more syllables have a Latin root and that the remaining 10% have a Greek root. Students have been scaffolded to the point at which whenever a new root is introduced, they immediately look for words to build from it. This week's root is *tract.* Mrs. McNaughton tells her students that *tract* means "to drag, or pull." Daniel immediately points out, "You mean like *tractor*?" With that encouragement, the students break into teams and are off and running. They use the affixes they've already learned, such as *con-, re-, dis-,* and *-tion,* and write the new words in spokes around the central root *tract.* Whenever a new word is created, a team member verifies it with a dictionary. After 15 minutes, the two boards are examined, discussed, and combined. Favorite new words are circled, and all the new words remain on the combined Root of the Week board. Throughout the week, students are urged to seek out the root of the week in print across content areas, to report back, and to use their new words in speech and written work.

Students are also encouraged to invent new words of their own, which get posted on Mrs. McNaughton's Shakespeare's Envy list, so called because Shakespeare is said to have invented 8% of the words that appeared in his plays. The students, therefore, get to identify with the bard and come to understand that large, seemingly complicated words are, in fact, quite manageable. Mrs. McNaughton finds that this "divide, conquer, and re-create" approach to vocabulary not only has increased students' word power, but has also created excitement among her students about playing with words and seeing language in a new light.

Given that one root or affix can help students decode and make sense of 10 or more English words, it makes good sense to incorporate them into a word recognition and word study program. Many people who have taken Latin in high school know that their knowledge of Latin has helped them immensely in their knowledge of English words. The problem is that in elementary school these roots are often invisible to students. Exposing students to these roots in quick and simple ways, such as a Word Spoke Chart, helps to make these word patterns visible to students for use in their own reading and writing.

Guided Word Building

Students are more likely to learn a competency if they are actually involved in co-constructing the learning task under the guidance of a teacher. In building words, students work with a limited set of letters to make a number of words predetermined by the teacher. McCandliss, Beck, Sandak, and Perfetti (2003) described a word-building instructional routine in which primary-grade students began with a word such as *pot* and proceed to change, add, or subtract one letter at a time to make a set of new words—for example, *tot, cot, cat, scat, spat, pat, bat, bad, bed, red*. As each word is made by students manipulating individual letter cards, the teacher engages students in an instructional conversation in which letter–sound relationships, letter–sound location with words, and meaning of words are discussed. McCandliss and colleagues reported that students demonstrated significant improvements in measures of word decoding, phonemic awareness, and comprehension.

Cunningham and Cunningham's (1992) Making Words is another form of word building in which students use a limited set of letters to make a series of increasingly challenging words. For example, given the vowels *a, a, e, i*, and the consonants *l, n, p, r*, with each letter on a letter card, students are guided by the teacher to make the following words: *pen, pan, ran, rain, rail, nail, pail, pain, plain, plane, airplane*. As the words are made by students, arranging and rearranging the limited set of letters, the teacher points out sound–symbol relationships and word patterns and elaborates on the meaning of the words. The final word of each lesson is a motivational device as it is a word that uses all the letters. Throughout the activity, students attempt to determine the final word without clues from the teacher.

Making Words can be made appropriate for students in grades 3–5 by increasing the number of letters used for each lesson (choose a final word that is made up of 10 or more letters; see Cunningham, Hall, & Heggie, 2001). Rasinski (1999a, 1999b) added a multisensory feature to Making Words in his Making and Writing Words activity. In this version, students write the words on a form as they work through each lesson with their teacher (see Figure 4.2).

Vowels		Consonants	
1	6	11	
2	7	12	
3	8	13	
4	9	14	
5	10	15	

Transfer

T-1	T-2	T-3
T-4	T-5	T-6

FIGURE 4.2 Making and Writing Words Form.

Following is a vignette demonstrating how one teacher uses Making and Writing Words on a regular basis with his class; in this example, one of the words from the class's science lesson is the basis of their word work.

FOUNDATIONAL SKILLS STANDARDS IN ACTION: PHONICS AND WORD RECOGNITION

Mr. Schubert's third-grade class comes in from recess with energy and enthusiasm. They are excited because it's time to play Making and Writing Words, and they know from past experience that this is fun. The students begin with a sheet that has two boxes at the top to accommodate the letters being used today. One box is for the vowels and the other for the consonants. The rest of the page has boxes numbered from 1 to 15 in which the students will write words derived from Mr. Schubert's clues. Mr. Schubert begins by instructing the students to write the following letters in the appropriate boxes: the vowels *a* and *e* and the consonants *c*, *r*, *r*, and *t*. Many of the students are already working to make words from the letters. Today's chosen topic is the automobile.

Modeling on the overhead projector, Mr. Schubert says, "OK, in box number 1, write a three-letter word that is another word for an automobile." After the students fill in the word, Mr. Schubert completes his own box sheet with the word *car* and models his work—for this and subsequent steps—using the overhead projector for wide-scale viewing.

"Good! Now change one letter to make a word for the sticky stuff they use to repair roads, and write this word in box 2." (*tar*)

"In box number 3, add a letter to *tar* to make a word that you make when you cry." (*tear*)

"Now in box 4 use any five letters to make a word that describes when you make a drawing of a picture by putting a transparent sheet of paper (paper you can see through) over the picture and then draw a copy of the original." (*trace*)

"In box 5, write the word *ace*. Does anybody know what the word *ace* means?" (The class discusses its meaning.)

"Now in box 6 add a letter to the beginning of *ace* to make a word that describes something that drivers of fast cars might do." (After a few moments of discussion, Mr. Schubert prompts, "That's right, the word is *race*."

Mr. Schubert now chooses to ask students for other examples of words that use the rimes *ar*, *ace*, and *ear*. He instructs them to write an example of another word that uses the rime *ace* and another that uses the rime *ear*. He continues guiding the class through other three-, four-, and five-letter words, such as *art*, *cart*, *rate*, *rare*, and *cater*.

Rather than provide a series of clues for the final word in the lesson, Mr. Schubert tells students that it uses all the vowels and consonants in the boxes at the top of their papers. Several students get the word *crater* on their own. Mr. Schubert affirms this word and indicates that they will be encountering this word in science later that day. Mr. Schubert knows that although the Making and Writing Words sheet has 15 boxes, he can stop at any time or extend the lesson when teaching moments present themselves.

In the transfer boxes at the bottom of the page, Mr. Schubert guides students in making additional words using some of the word patterns they have just covered. However, students are not restricted to the initial set of letters in the transfer boxes; instead, they can use any letter of the alphabet. At this point in the lesson, students are guided to make the words *artist*, *started*, *beware*, *careful*, *place*, and *replace*.

Students who do Making Words or Making and Writing Words or other word-building activities such as Word Ladders (Rasinski, 2005a, 2005b) may think of them as games. The notion that word recognition instruction should be gamelike is appealing—just think of all the games that children and adults play that involve word exploration in some way, whether as a board game or on a computer. We believe that beyond their gamelike nature, though, word-building activities allow various features of words and word parts to be highlighted for students. Using a limited set of letters also ensures that students, especially those who struggle, will not be overwhelmed by all 26 letters in the English orthography.

Fluency

4. Read with sufficient accuracy and fluency to support comprehension.

   Grades 3–5:

   a. Read on-level text with purpose and understanding.

   b. Read on-level prose and poetry orally with accuracy, appropriate rate, and expression on successive readings.

   c. Use context to confirm or self-correct word recognition and understanding, rereading as necessary.

Fluency, the second foundational anchor standard for grades 3 through 5, refers to the ability to read words in text automatically as well as accurately, so that readers can use their cognitive abilities to construct meaning instead of decoding. Fluency also refers to the ability to read the words in texts with expression that reflects and enhances the reader's understanding of the passage. Two principles that guide the development of fluency in reading are wide practice and deep practice in reading.

Wide Reading

Developing fluency in any human endeavor requires practice—engaging the competency to be learned often enough so that it can be done with a high degree of accuracy and automaticity (allowing the competency to become second nature). In reading, such practice is normally associated with wide reading (e.g., Kuhn, Schwanenflugel, & Meisinger, 2010), where the goal is to maximize one's reading ability by reading multiple texts, one after another. Adults normally engage in wide reading as they read one book (or other text) and follow it up with a new and different book.

In schools, wide reading is often found in the silent reading of textbooks or trade books where students read a large number of texts sequentially. The teacher provides background, guidance, and elaboration on the texts that are read. Research and reviews of research have concluded that wide reading can lead to improvements in students' reading, especially when the level of support provided by the teacher is matched to the difficulty of the text (Kuhn et al., 2006, 2010; Morgan, Mraz, Padak, & Rasinski, 2008).

Independent silent reading is one way wide reading can be integrated into the classroom; on the other hand, it has been criticized both because of the lack of student accountability for the time spent reading and because students often make inappropriate text choices (e.g., National Reading Panel, 2000). In response to these critiques, Reutzel, Jones, Fawson, and Smith (2008) devised a wide reading approach called scaffolded silent reading. In this approach, the teacher plays a more proactive role in, among other things, helping students make appropriate choices in texts to be read and holding students accountable for the time devoted to wide reading. Notably, Reutzel and colleagues reported promising results from the implementation of their scaffolded silent reading approach. In the following anecdote, Mr. Bascom has adapted scaffolded silent reading for his fourth-grade class.

FOUNDATIONAL SKILLS STANDARDS IN ACTION: FLUENCY

Mr. Bascom's fourth-grade class settles in for silent reading time. Jacob, who came to this school a struggling reader, says this is his favorite time of day: "I get to read books that I like that aren't too hard, and Mr. Bascom always asks me about the story and how I like it and stuff." Mr. Bascom has taken an established reading routine—silent reading—and modified it to ensure all of his readers are able to benefit from it. "We used to believe that just allowing the kids 20–30 minutes a day to read what they wanted was sufficient to increase their engagement with reading and improve overall reading ability," he says. "And we were told that the best thing we could do during this time was to provide a good model by reading something enjoyable ourselves. But we discovered that the students weren't wise in their self-selections, often choosing books at their frustration level and not really reading at all. I had at least half a class of students who became experts at faking their silent reading. I wanted to do something that wouldn't take away their freedom to choose or make silent reading time a chore." His solution? Guided silent reading or scaffolded silent reading, where students still get to choose their silent reading books but are guided toward reading widely at their independent level. Books in Mr. Bascom's classroom library are categorized by genre (including informational texts on science and social studies topics) as well as by reading level.

Mr. Bascom began the school year by explaining how the system worked. On the wall he put a large poster that displayed what at first pale appeared to be a large pizza cut into 12 slices. In reality, each slice of the "pie" contained one of the genres that the students would be reading during silent reading time. Books were sorted in the classroom library and color-coded to different levels. Each level contained at least three books of the various genres. Knowing the reading levels of his students allowed Mr. Bascom to confer with each to identify his or her color. Students were given reading folders that included a copy of the genre wheel for them to keep track of how many different genres they read at their level.

Every day guided silent reading begins with a 5- to 8-minute mini-lesson, with Mr. Bascom modeling the steps for his students. Today's lesson: using context clues to figure out unknown words. Mr. Bascom starts his mini-lesson by picking a word he doesn't know from the text he is reading and skipping over it in the text to see whether reading ahead makes the unknown word clear. If that doesn't work, he then looks for parts of the word he might recognize to see if he can make sense of it that way. Failing that, he looks up the word in the dictionary, which all students have access to, and then adds the term and its definition to his personal dictionary at the back of his reading folder.

After this short lesson, the students take a new or previously selected book and find a cozy place in the room to read for the next 20 minutes. Students are urged to use the three-finger method to determine whether the book is at an appropriate reading level. With this method, students hold up one finger each time they come to a word they don't know. If they end up with three or more fingers by the end of a page this signals that the book is at a frustrational level, and they should find a different book to read. During reading time, Mr.

Bascom confers with individual students, the hallmark of guided silent reading. In these brief (approximately 5-minute) meetings, students read aloud from their books so that Mr. Bascom can get a sense of their rate, accuracy, and prosody. To monitor comprehension, he asks them about what they just read; if the text is informational, he may ask them questions about facts related to the topic. Mr. Bascom then asks when they expect to be finished with their book. Students' responses are written into the running record on the clipboard Mr. Bascom carries with him.

By conferring with four to five students a day, Mr. Bascom is able to keep a finger on the reading pulse of classroom. Students count on his personal interest and are excited to tell him about what they are reading. When they finish a book, students get to choose how they share what the book is about from a menu of response projects, ranging from a graphic organizer to a movie-type poster.

With the 20-minute scaffolded silent reading time now coming to an end, students quietly return the books to their leveled bins, and their folders containing the genre wheel and their personal response projects are put away until tomorrow's eagerly awaited lesson.

By guiding students to appropriately leveled texts and holding them accountable for the 20 minutes devoted to silent independent reading, students are actually reading from a variety of genres (some more personally challenging than others). They are no longer frustrated with materials that are too difficult or perseverating on only one genre or type of text. In fact, the design of the approach ensures students are exposed to a range of genres, from science fiction to science fact and from historical fiction to historical nonfiction or informational texts. Ideally, this will expose students to types of text they might not select if left to choose entirely on their own, many of which they may unexpectedly find enjoyable. Furthermore, highly engaging wide reading practice will indeed lead to improved reading. Although 20 minutes per school day may not seem to be much time, over the course of a 180-day school year, this daily silent reading time adds up to 60 hours of engaged reading. That amount of reading will definitely make a positive difference in students' fluency and overall reading achievement.

Deep Reading—Repeated Reading

It is not unusual for students to read material that is somewhat challenging. However, their initial reading of that text is unlikely to be good; word recognition is slow and labored, and prosody is nonexistent as students engage in word-by-word, monotone reading. In these cases, students need to move beyond wide reading (reading the text once) to deep or repeated reading, where a passage is rehearsed several times until the reader can read it with high levels of accuracy, automaticity, and expression. Not only can this be helpful with complex narrative text, but it is a particularly useful strategy with informational text that is likely to be introducing new concepts as well as new vocabulary.

Research into repeated or deep reading over the past 30 years or more has demonstrated that this form of practice also yields improvements in students' reading fluency and overall reading achievement (Rasinski, Reutzel, et al., 2011). Some repeated reading and fluency practices and assessments have been criticized as overly focused on reading speed, with minimal attention to prosody and comprehension (Rasinski, 2006; Rasinski & Hamman, 2010; Samuels, 2007). Although repeated reading is a proven method for improving fluency, care must be taken in how repeated reading is actually implemented in classroom settings. Just as actors rehearse a written text for the purpose of performing the text for an audience, students can engage in repeated readings (or rehearsal) of texts that will eventually be performed for an audience. By repeatedly reading the text, students will develop word recognition accuracy and automaticity. However, since their rehearsal is aimed at an eventual performance, students' goal is an oral reading that is filled with expression, one that reflects and enhances the meaning of the reading for a listening audience. Texts that lend themselves to deep practice and performance include poetry, Reader's Theatre scripts, famous speeches from history, and written portions of more extended texts written with a strong voice that allows for expressive reading. Research into this practice and performance approach to deep reading has shown very promising results beyond second grade (Rasinski, Reutzel, et al., 2011).

Clearly, students who engage in deep practice of their assigned text will improve in their reading of that text. However, research has shown that the improvement generalizes to new, never-before-read texts. And, when engaged in on a regular basis, students will make great strides in fluency and overall reading achievement through regular deep reading that involves practice and performance.

Interestingly, Stahl, Heubach, and Holcomb (2005) found that students who engaged in repeated reading of more challenging materials made greater progress than those who engaged in repeated reading at their instructional level. If students are asked to repeatedly read a passage and are given support in their rehearsal, it makes good sense that they will be able to handle more challenging materials. The Common Core State Standards (NGA and CCSSO, 2010) calls for teachers to engage students in more challenging reading, and the use of repeated readings is one method that effectively engages students in mastering more demanding materials. In doing so, we may also expect students to accelerate their reading progress.

For students who need a more intensive form of repeated readings, there is the fluency development lesson (FDL; Rasinski, Padak, Linek, & Sturtevant, 1994), a daily 20-minute instruction in which students master a 100- to 200-word passage. Not only does it involve repeated readings (in school and at home), but it also involves word study, teacher modeling of the reading, and a brief discussion of the passage, the text is read with the assistance of classmates and the teacher. The FDL is the core reading lesson used, with great success, in the Kent State University Reading Clinic.

FOUNDATIONAL SKILLS STANDARDS IN ACTION: FLUENCY

Ms. Martin loves to read aloud to her third-grade students, most of whom struggle in reading. During her daily FDL, she models good expressive reading in an interactive activity that delights the students. Ms. Martin starts each lesson by introducing a new short text: either a poem, a segment from a basal passage, or a trade book selection. Today she chooses Shel Silverstein's poem "One Inch Tall." All the students have a copy in front of them, and Ms. Martin also displays the poem for large-scale viewing using the overhead projector. She reads the poem several times as the students follow along silently. During her readings, Ms. Martin models both fluent and disfluent renditions and asks the students which versions they prefer. As part of their discussion of the nature and content of the poem, the class becomes divided over whether or not it would be really cool to be an inch tall. Then with Ms. Martin leading, the class reads the passage chorally several times. To keep it interesting, today she has the boys and girls antiphonally read alternate lines. At other times, she will use call and response or direct the students to read specific lines at different volumes.

After the readings, Ms. Martin organizes her class into groups of two and three. Each student practices the poem two or three times while the partners listen and provide support and encouragement. Today the groups are performing for the vice principal, who enjoys coming to the class to hear students read their poem. After the performances, the students choose a number of words from the poem they especially like. This time, they choose *teardrop, fluff, surf,* and *beast,* while Ms. Martin adds the words *crumb, thread,* and *thimble.* The students also add their favorite words to their individual word banks, and the words will later be displayed so that they are accessible to the class.

For the next 10 minutes, Ms. Martin takes sets of words she had pulled from the poem earlier and passes them out for the students to sort into categories of their choosing. She knows that interaction with words and word associations develop higher level thinking. On different days, she plans other activities such as word games, flash card practice, definitions matches, or crossword puzzles.

Ms. Martin instructs her students to take home the poem and encourages them to practice it with family members or friends. Tomorrow they will get a chance to read the poem one more time for either Ms. Martin or another student for accuracy, fluency, and expression. Words from today and previous days will be revisited through more word play activities. After rereading the previous day's poem, Ms. Martin and her students will begin the FDL routine once again.

Because the FDL is a daily routine, students know exactly what is expected of them each day. Very little instructional time is used for explanation of procedures. Through this form of daily fluency instruction, striving students are able to read a text accurately, automatically, expressively, and with good comprehension on a daily basis. The FDL's impact on students' fluency, reading achievement, and attitude toward reading in the Kent State University Reading Clinic has been remarkable (Zimmerman & Rasinski, 2012).

USING THE FOUNDATIONAL SKILLS STANDARDS THROUGHOUT THE SCHOOL DAY

Although some models of reading development posit that foundational skills in reading should be mastered by grade 2 (e.g., Chall, 1996), it is clear that many students in grade 3 and beyond have yet to achieve sufficient mastery in word recognition and fluency. As a result, they are unlikely to be able read grade-level materials or materials from less familiar genres fluently and with good comprehension. Moreover, because reading materials become more complex as students enter the upper elementary grades and the words they encounter in their academic and other reading are progressively more challenging, it seems clear that instruction in foundational skills should continue for most students. Although we recognize that there is no one way to teach the foundational Common Core standards, we present successful approaches that we have observed.

In Cunningham's (2006) four-block reading curriculum, one block of daily time is reserved for word study. Although initially viewed as a model for the primary grades, Cunningham suggests that it is also appropriate for the upper elementary grades. We

TABLE 5.1. *(cont.)*

Grade 3	Grade 4 (changes)	Grade 5 (changes)
b. Use dialogue and descriptions of actions, thoughts, and feelings to develop experiences and events or show the response of characters to situations.	Use dialogue and description to develop experiences and events or show the responses of characters to situations.	Use **narrative techniques, such as** dialogue, description, **and pacing,** to develop experiences . . .
c. Use temporal words and phrases to signal event order.	Use **a variety of transitional words and phrases to manage the sequence of events.**	
	Use concrete words and phrases and sensory details to convey experiences and events precisely.	(no change)
d. Provide a sense of closure.	Provide a **conclusion that follows from the narrated experiences or events.**	(no change)

Note. Changes from one grade to the next are in bold.

As noted earlier, the standards for opinion, informative, and narrative writing focus on the basic genre elements and structure for each type of writing. Changes from one grade level to the next are relatively minor, often involving a further specification on the quality or structure of a specific element. Examples include how ideas are presented ("clearly") or ordered ("related ideas presented together"), what types of vocabulary ("concrete words") and linking words ("consequently") are used by the writer, and what needs to be added to the text ("facts and details").

A tested evidence-based writing practice that is effective in helping students in grades 3–5 write the type of text emphasized in the CCSS is to teach them directly about the characteristics of such text (Graham et al., in press). This involves exposing them to the basic structural elements of a genre such as story writing and then encouraging them to write papers where they include these elements. The elements can be genre specific (e.g., opinion, reasons to support opinions), generic (e.g., words that sparkle, vary sentence structure), or both. This practice can be repeated at each grade level for each type of writing, with teachers reinforcing characteristics, elements, and structures presented in the previous grade and introducing new attributes that address and even surpass the specifications put forth in the CCSS. Such instruction provides models for students' writing and develops a common language for students and teachers to use when discussing writing. A list of books that provide models for narrative, persuasive, and informative text are presented at the end of the chapter. It is important to note that these texts are much longer than what students in grades 3–5 normally write, but they can be used to illustrate the basic elements of these three types of writing.

WRITING STANDARDS IN ACTION: TEACHING STUDENTS ABOUT THE CHARACTERISTICS AND STRUCTURE OF TEXT

Mr. Longmire initiates a discussion with his third graders about the characteristics of good stories. As they generate their ideas, he lists them on the white board, providing a label for common narrative elements such as "narrator" and "event sequence." Next, they read a story together and talk about the characteristics of the story that made it so enjoyable. Then they conduct a "story hunt" to find and discuss other story elements that were listed on white board and to add any new elements, characteristics, or structures they identified. Again, Mr. Longmire provides labels for these elements or characteristics (e.g., "sensory details").

Over the next 2 days, the class reads and discusses the characteristics of four additional stories, using the vocabulary they developed on Day 1 to analyze and evaluate these stories. Special emphasis is placed on what the writer did to make the stories interesting and meaningful. The last two stories were written by third- and fourth-grade children and contain the basic elements emphasized in the CCSS for third grade. Students are asked to use one or more of these stories as a model in generating their own narrative. They share their stories with one or more peers (and in some instances with the class), receiving feedback on what worked and how they could make their story even better. As they develop new stories, they are encouraged to go beyond the initial models they used as a guide.

PRODUCTION AND DISTRIBUTION OF WRITING

The basic goal for Production and Distribution of Writing is for students to produce and publish (using traditional and electronic writing tools) well-organized text appropriate to their task and purpose using planning, revising, editing, and collaboration as mechanisms for crafting and strengthening their written ideas. Table 5.2 presents Production and Distribution of Writing standards for grades 3–5. The standards for grade 3 are presented in their entirety. For grades 4 and 5, only the part of the standard where a change was made is presented, with all changes in bold print.

A primary change from one grade to the next in the CCSS for Production and Distribution of Writing involves the amount of guidance and support provided by teachers and peers, with diminishing support provided in higher grades (see Table 5.2). The only exception to this involves strengthening writing through planning, revising, and editing, where support from teacher and peers remains constant. While students clearly need teacher and peer support to meet these standards, I encourage you to work toward independent mastery of these goals at each grade level. For example, my colleagues and I have found that with appropriate instruction students in these and earlier grades can learn to apply planning, drafting, and other writing strategies effectively and independently (see Graham, Harris, & Mason, 2005; Harris, Graham, & Mason, 2006).

A tested evidence-based writing practice that is effective in helping students plan, revise, edit, and rewrite text so that they produce and publish well-organized persuasive, informative, and narrative text is strategy instruction (Graham et al., in press). With strategy instruction, students are explicitly and directly taught strategies for planning, drafting, revising, and editing text. While these strategies can be generic, such as brainstorming and semantic webbing, they typically involve techniques that are tied directly to the basic features of the type of text students are creating. For instance, a planning strategy for helping students generate possible ideas for story writing involves thinking about the goals of the main character in a story, where the story takes place, what happens as characters try to achieve their goals, the reactions of characters as the story proceeds, and how the story ends (Harris et al., 2006).

At a minimum, strategy instruction involves the following three instructional processes:

1. Teachers describe the strategy to students and discuss with them its purpose, how it will strengthen their writing, and when and where to apply it.
2. Teachers model how to use the strategy (often more than once).
3. Teachers support students' use of the strategy until they can apply it effectively and independently. This support can range from the teacher and students applying the strategy conjointly, to peers working together to apply it, to students applying it independently, receiving only assistance from teacher and peers as needed.

An important goal in strategy instruction is for students to apply the strategies they are taught in a flexible manner. As students learn new strategies for planning and writing, they should be encouraged to think about when, how, and where they can use what they have learned. We have found that such transfer can be facilitated by having students' set goals for using specific strategies in new situations or combinations, considering how the strategies need to be modified to be successful to these new applications and evaluating how their efforts to use strategies in these new ways fared (see Graham et al., 2005).

It is beyond the scope of this chapter to present the full range of strategies that have been validated for planning, drafting, revising, editing, and rewriting text. Such

TABLE 5.2. Writing Standards: Production and Distribution of Writing (Noting Changes across Grades)

Grade 3	Grade 4 (changes)	Grade 5 (changes)
4. With guidance and support from adults, produce writing in which the development and organization are appropriate to task and purpose.	(**With guidance and support** removed), produce **clear and coherent writing in which** the development and organization are appropriate to task, purpose, **and audience**.	(no change)
5. With guidance and support from peers and adults, develop and strengthen writing as needed by planning, revising, and editing.	(no change)	. . . strengthen writing as needed by planning, revising, editing, **rewriting, or trying a new approach**.
6. With guidance and support from adults, use technology to produce and publish writing (using keyboarding skills) as well as to interact and collaborate with others.	With **some** guidance and support from adults, use technology, **including the Internet,** to produce and publish writing (**using keyboarding skills** removed) as well as to interact and collaborate with others; **demonstrate sufficient command of keyboarding skills to type a minimum of one page in a single sitting**.	. . . demonstrate sufficient command of keyboarding skills to type a minimum of **two pages** in a single sitting.

Note. Changes from one grade to the next are in bold.

evidence-based practices for elementary-grade students, along with procedures for teaching them, have been collected in *Writing Better* (Graham & Harris, 2005) and *Powerful Writing Strategies for All Students* (Harris, Graham, Mason, & Friedlander, 2008).

Similar to the suggestion for teaching text structure presented in the previous section, strategies for planning, revising, and editing should be upgraded over time. For example, students might be taught a general peer revising strategy in grade 3, where they provide feedback to another student on the parts of text that are unclear and points where more information is needed. As students become comfortable and effective with this strategy, additional criteria can be added that address factors such as voice, organization, vocabulary, sentence structure, mechanics, or basic elements of a genre.

WRITING STANDARDS IN ACTION: MODELING HOW TO PLAN AND WRITE AN OPINION PAPER

Ms. Bishop models for her third graders how to plan an opinion essay. She asks her class to review with her the purpose of opinion essays ("to convince others") and to help her identify the characteristics of such writing (e.g., "clearly stated opinion, reasons that support the opinion, linking words to connect opinion and reasons, a strong conclusion").

She tells the class she wants them to help her write a letter to the head of the schools explaining why her students need to have physical education several times a week (the district had just eliminated almost all physical education from the curriculum). The teacher and students discuss the purpose of the letter and the intended audience and decide to send it to the school principal too.

The teacher and students brainstorm as many reasons they can think of to support why physical education is needed at their school, writing them on a white board. After compiling a lengthy list of ideas, they analyze each one to identify those that made the strongest case for their claim. Next, with Ms. Bishop taking the lead, they discuss possible explanations/examples for the strongest reasons. They discard several more reasons that are viewed as weak once they had thought about them further.

At this point, the teacher and students make a tentative outline for the letter and begin to write it as a group. As they write, the teacher emphasizes the use of linking words and making clear and simple statements. Ms. Bishop keeps the process of planning going during the drafting process, as she adds two other supporting reasons to the letter and the class drops one they had planned to use as it became clear that it was relatively weak.

After further revising and polishing the letter later in the week, they send it to the school superintendent and their principal.

The Production and Distribution of Writing standards also emphasize technology as a tool for writing, including using the Internet to produce, collaborate, and publish writing and develop sufficient keyboarding skills to produce short electronic papers in a single setting (see Table 5.2). For many teachers, meeting these goals will be a challenge because of the limited availability of computers (Cutler & Graham, 2008; Gilbert & Graham, 2010). One way of addressing this limitation is for schools to construct a computer labs where students can work on specific writing projects. Another is for the school to invest in rolling labs, where 20 or 30 laptops can be moved from one class to the next. A third is for teachers to devise innovate ways to use the limited number of computers in their classroom so that students can develop needed keyboarding skills and work in groups to use electronic resources to write. Of course, the ideal solution is one computer for each child.

RESEARCH TO BUILD AND PRESENT KNOWLEDGE

In support of the Research to Build and Present Knowledge standards for grades 3–5, the CCSS emphasize short and focused research projects on a single topic. These short reports become more complex over time, as students are expected to address multiple aspects of a topic and consult multiple sources by the end of the elementary grades (see Table 5.3). The processes for gathering, recording, analyzing, organizing, and presenting information for the report are also emphasized and involve multiple sources, including recalling information from experience as well as gathering information from printed and digital sources. The processes of handling this information moves from taking brief notes and sorting information into provided categories in grade 3 to taking more extensive notes, categorizing obtained information, and summarizing it in notes and finished work in grade 5. Starting in grade 4, students are also expected to use writing to support their analyses of literature and informational text (discussed in greater detail later).

Teaching students how to write research reports to build and present knowledge involves the same basic instructional principles used to teach strategies for planning, revising, and editing (see previous section). The teacher should establish the purposes for conducting research reports with the class, describe and discuss the procedures students will use for completing the report, and model the use of these procedures to complete a research report; and students should conduct their own research with teacher and peer assistance. The goal for teaching students how to write research reports is identical to the goal for strategy instruction. Students should learn how to write informative and insightful research reports independently.

WRITING STANDARDS IN ACTION:
TEACHING STUDENTS HOW TO WRITE A RESEARCH PAPER

Ms. Little, a fourth-grade teacher, taught her students to use the following set of strategies for writing a research report.

- Brainstorm what you know and what you want to learn.
- Organize this information on a web so you can see how your ideas are related and what you still need to learn.
- Gather new information from books or the Internet, make notes, and keep track of your sources.
- Revise your web, adding useful new information and reorganizing ideas as needed.
- Use your web as a guide as you write.
- Keep thinking and planning as you write.
- Once your first draft is done, check your web: Did you write what you wanted to?

TABLE 5.3. Writing Standards: Research to Build and Present Knowledge (Noting Changes across Grades)

Grade 3	Grade 4 (changes)	Grade 5 (changes)
7. Conduct short research projects that build knowledge about a topic.	. . . build knowledge through investigation of different aspects of a topic.	Conduct short research projects that **use several sources to** build knowledge . . .
8. Recall information from experiences or gather information from print and digital sources; take brief notes on sources and sort evidence into provided categories.	Recall **relevant** information from experiences or gather **relevant** information . . . take notes on sources; **and categorize information, and provide a list of sources.**	. . . from print and digital sources; **summarize or paraphrase information in notes and finished work** . . .
(Begins in grade 4)	9. Draw evidence from literary or informational texts to support analysis, reflection, and research.	(no change)
	a. Apply *grade 4 Reading standards* to literature (e.g., "Describe in depth a character, setting, or event in a story or drama, drawing on specific details in the text [e.g., a character's thoughts, words, or actions]").	Apply *grade 5 Reading standards* to literature (e.g., **"Compare and contrast two or more characters, settings, or events in a story or a drama, drawing on specific details in the text [e.g., how characters interact]"**).
	b. Apply *grade 4 Reading standards* to informational texts (e.g., "Explain how an author uses reasons and evidence to support particular points in a text").	Apply *grade 5 Reading standards* to informational texts (e.g., ". . . uses reasons and evidence to support particular points in a text, **identifying which reasons and evidence support which point[s]**").

Note. Changes from one grade to the next are in bold.

RANGE OF WRITING

The most poorly specified writing standard in grades 3–5 falls under the Range of Writing domain. The same standard is applied at all three grade levels:

> Write routinely over extended time frames (time for research, reflection, and revision) and shorter time frames (a single sitting or a day or two) for a range of discipline-specific tasks, purposes, and audiences.

This standard indicates students will use both brief and extended writing tasks to accomplish a range of purposes in content-subject areas, including the language arts. I interpreted the standard to mean that students will use writing to help them learn and better understand content material from lectures, classroom exercises, and print and electronic text.

A variety of tested evidenced-based writing activities have been shown to improve students' learning of content materials (Bangert-Drowns et al., 2004; Graham & Hebert, 2010). For example, students' comprehension of text is enhanced when they are asked to answer questions in writing, create their own written questions, take notes or complete graphic organizers, create a written summary, and engage in more extended writing tasks where they personalize, apply, or analyze what was read. The use of such writing tasks is likely to be most effective when students are taught how to apply them within specific domains (Graham & Hebert, 2011). For example, the process of developing and defending a written opinion for science and for social studies differs in that what counts as evidence and how it is presented is not the same in the two subject areas.

WRITING STANDARDS IN ACTION: USING WRITING TO FACILITATE LEARNING IN SCIENCE

Mrs. Morgan, a fifth-grade teacher, begins an experiment on buoyancy by directing students to look at the various objects they will test (rock, Styrofoam, rubber ball, wood, key, and celery stick) and asking them to partner with another student to write a prediction for each item: whether it will sink to the bottom in a tank of water, float on top of it, or be suspended between. Each prediction is accompanied by a written explanation. After discussing their predictions as a class, students conduct the experiment, making notes about what happened to each item as it is placed in the water. Student partners then reexamine their predictions and explanations, revising them in writing as necessary. The class discusses the experiment, their revised predictions, and explanations, drawing several general observations about buoyancy, which students record in their journal.

It is especially important that writing is included as an integral part of content instruction in disciplines like science, social studies, and mathematics. For example, when students write informative papers about the content they are learning in social studies (the consequences of the westward movement in American history as illustrated through the Oregon Trail, for instance), it forces them to make decisions about (1) what information is most important; (2) what consequences were positive, negative, or both; and (3) how their findings should be organized and presented. Such analyses and interpretation force students to wrestle with the content, especially if they have to defend the choices they made (e.g., why were the consequences they presented important).

WRITING STANDARDS IN ACTION: USING WRITING TO FACILITATE LEARNING IN SOCIAL STUDIES

Ms. Morretti works with her fourth-grade class to understand the issues surrounding the American Revolution and the quest for independence. She begins this discussion by reading aloud an argument by a colonial American who was in favor of independence and another by a loyalist against independence. Ms. Morretti tells students she has several other arguments for and against independence that she wants them to read, and asks them to form a committee with one or two other students to create a written argument supporting one position or the other. Once students complete their written argument, they convert it into a 5-minute speech, which they deliver to the class.

CONCLUSION

The demanding and complex writing applications specified in the Common Core require sustained instruction on the part of teachers. Just describing or modeling how to carry out a specific application in a single session will not be enough for many students. They need more extended assistance and support from teachers and their peers to apply such applications effectively. Moreover, as they learn to use writing and writing strategies for different tasks, purposes, and audiences, they need guidance in thinking about how to apply what they know in a strategic manner, structuring and honing the writing tasks and process learned to better fit their intentions. They are more likely to master these writing applications if the environment in which they write is encouraging, pleasant, and supportive.

BIBLIOGRAPHY OF BOOKS ILLUSTRATING GOOD NARRATIVE, PERSUASIVE, AND INFORMATIVE WRITING

Do Tornadoes Really Twist? Questions and Answers about Tornadoes and Hurricanes, by Melvin and Gilda Berger. This informative book answers a variety of questions about two of the most destructive natural disasters. (model for expository text)

A Drop of Water, by Walter Wick. This book explores the many forms of water. (model for expository text)

Saving the Buffalo, by Albert Marrin. The author explores the fate of the American buffalo, from king of the plains to near extinction. (model for expository text)

Caddie Woodlawn, by Carol Ryrie Brink. This historical fiction portrays American pioneer life through the eyes of a woman who settles in Wisconsin in the 1800s and learns about Native Americans. (model for narrative text)

The Ordinary Princess, by M. M. Kaye. A princess gets the best gift of all—being ordinary. (model for narrative text)

Dragon's Egg, by Sarah Thomson. This story presents the adventures of a girl who dreams of giant fire-breathing dragons. (model for narrative text)

City Green, by DyAnne DiSalvo-Ryan. A youngster cleans up a vacant lot and improves the neighborhood at the same time. (model for narrative and persuasive text)

More Than Anything Else, by Marie Bradby. What Booker T. Washington wants more than anything else is to be able to read. (model for persuasive, expository, and narrative text)

Why Alligator Hates Dog, by J. J. Reneaux. Alligator, who is the king of the swamp, does not like it when Dog tricks him. (model for persuasive and narrative text)

Egg-Drop Blues, by Jacqueline Banks. A boy with dyslexia convinces his brother to help him with a school project to earn extra credit. (model for persuasive text)

QUESTIONS AND ACTIVITIES

1. In addition to the four writing applications included in the CCSS writing for grades 3–5, what other writing skills will you need in your work with students in one of these grades to ensure that they grow as writers?

   Activity: Pair with one or more teachers (or prospective teachers) in your school (or class). Select a grade level to focus on. Examine the CCSS for foundational skills in kindergarten to grade 5 to identify which writing skills are emphasized. Make a list of the skills you think some or all of the students in the grade you selected are still in the process of acquiring (i.e., have not been mastered). Consider whether there are other writing skills that your students need that are not included in the CCSS. Make a plan for how these skills will be taught along with the four writing applications.

2. How can you infuse writing into the teaching of social studies, sciences, mathematics, and other content classes in grades 3 to 5?

   Activity: Form a study group with other teachers (or students in your class). Make a list of all of the different types of writing that your group thinks can be used to improve students' learning of content material. For each type of writing, list why you think it facilitates learning. Select at least four writing activities that can be applied in science, social studies, and mathematics. Develop a plan (and implement it if you are a teacher) for integrating at least two writing activities into each of these content areas. Also indicate how you will determine the effectiveness of each writing activity in each of the content areas.

3. How would you design an evaluation tool to help students revise either a persuasive, narrative, or informative text that meets or go beyond the CCSS standards for text types and purposes in grades 3, 4, or 5?

   Activity: Select a type of writing: persuasive, narrative, or informational. Read a high-quality model of this type of text to your class (or to the students in your practicum). Have the students help you identify what makes the text so good. Read another model composition to the class and ask them if each of the factors they identified earlier were present in this text also. Add other factors to your list that the students identified for this second reading. Do this with additional compositions until the class reaches consensus on the characteristics of a model text in this genre. Select four to six attributes with the students' help and build a genre-specific rubric that you and they can use to evaluate their writing.

4. What can you do to differentiate instruction in the four writing applications included in the CCSS writing in grades 3–5 so that it meets the needs of all of the students in your class?

   Activity: Develop an outline for how you will either teach or facilitate the use of one of the four writing applications emphasized in CCSS writing for the students in your class (or practicum). Be as specific as possible. Then consider the students in your class and identify who will need extra assistance and who will already be able to apply the writing application without assistance. Identify the supports and scaffolds that you will use with the former as well as how you will modify what you are doing for the latter so that the use of the application interests and challenges them.

5. Decide what skills students in grades 3, 4, or 5 will need to be able to apply to write a research report in a content area.

   Activity: Design a research project that your students (or students in your practicum) will conduct in science, social studies, mathematics, or language arts. Complete a task analysis of what skills students must possess in order to complete this assignment. Share this list with your students and ask them to identify which skills they can already do well as well as other skills they think they still need in order to complete the research report. Develop a plan for teaching the needed skills and implement it.

REFERENCES

Bangert-Drowns, R. L., Hurley, M. M., & Wilkinson, B. (2004). The effects of school-based writing-to-learn interventions on academic achievement: A meta-analysis. *Review of Educational Research, 74,* 29–58.

Bereiter, C., & Scardamalia, M. (1987). *The psychology of written composition.* Hillsdale, NJ: Erlbaum.

Cutler, L., & Graham, S. (2008). Primary grade writing instruction: A national survey. *Journal of Educational Psychology, 100,* 907–919.

Gilbert, J., & Graham, S. (2010). Teaching writing to elementary students in grades 4 to 6: A national survey. *Elementary School Journal, 110,* 494–518.

Graham, S. (2010). Teaching writing. In P. Hogan (Ed.), *Cambridge encyclopedia of language sciences* (pp. 848–851). Cambridge, UK: Cambridge University Press.

Graham, S., & Harris, K. R. (2005). *Writing better: Teaching writing processes and self-regulation to students with learning problems.* Baltimore: Brookes.

Graham, S., Harris, K. R., & Mason, L. (2005). Improving the writing performance, knowledge, and self-efficacy of struggling young writers: The effects of self-regulated strategy development. *Contemporary Educational Psychology, 30,* 207–241.

Graham, S., Harris, K. R., & McKeown, D. (in press). The writing of students with LD, meta-analysis of SRSD writing intervention studies, and future directions: Redux. In H. L. Swanson, K. R. Harris, & S. Graham (Eds.), *Handbook of learning disabilities* (2nd ed.). New York: Guilford Press.

Graham, S., & Hebert, M. (2010). *Writing to reading: Evidence for how writing can improve reading.* Washington, DC: Alliance for Excellence in Education.

Graham, S., & Hebert, M. (2011). Writing to read: A meta-analysis of the impact of writing and writing instruction on reading. *Harvard Educational Review, 81,* 710–744.

Graham, S., Hebert, M., & Harris, K. R. (2011). Throw em' out or make em' better? High-stakes writing assessments. *Focus on Exceptional Children, 44,* 1–12.

Graham, S., Kiuhara, S., McKeown, D., & Harris, K. R. (in press). A meta-analysis of writing instruction for students in the elementary grades. *Journal of Educational Psychology.*

Graham, S., & Perin, D. (2007). *Writing next: Effective strategies to improve writing of adolescent middle and high school.* Washington, DC: Alliance for Excellence in Education.

Harris, K. R., Graham, S., & Mason, L. (2006). Improving the writing knowledge and motivation of struggling young writers: Effects of self-regulated strategy development with and without peer support. *American Educational Research Journal, 43,* 295–340.

Harris, K. R., Graham, S., Mason, L., & Friedlander, B. (2008). *Powerful writing strategies for all students.* Baltimore: Brookes.

Hayes, J. (1996). A new framework for understanding cognition and affect in writing. In M. Levy & S. Ransdell (Eds.), *The science of writing: Theories, methods, individual differences, and applications* (pp. 1–27). Mahwah, NJ: Erbaum.

Hayes, J., & Flower, L. (1980). Identifying the organization of writing processes. In L. Gregg & E. Steinberg (Eds.), *Cognitive processes in writing* (pp. 3–30). Hillsdale, NJ: Erlbaum.

MacArthur, C., Schwartz, S., Graham, S., Molloy, D., & Harris, K. R. (1996). Integration of strategy instruction into a whole language classroom: A case study. *Learning Disabilities Research and Practice, 11*, 168–176.

Morphy, P., & Graham, S. (2012). Word processing programs and weaker writers/readers: A meta-analysis of research findings. *Reading and Writing, 25*, 641–678.

National Governors Association Center for Best Practices and Council of Chief State School Officers. (2010). Common Core State Standards for English language arts & literacy in history/social studies, science, and technical subjects. Retrieved from *www.corestandards.org.*

Rijlaarsdam, G., & van den Bergh, H. (2006). Writing process theory: A functional dynamic approach. In C. A. MacArthur, S. Graham, & J. Fitzgerald (Eds.), *Handbook of writing research* (pp. 41–52). New York: Guilford Press.

CHAPTER 6

Speaking and Listening Standards

Douglas Fisher
Nancy Frey
Diane Lapp

What does it mean to communicate? Typical dictionary definitions suggest that communication is a process by which information is exchanged between individuals through a common system of symbols, signs, or behaviors shared through speaking, listening, and nonoral systems such as reading, writing, and gestures. Communication can occur in ways not typically considered. For example, insects "communicate" with pheromones, or secreted chemicals. Animals communicate by urinating on objects to mark their territory. Fortunately, humans do not need to rely on these unconventional means! Instead, we speak and listen. We've adopted the speaking and listening definitions forwarded by Cooper and Morreale (2003, p. x), namely:

> *Speaking*: Speaking is the uniquely human act or process of sharing and exchanging information, ideas, and emotions using oral language. Whether in daily information interactions or in more formal settings, communicators are required to organize coherent messages, deliver them clearly, and adapt them to their listeners.

> *Listening*: Listening is the process of receiving, constructing meaning from, and responding to spoken and/or nonverbal messages. People call on different listening skills depending on whether their goal is to comprehend information, critique and evaluate a message, show empathy for the feelings expressed by others, or appreciate a performance. Taken together, the communication skills of speaking and listening, called oral language, form the basis for thinking.

Speaking and listening—oral language—must be taught like all the other content of school. Nearly every state has had content standards related to speaking and listening, but since they were not tested, little instructional attention has been devoted to these critical skills. The Common Core State Standards (CCSS; National Governors Association [NGA] Center for Best Practices and Council of Chief State School Officers (CCSSO), 2010), however, change that. The architects of these standards noted that speaking and listening are critical skills that build the foundation for college and career readiness. In the language of the standards:

> To build a foundation for college and career readiness, students must have ample opportunities to take part in a variety of rich, structured conversations—as part of a whole class, in small groups, and with a partner. Being productive members of these conversations requires that students contribute accurate, relevant information; respond to and develop what others have said; make comparisons and contrasts; and analyze and synthesize a multitude of ideas in various domains. (p. 22)

DEFINING THE SPEAKING AND LISTENING STANDARDS

The Common Core standards for speaking and listening are divided into two categories: Comprehension and Collaboration and Presentation of Knowledge and Ideas. As with other focus areas, the speaking and listening standards are organized into anchor standards that cross grade levels. The six anchor standards related to speaking and listening include:

Comprehension and Collaboration

1. Prepare for and participate effectively in a range of conversations and collaborations with diverse partners, building on others' ideas and expressing their own clearly and persuasively.
2. Integrate and evaluate information presented in diverse media and formats, including visually, quantitatively, and orally.
3. Evaluate a speaker's point of view, reasoning, and use of evidence and rhetoric.

Presentation of Knowledge and Ideas

4. Present information, findings, and supporting evidence such that listeners can follow the line of reasoning and the organization, development, and style are appropriate to task, purpose, and audience.
5. Make strategic use of digital media and visual displays of data to express information and enhance understanding of presentations.
6. Adapt speech to a variety of contexts and communicative tasks, demonstrating command of formal English when indicated or appropriate.

For each of these anchor standards, there are grade-level specific expectations. For example, the third anchor standard focuses on the speaker's point of view, reasoning, and use of evidence and rhetoric. This is clearly related to the reading and writing students are expected to do as they must identify evidence from the text and use evidence in their writing (see Chapters 2, 3, and 5, this volume). In grades 3, 4, and 5, students are expected to master the following to meet the anchor standard:

Grade 3: Ask and answer questions about information from a speaker, offering appropriate elaboration and detail.

Grade 4: Identify the reasons and evidence a speaker provides to support particular points.

Grade 5: Summarize the points a speaker makes and explain how each claim is supported by reasons and evidence.

Table 6.1 contains a list of all of the speaking and listening standards in grades 3–5. It is critical that teachers address these standards so that students' thinking is fostered and their reading and writing skills progress.

The Relationships among Speaking, Listening, Reading, and Writing

A significant body of research has been developed to support the notion of interrelatedness among and between literacy processes (speaking, listening, reading, and writing). For example, Burgess (2002) noted the relationship between oral language development and subsequent growth in phonological sensitivity, a predictor of reading ability. Similarly, Cooper, Roth, Speece, and Schatschneider (2002) reported that oral language development positively contributes to progress of early reading through specific influence on development of phonological awareness. Although it seems obvious, it is important to note that poor listening skills are associated with lower academic achievement (Ross, 1964) and low levels of reading comprehension (Devine, 1978). Furthermore, increasing oral language skills is associated with improved reading and writing achievement (Harste & Short, 1988). As Fisher (2003) noted with her students, "If we can talk about it, we can write about it; if we can write about it, we can read about it" (p. 6).

Oral Language Development

As with reading and writing, language follows a developmental path. A series of developmental phases describe the progression of children as they learn to use language in increasingly sophisticated ways. The following eight phases of language development describe this progression (Education Department of West Australia, 1994a, 1994b).

Beginning Language

As children enter the world, they immediately begin learning language. Using cries, coos, and other sounds, infants make their needs and wants known. Over time, they produce single words and then two-word combinations, such as *car go* or *daddy up*. As their understanding of language develops, children in this phase also understand simple questions and directions and enjoy language games and songs (such as *I'm a Little Teapot*).

Early Language

At the early language phase, children begin to experiment with sound through rhymes and repetition. They begin to use prepositions, often confuse pronouns, and start to read

TABLE 6.1. Speaking and Listening Standards

Grade 3 students	Grade 4 students	Grade 5 students
Comprehension and Collaboration		
1. Engage effectively in a range of collaborative discussions (one-on-one, in groups, and teacher led) with diverse partners on grade 3 topics and texts, building on others' ideas and expressing their own clearly.	1. Engage effectively in a range of collaborative discussions (one-on-one, in groups, and teacher led) with diverse partners on grade 4 topics and texts, building on others' ideas and expressing their own clearly.	1. Engage effectively in a range of collaborative discussions (one-on-one, in groups, and teacher led) with diverse partners on grade 5 topics and texts, building on others' ideas and expressing their own clearly.
a. Come to discussions prepared, having read or studied required material; explicitly draw on that preparation and other information known about the topic to explore ideas under discussion.	a. Come to discussions prepared, having read or studied required material; explicitly draw on that preparation and other information known about the topic to explore ideas under discussion.	a. Come to discussions prepared, having read or studied required material; explicitly draw on that preparation and other information known about the topic to explore ideas under discussion.
b. Follow agreed-upon rules for discussions (e.g., gaining the floor in respectful ways, listening to others with care, speaking one at a time about the topics and texts under discussion).	b. Follow agreed-upon rules for discussions and carry out assigned roles.	b. Follow agreed-upon rules for discussions and carry out assigned roles.
c. Ask questions to check understanding of information presented, stay on topic, and link their comments to the remarks of others.	c. Pose and respond to specific questions to clarify or follow up on information, and make comments that contribute to the discussion and link to the remarks of others.	c. Pose and respond to specific questions by making comments that contribute to the discussion and elaborate on the remarks of others.
d. Explain their own ideas and understanding in light of the discussion	d. Review the key ideas expressed and explain their own ideas and understanding in light of the discussion.	d. Review the key ideas expressed and draw conclusions in light of information and knowledge gained from the discussions.
2. Determine the main ideas and supporting details of a text read aloud or information presented in diverse media and formats, including visually, quantitatively, and orally.	2. Paraphrase portions of a text read aloud or information presented in diverse media and formats, including visually, quantitatively, and orally.	2. Summarize a written text read aloud or information presented in diverse media and formats, including visually, quantitatively, and orally.
3. Ask and answer questions about information from a speaker, offering appropriate elaboration and detail.	3. Identify the reasons and evidence a speaker provides to support particular points.	3. Summarize the points a speaker makes and explain how each claim is supported by reasons and evidence.
Presentation of Knowledge and Ideas		
4. Report on a topic or text, tell a story, or recount an experience with appropriate facts and relevant, descriptive details, speaking clearly at an understandable pace.	4. Report on a topic or text, tell a story, or recount an experience in an organized manner, using appropriate facts and relevant, descriptive details to support main ideas or themes; speak clearly at an understandable pace.	4. Report on a topic or text or present an opinion, sequencing ideas logically and using appropriate facts and relevant, descriptive details to support main ideas or themes; speak clearly at an understandable pace.

(cont.)

TABLE 6.1. *(cont.)*

Grade 3 students	Grade 4 students	Grade 5 students
5. Create engaging audio recordings of stories or poems that demonstrate fluid reading at an understandable pace; add visual displays when appropriate to emphasize or enhance certain facts or details.	5. Add audio recordings and visual displays to presentations when appropriate to enhance the development of main ideas or themes.	5. Include multimedia components (e.g., graphics, sound) and visual displays in presentations when appropriate to enhance the development of main ideas or themes.
6. Speak in complete sentences when appropriate to task and situation in order to provide requested detail or clarification.	6. Differentiate between contexts that call for formal English (e.g., presenting ideas) and situations where informal discourse is appropriate (e.g., small-group discussion); use formal English when appropriate to task and situation.	6. Adapt speech to a variety of contexts and tasks, using formal English when appropriate to task and situation.

environmental print. Still very egocentric and focused on their own life and experiences, they produce questions such as "I go to the store?"; children very much enjoy imaginative play, retelling events and stories, and love to ask question after question during this phase.

Exploratory Language

Later in their development, children use language to contribution to conversations, engage others, and predict future events. They have developed a good sense of grammar, although they still make overgeneralizations with tenses and plurals, such as *goed* and *mouses*. Their questioning becomes more focused, and they often utilize a "who, what, where, when, why, and how" format. Parents everywhere recall the insistence of the toddler demanding to know "Why is the sky blue?," "Where do fish sleep at night?," and on and on! At this phase, children become more reflective in their thinking and their resulting use of language.

Emergent Language for Learning

Many children entering school are somewhere near this phase of oral language development. Students know when spoken sentences are grammatically correct and can adapt their speech and writing to ensure that tenses and verbs agree. In terms of speech, students begin to develop a sense of tone, volume, pace, intonation, and gestures to complement the content they wish to present. Furthermore, they are expanding their vocabulary and use words for different purposes. They also understand that they can use language to persuade, inform, and reason with their peers, teachers, and parents. Words like *because* figure prominently in the emergent language user's vocabulary as they seek to persuade, inform, and reason!

Consolidated Language for Learning

By this phase, students in the primary grades can communicate effectively, offer advice and opinions, and interpret messages for different layers of meaning. They are developing the ability to make inferences and judgments based on the information provided. Furthermore, they have become skilled at using slang with their peers and switching to more formal registers with adults.

Extended Language for Learning

Building on the skills acquired at the consolidated language for learning phase, primary and intermediate students subsequently develop an ability to summarize information effectively and efficiently, use language to form hypotheses, and engage in constructive criticism. They also can use language in novel ways to engage their audiences and to create mental images for their listeners.

Proficient Language Use for Learning

Once proficient, intermediate-grade students learn to adjust their language to include or exclude individuals from the conversation by adding or deleting details, word choice, and paraphrasing. They also have developed a sense of main idea and can easily take notes during spoken conversations and lectures. Finally, they can use language to reflect on their own ideology or position on an issue.

Advanced Language Use for Learning

The final phase identified in the first steps framework includes the development of a very sophisticated understanding of the power of language to cause emotional reactions. Advanced language users in intermediate and middle school grades can analyze spoken messages for cultural relevance, values, attitudes, and assumptions. They can also interpret the speaker's tone to make inferences. Speakers at the advanced language use phase have the ability to immediately modify their content and style based on verbal and nonverbal feedback they receive from their audience. (Education Department of Western Australia, 1994a, 1994b).

   As you read about the developmental phases of oral language, were you struck by the similarities to the reading and writing skills and strategies we teach throughout the elementary-school years? Understanding these similarities illuminates the intricate relationships among language processes.

PUTTING THE SPEAKING AND LISTENING STANDARDS INTO PRACTICE

Speakers of all ages must develop interaction skills in order to be understood by listeners. In addition, interactions need to be respectful and efficient in purpose. These interaction skills permeate conversations in and out of school and begin to develop long before a child enters the classroom. Pinnell and Jaggar (2003, pp. 889–892) have noted that as one's interaction skills become increasingly sophisticated, so too does the use of other literacies.

- *Conversational discourse.* Speakers understand the ways in which conversations occur, including turn-taking, listening and responding, and maintaining interest.
- *Sensitivity to audience.* Understanding that language changes depending on who is listening is also important. Children learn that they change their speech and language registers depending on the social context, background knowledge of the listeners, age of the listeners, and the expectations for the setting. Speech registers involve the level of formality in presenting information. For example, we use different registers to explain directions to a toddler and to a teenager.
- *Arguing, persuading, and controlling others.* Another function of language is to make your perspective known and to attempt to influence the thinking of others. Persuasion is an important skill and is often the focus of writing instruction. This function is also important as students develop skills in conflict resolution.
- *Making requests and asking for information.* Over time, children learn how to ask for things and information with direct statements. They also develop their skills in using questions to gain information they want.
- *Informing.* People also use language to inform others. Effectively providing information requires skills in organizing thinking and sharing information in a way that allows the listener or reading to follow the logic and flow of ideas.
- *Imagining.* This function encourages children to assume different characters and roles as they engage in play. As they do so, they become skilled in using descriptive language to share their thoughts. Interestingly, the development of imagining is related to understanding narrative stories and story grammar (Galda, 1984).
- *Telling stories and narrative discourse.* To tell a story, students must learn the conventions of story grammar and the idea that all stories have specific parts. In the stories and narrative discourse, children learn to sustain longer monologues and to focus on their audience and the audience's interest. Importantly, stories provide students an opportunity to reflect on and present their own language, ethnicity, culture, religion, and experience with the world.
- *Inquiry.* As Vygotsky (1986) noted, learning requires that students use inquiry and "inner speech" as they solve problems, acquire new information, and modify what they already know. Inquiry, as a process, allows children to continuously make sense and understand their world.

These types of interactions are used throughout the day both in and out of school, and some, such as informing and inquiring, are used frequently during the school day. In the classroom, these interactions are most commonly conducted in the formal and consultative registers. This talk between and among students and the teacher is referred to as classroom discourse. Oral language development occurs in part when teachers foster meaningful classroom discourse through intentional instruction.

Arguably the most important teaching tool at a teacher's disposal is talk. Teachers rely on talk, both their own and their students', to drive instruction. It should, therefore, come as no surprise that classroom teachers deliver most of the information during the day orally. The oral language demands of school are intense. There are, however, good and not so good ways to use speaking and listening in the classroom. In particular, the questioning habits of teachers can increase or suppress classroom discourse.

Effective Questioning Habits

Reading researchers report from their classroom observations at the elementary level that the majority of questions used in classroom discourse on a daily basis are teacher generated and explicit and require only one correct answer (Block, 2001). Cazden (1988) conducted an important series of studies on the questioning habits of teachers. Like others before her, she found that classroom instruction is dominated by a particular cycle of questioning known as IRE: *Initiate*, *Respond*, and *Evaluate* (Mehan, 1979). The IRE pattern of questioning is familiar to all—the teacher initiates a question, students respond, and then the teacher evaluates the quality and accuracy of the responses. For example:

> Teacher: "Why did the plants with both water and sun grow the best?" (Initiate)
>
> Student: "They used photosynthesis." (Response)
>
> Teacher: "Good. (Evaluate) Why else?" (Initiate)

Here's the difficulty with that question: The student could have also answered that water contains nutrients needed by the plant, that plants can convert sunlight into chemical forms of energy, or a host of other answers. The question is a low-level, teacher-directed query that excludes any discussion or debate among students. A classroom where IRE is the dominant form of discourse quickly becomes a passive learning environment dependent on the teacher for any kind of discussion. The danger, of course, in the overuse of an IRE pattern of questioning is that the teacher alone becomes the mediator of who will speak and who will not (Mehan, 1979). The students learn that the only questions worth considering are those formulated by the teacher. Ironically, the teachers in Cazden's (1988) study reported that they wanted a student-centered, constructivist classroom, yet clung to IRE as their dominant instructional method for inquiry. If you doubt the pervasiveness of this questioning pattern, then eavesdrop on kindergartners "playing school." Invariably, the 5-year-old "teacher" will engage in this questioning pattern with his or her "students." If only all teaching behaviors were this easy to teach!

Factors Impacting Classroom Discourse

Of course, fostering meaningful classroom discourse can be challenging. Many teachers have had the experience of posing a question to a class only to be greeted with silence. *What's wrong with them?*, the teacher thinks. *Don't they know any of this? Haven't they been listening?* This is usually immediately followed by *What's wrong with me? Am I that ineffective as a teacher?* Blame for not learning or teaching is not the culprit. Instead, a mixture of complex factors may be at play, among them:

- Academic factors: lack of prior knowledge, lack of understanding of current content of study.
- Language factors: difficulty in utilizing academic language to answer the question posed or lack of understanding of the question itself.

- Intrinsic factors: the student may be shy, uncomfortable speaking in front of the group, uncomfortable with his or her language skills, or unmotivated to participate in the activity.
- Extrinsic factors: fear of the perceptions of specific members of the class or the class as a whole.

As you can see, this adds up to a mélange of reasons why the same handful of students seem to answer teacher questions. This is borne out in research as well. According to several studies collected in classrooms of various ages, boys are up to eight times more likely to call out and answer than girls and, therefore, gain more of the teacher's attention (Holden, 1993). Moreover, teachers need to be mindful of more than just the types of questions asked. There is evidence that teachers call on boys to talk in class significantly more often than girls (Sadker & Sadker, 1995).

Cazden (2001) suggests that all teachers ask themselves two questions about classroom discourse:

- How do patterns of talk in classrooms affect the equality of students' educational opportunities and outcomes?
- How is discourse used as a support for deeper student learning?

Focusing on these questions as you establish your classroom will ensure that students are engaged in meaningful ways and that you achieve both excellence and equity as you develop the skills students need to be successful. However, changes to questioning habits alone will not automatically foster more meaningful classroom discourse. Students also need to be taught how to communicate effectively in the classroom in order to support their own learning through creative and critical thinking. This is called "accountable talk."

What Is Accountable Talk?

Recall some of the classrooms in which you have participated. Were you held accountable for what you thought and said? Were you allowed to sit quietly and not participate in any way in the class activities and lessons? If so, how much did you learn? "The shy, quiet and reserved child may seem like a model of good behavior—but that child may be cause for concern, not celebration. *All* children need opportunities to talk *a lot* to develop word knowledge and language skills" (National Center on Education and the Economy, 2001, p. 12).

Accountable talk is the practice of fostering classroom discourse about learning through partner conversations and whole-group discussions. This term was developed and researched by Lauren Resnick and her colleagues at the University of Pittsburgh's Institute for Learning to describe high levels of engagement in creative and critical thinking among learners. Although the term seems to suggest that it is about speaking, listening is essential to accountable talk because the discourse springs from careful listening to the conversation. A focus on accountable talk provides teachers and students with expectations for their conversations and discussions. The basic principles of accountable talk include:

- Accountability that discussions are on topic
- Accountability to use accurate information
- Accountability to think deeply about what is being discussed

Although not easy to achieve, an excellent indicator of accountable talk is when discussion in the classroom ceases to be brokered by the teacher and becomes a series of interchanges among students. When this occurs, the teacher no longer has to be the originator of all the questions (recall IRE) because students are asking and responding to the inquiries and comments of classmates.

Indicators of Accountable Talk

Accountable talk is developed through modeling the kinds of questions and follow-up probes used in meaningful classroom discourse. The purpose of these follow-ups is to encourage creative and critical thinking. Following up student responses with an additional probe is an excellent means for modeling how meaningful exchanges can occur. The Institute for Learning at the University of Pittsburgh has identified specific indicators of accountable talk required of teachers and students as follows (with examples in italics after each to illustrate):

- Press for clarification and explanation: *Can you tell me more about that?*
- Require justification of proposals and challenges: *What facts support your idea?*
- Recognize and challenge misconception: *I don't agree because _____.*
- Demand evidence for claims and arguments: *Can you give me an example?*
- Interpret and use each other's statements: *Tino's idea reminded me of _____.*

Teaching Accountable Talk

Accountable talk is used throughout the language arts workshop. Focus lessons and guided instruction are ideal times to provide intentional instruction on listening carefully to one another in order to participate in meaningful discussion. Accordingly, accountable talk is fostered through multiple opportunities to interact with a partner. For instance, the beginning of a focus lesson might begin with each student identifying a classmate for partner talk. Throughout the lesson, the teacher pauses and instructs students to "turn to a partner and . . . " followed by a discussion prompt. While students discuss the prompt with one another, the teacher moves about, listening for accountable talk and interjecting when necessary to coach higher quality conversation.

Accountable talk is an integral element of the language arts workshop because conversations, discussions, and dialogues are critical to the learning process. Therefore, it is necessary for the teacher to create a climate and culture in which students are respected when they speak. In addition, the learning environment must be one in which asking questions and challenging ideas is valued.

SPEAKING AND LISTENING STANDARDS IN ACTION: TEACHING ACCOUNTABLE TALK

Mr. Anderson knows that his students need support in talking with their peers, especially in the area of argumentation. He provides his students a number of sentence frames that they can use with each other as they solve problems. He models the use of each frame and then invites students to collaborate with their peers, reminding them to use the frames as they interact. Some of the frames he uses to facilitate students' skills in argumentation include:

I think _____ is important because _____.

I agree/disagree with _____ because _____.

They say _____ and/but I say _____ because _____.

INTEGRATING THE SPEAKING AND LISTENING STANDARDS ACROSS THE DAY

Different phases of instruction provide teachers with myriad opportunities for developing the speaking and listening skills of students. The emphasis is on offering a variety of strategies for using language to foster creative and critical thinking. Students also have numerous opportunities to talk with partners to develop the skills of accountable talk. Throughout this section, we provide examples of children's literature that promotes listening and speaking (see Children's Literature list). The box below includes a number of texts that are useful in developing students' oral language proficiency. In addition,

---

TEXTS FOR FACILITATING ORAL LANGUAGE PROFICIENCY

Narrative

Tuck Everlasting, by Natalie Babbitt
Bud, Not Buddy, by Christopher Paul Curtis
Sarah, Plain and Tall, by Patricia MacLachlan
The Raft, by Jim LaMarche
The Cricket in Times Square, by George Selden

Poetry

"Weather," by Eve Merriam
"Who Has Seen the Wind?," by Christina Rossetti
"Fog," by Carl Sandburg
"Eating While Reading," by Gary Soto
"Casey at the Bat," Ernest Lawrence Thayer

Informational

Throw Your Tooth on the Roof: Tooth Traditions Around the World, by Selby Beeler
The Story of Ruby Bridges, by Robert Coles
A History of US, by Joy Hakim
If the World Were a Village: A Book about the World's People, by David J. Smith
So You Want to Be President?, by Judith St. George
Toys! Amazing Stories Behind Some Great Inventions, by Don Wulffson

students at this grade level will also talk about menus, advertising, directions, Web pages, and a host of other texts.

Focus Lessons

Focus lessons provide a time when the teacher can model, coach, and scaffold instruction for oral language development. When using these strategies, remember to pause from time to time to tell students about the language you are using. This makes the purpose of instruction more explicit to students.

Think–Pair–Share

One of the most transportable teaching strategies, Think–Pair–Share (Lyman, 1981), introduces an intermediate stage between when the question is asked and when the answered is delivered and serves as an important strategy for developing accountable talk (Resnick, 1995). After asking the question, the teacher invites students to think about the possible answers. When a short amount of time has elapsed (30 seconds or so), the teacher then instructs them to turn to a partner and discuss their answers. After allowing a few minutes for discussion, the teacher then invites students to offer answers. Invariably, more hands go up because they have had some time to consider their answer, listen to someone else, and refine their response. In addition, the answers are likely to be rich and detailed because of this intermediate step.

There is another compelling reason for using Think–Pair–Share, and it has to do with oral language and engagement. For reasons cited previously, some students are reluctant to participate in large-group discussion, and some may remain silent during the whole-class conversation. However, when Think–Pair–Share is utilized, *every student participates*. Thirty students answer, not just one, because they have responded to another classmate.

One variation of Think–Pair–Share is Read–Write–Pair–Share. The difference lies in what students do before discussing with a partner. Students first read a question that has been posted on the board or a brief piece of text and then write a response. After a few minutes of writing, pairs of students discuss what they have written. Finally, students are invited to share their own as well as their partner's ideas.

SPEAKING AND LISTENING STANDARDS IN ACTION: THINK–PAIR–SHARE

Ms. Jacobs uses a variation of Turn to Your Partner called Think–Pair–Square. She wants to teach her students to interact in increasingly larger group settings, so she uses this approach to expand students' repertoire. To begin, she provides a statement or question and invites students to talk with their partners. After the allotted time, she asks each partnership to join another and "square up and talk with each other." For example, during a discussion about the text they were reading, Ms. Jacobs asks students, "What does the author do to help readers understand confusing words?" Micah and Dale talk about the way that the author provided context clues, so Micah responds, "I like that the author uses punctuation, like these commas right here, to help us know what the word means." Dale adds, "Yeah, and sometimes when the author just gives another word, like a synonym, to help." Dale and Micah are then joined by Andrea and Roberto, who add information about bold words, a glossary, and prefixes to the conversation.

Shared Writing

The language experience approach (LEA) allows the teacher to engage students in conversation about a book or experience and invite them to orally compose a message (Ashton-Warner, 1963). In LEA, the teacher writes down everything the children say, reinforcing speech-to-print connections. These writings then become reading material for the students during subsequent instruction.

A version of LEA for use with groups is called shared writing (McKenzie, 1985). As in LEA, children's speech is written on chart paper for all to see. However, in shared writing the teacher takes a more active role in shaping the composition of the message as the group is helped toward consensus on the text. Because LEA and shared writing result in a written product, it is easy to overlook the role of oral language development in this activity. However, much of the value of shared writing lies in the oral composition, as students alternately offer ideas, listen to others, and use their words to persuade. Recall from earlier in this chapter the importance of these interaction skills. In shared writing, it is important not to rush through the oral composition in an effort to get the text written down on the page.

A popular version of shared writing is Daily News. This may be done inside of the language arts workshop, as in a focus lesson, or during the morning circle routine of the classroom. In Daily News, students are asked about an event that will occur that day, such as an assembly or a visitor to the classroom, or another noteworthy incident that happened in the community. After discussing the event, selecting and refining the message, and developing word choices, the agreed message is written on the chart or board along with the date. You can use an 18″ × 24″ tablet labeled "Daily News" and make it available for collaborative reading. These collections are popular with the students, who enjoy seeing a chronicle of their school year develop over time.

Developing K-W-L Language Charts

One of the most widely used instructional activities used by classroom teachers is the K-W-L ("what we know, what we want to know, what we learned") chart (Spor & Schneider, 1999). The K-W-L chart (Ogle, 1986) is developed through discussion with the class at the beginning and end of a book or unit of study. Before the reading or topic of study, the class discusses the first question to activate background knowledge about a subject. Development of K-W-L charts is highly regarded in part because it mirrors an approach to research that begins with reviewing what is known, developing questions to guide the study, and then evaluating what has been learned (Ogle, 1986), making this approach useful for developing creative and critical thinking skills.

SPEAKING AND LISTENING STANDARDS IN ACTION:
USING K-W-L CHARTS

In Ms. Hart's classroom, students are learning about spiders. Ms. Hart engages the class in listing all the things they know about spiders. She elicits their comments through a series of questions prepared in advance.

- Have you ever seen a spider?
- What do they look like?

- Where do they live?
- What do they eat?
- What about poisonous spiders?

(Some teachers feel more comfortable entitling this portion "What do we think we know?" in order to allow for incorrect statements.)

Once students thoroughly discuss their background knowledge about the topic, the conversation moves to the next level: What do we want to know? During this phase, the teacher's role is to assist the class in formulating questions. This portion of the K-W-L is critical because it encourages students to anticipate information they are likely to encounter during the reading and fosters inquiry as an interaction skill.

Students then work in literature circles to read the spider books. They use the K-W-L language chart they created to confirm or disconfirm their beliefs and predictions about the topic. The last column, What have we learned?, is intended to solicit answers to the questions developed during the "W" portion of the activity. Of course, it is possible that not all questions will be answered during the subsequent reading; these can be used to extend the experience later for further study through a process called K-W-L Plus (Carr & Ogle, 1987). The "plus" portion represents a fourth question: *What do we want to know next?* Figure 6.1 contains a completed K-W-L chart on spiders.

Oral language development is a key component in developing a K-W-L chart on a topic. Student participation can be enhanced by using a think–pair–share approach to foster student engagement. As well, students participating in K-W-L benefit from opportunities to formulate and refine questions and craft answers that are accurate and succinct.

Know?	Want to Know?	Learned?
Spiders are scary	What do spiders eat?	Most spiders are harmless to people
Have 8 legs	What if you get bit by a poisonous spider?	They are useful because they control insects
Make spider webs	What kinds of spiders live here?	Some spiders eat small animals
They bite	How many spiders are there in the world?	Not all spiders make webs (trapdoor spider)
Eat bugs		Tarantulas are not very poisonous
Tarantulas are poisonous		Black widow spiders are more poisonous
Some are hairy		
Live in the garden		
"Charlotte's Web"		

FIGURE 6.1. K-W-L chart on spiders.

Guided Instruction

During guided instruction, the teacher works with students in a small group to give attention to a particular skill or strategy. Guided instruction is an excellent time for oral language development because students have many opportunities to use speaking and listening skills.

Oral Cloze Method

Have you wondered why some teachers seem to pause before a key word in a statement? For example, a teacher might say, "The punctuation mark we use to end a sentence is called a _____." The students complete the statement with the word *period*. This "fill in the blank" technique is called an *oral cloze method*. By posing such questions (and they really are questions despite their declarative appearance), teachers are able to accomplish several goals:

- Check for understanding
- Increase engagement through active participation
- Rehearse vocabulary and concept knowledge

Unlike many of the other strategies in this chapter, oral cloze should not be the focus of your lesson. Rather, it is a simple technique for increasing response rates among students while giving them an opportunity to practice academic language. Students who are English language learners can benefit from this technique, especially if they are uncomfortable with their pronunciation of unfamiliar words. Like Think–Pair–Share, this is a transportable teaching strategy that is useful in all content areas. It is transportable across the language arts workshop as well, especially during focus lessons.

ReQuest

ReQuest is an instructional procedure for developing comprehension through developing questions about a reading (Manzo, 1969). ReQuest is typically done between a teacher and a group of students, although it was initially intended to be completed with an individual student. The steps for ReQuest are simple to follow:

1. Select a text for reading and assign roles as questioner and responder. The students and teacher read silently and formulate possible questions for the first section of the reading.
2. The responder closes the book while the questioner asks a question about the passage.
3. The responder answers the question and then checks the passage for accuracy.
4. Select the next passage, and have students change roles. After several rotations, the teacher invites predictions about the rest of the reading. The students continue to read to the end of the text.

Task cards can assist students in remembering each of the steps. The ReQuest procedure requires students to listen carefully to one another and use the interaction skills of inquiring and informing.

Collaborative Learning

The collaborative phase of the workshop is a time when students work together to support the learning of one another. The use of accountable talk is critical to activities conducted during this time.

Book Clubs and Literature Circles

These peer-led reading groups meet during the course of several weeks to discuss a single text (Daniels, 2002). Students benefit from guidelines regarding how the literature circle should function and often respond well to the assignment of specific roles within the group, for example (Daniels, 2002):

- Discussion director
- Vocabulary enricher
- Passage picker
- Real-life connector
- Illustrator

Accountable talk is an important aspect of an effective literature circle. In each role, students should guide their discussion using the expectations associated with accountable talk, including supplying evidence, using the statements of others, and asking follow-up questions to clarify understanding (Resnick, 1995).

In addition to the roles assumed by each member of the group, the composition of students must be considered as well. Will these groups be homogeneous or heterogeneous in nature? According to what elements? It is not uncommon to form groups based on reading ability; this is perhaps the most popular way. However, there are other factors that influence the success of group interactions. You will recall from earlier in this chapter that academic, language, intrinsic, and extrinsic factors can negatively impact whole-class discussions. The same is true for peer discussions in literature circles. Wiencek and O'Flahavan (1994) suggest considering the relative abilities of each student in three skill sets when creating literature circles and book clubs.

- Social ability: Is the student very quiet during group discussions? Is the student very vocal and often the leader?
- *Interpretive ability.* Do the students comprehend text and share their ideas with others? Do they have difficulty locating evidence to support their assertions?
- *Reading ability.* Will this text be at the students' independent, instructional, or frustration level? Independent = accuracy of 95% or above and 90% comprehension; instructional accuracy = 90–94% and 75% comprehension; frustration = 89% or below in accuracy.

The researchers suggest rating each child on a scale of 1–3 for each dimension and composing groups of five to six students with a mixed range of abilities for these skills (Wiencek & O'Flahavan, 1994). In this way, oral language development can be enhanced through the use of accountable talk with peers.

Jigsaw

Book clubs and literature circles promote discussion of a single text, but at other times students need to analyze multiple texts at the same time. When a group of readers is presented with information from several texts, they are more likely to make connections between those readings, called *intertextuality* (Bloome & Egan-Robertson, 1993). However, it can be difficult to organize multiple readings for use in a discussion. One instructional arrangement for doing so is a jigsaw (Aronson, 1978).

The readings used in a jigsaw may be chosen because they each offer similar perspectives of the same concept or event (*complementary*), or because they present very different views (*conflicting*) (Hartman & Allison, 1996). A third arrangement divides a concept or idea into smaller elements so that the topic is only fully understood after all the readings have been discussed (Aronson, 1978).

The jigsaw is accomplished through two types of groups: the home group and the expert group. First, members of a home group divide the task of reading multiple texts among themselves. Each reader is responsible for identifying the important elements of the text to report to the home group. They then meet in an expert group of students reading the same text to discuss the reading and take notes for use with the home group. Finally, students reconvene in their home group to learn and share information from each of the readings. A procedural map for jigsaw is illustrated in Figure 6.2.

SPEAKING AND LISTENING STANDARDS IN ACTION: USING A JIGSAW

Ms. Matheson's students are reading different perspectives of people who traveled west during the Gold Rush. She wants her students to talk about the various perspectives and uses a jigsaw to ensure that they will actively listen to the other members of their group. There are a total of six different readings, each about 600 words long. She assigns each student to a specific reading and asks them to read the text independently. The texts are somewhat leveled in that some are less conceptually dense than others, and Ms. Matheson assigns texts according to her assessment information, knowing that the assigned text would stretch the reader. Once students finish reading their assigned text, they meet in expert groups with others who read the same text. They discuss their shared text, talking about the major points raised by the writer and how this person fared during his or her travels. The students then meet in home groups, with each member of the group having read a different text. As each person shares what they learned from reading and talking about the text, the other members of the group use a structured note-taking tool to record information. This information is used later, as students write compare-and-contrast papers, analyzing the different experiences of travelers during the Gold Rush.

Table Topics

This activity ensures that students have practice with organizing their thinking and presenting ideas orally. Sample table topics include (1) What's best on pizza? (2) Who should be class president and why? (3) Why does England have a queen? and (4) What does it mean to be a friend?

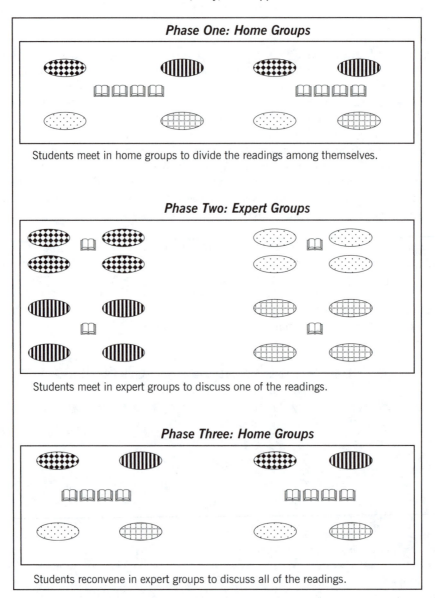

FIGURE 6.2. Jigsaw.

As students arrive at a center dedicated to table topics, they each select a numbered slip of paper from a container. Once they have randomly selected their table topics, students take a few minutes to make notes and organize their thinking. The person with the lowest number presents first. Remaining topics are presented in numerical order. Someone in the group sets the timer and the first person presents. Students know that they are to state their opinion or idea first, then provide two to four supporting details, facts, or points and then summarize or close. When the presentation is complete, other students in the group provide feedback. Again, a timer is used to ensure that each person in the group has an opportunity to share. The students know that this is not a time to disagree, that arguing over a position or opinion is not the point of this center. Rather, they focus on the speaking performance of the presenter and provide compliments and constructive criticism, duties that also require them to listen carefully in order to provide specific feedback, thus giving them practice with this skill.

Oral Composition before Writing

Emergent and early writers, while often eager to write, may not take as much time as they should to plan their writing. Brainstorming ideas and creating concept maps can be two useful strategies to encourage planning, although for the youngest writers this can sometimes be cognitively demanding. We encourage the use of peers to help students plan through *oral composition*. During collaborative writing, students meet with a peer to tell a story they are planning to write. The classmate listens to the story and then retells in his or her own words. The writer listens to the retelling to make sure the message was clear. At this point, the listener can ask clarifying questions and make suggestions. The intent of oral composition is to foster creative and critical thinking and give students opportunities to engage in narrative discourse. We keep a small poster to remind students about the steps for oral composition. See Figure 6.3.

Group Retellings

Students often find themselves reading the same material in order to complete a project or assignment. However, not all students in a group will comprehend the text equally. This is particularly true in heterogeneously constructed groups of students possessing a range of reading abilities. We encourage our students to use a group retelling when they are reading an assignment together. Group retelling is the student practice of reading a portion of the assignment and then stopping to retell what has been read to a partner (Wood & Jones, 1998). In this way, students can check each other's understanding, clarify difficult concepts, and ask questions. We advise introducing group retelling as a focus lesson, modeling the type of language used in a retelling. As students practice, the teacher should circulate and listen in on their retellings to provide guidance.

Tableau

As students move into the middle grades, they often become reluctant to perform in front of the class. For many, the potential for embarrassing themselves in front of peers outweighs any displeasure the teacher may show about their nonparticipation. An alternative to public performance is the tableau. Ironically, this is a silent activity that involves a group of students striking a group pose to dramatize a scene from a book. For example, students reading *Lord of the Flies* (Golding, 1954) can re-create the scene where the boys create rules for their life on the island, including the rule that the person who holds the conch shell gets to talk. The group reads the scene and discusses how it might look. They use simple props and the position of their bodies to illustrate the scene for the class while a narrator explains the tableau. The oral language development, of course, comes from the conversations within the group to plan the scene.

Oral Composition

	Writer's Job		Listener's Job
	Greet your partner.		Greet your partner.
	Tell your story to the listener. Try to tell it the way you want to write it.		Listen carefully and do not interrupt.
	Listen carefully and do not interrupt.		Retell the writer's story as best as you can.
	Ask your partner if there were any parts he or she did not understand. Listen carefully to the answers and do not interrupt.		Answer your partner's questions. Tell your partner about the parts you liked.
	Thank your partner for listening to your story.		Thank your partner for sharing their story.
	Use what you learned from your partner in your writing.		

FIGURE 6.3. Oral composition poster.

Independent Learning

How do you use oral language during independent learning? Remember that "independent" doesn't mean "isolated"; instead, it refers to times when students use the skills and strategies they have been learning to create original experiences. Therefore, this phase of the language arts workshop allows students to apply their listening and speaking skills in ways that are less structured than the collaborative learning activities.

Author's Chair

This is the time during the language arts workshop when writers share their work with others. Like other public performances, it is an opportunity for students to read and discuss their writing with classmates. Even emergent and early writers can share their work and take pride in their accomplishments. The actual chair itself is different from the others in the room (it may be a rocking chair, an ottoman, or other unique piece) and is placed in an area that allows for a small audience. Older students who may be more reticent about such public displays enjoy the "literacy lounge," a more intimate arrangement of pairs of students who read their work to one another while sharing hot chocolate or other treats. These experiences give students an opportunity to use conversational discourse while sharing their writing.

Extemporaneous Speaking

Many of us may recall a type of debate team competition called *extemporaneous speaking*. While we borrow the term, it is not performed as a competitive event in the language arts workshop; instead, we borrow the format:

- Three topics are drawn out of a jar and the speaker chooses one to focus on.
- The speaker is given 15 minutes to prepare talking points on the topic.
- Each speaker speaks for 3 minutes on the topic using notes.

Topics should be general in nature and developmentally appropriate. For example, topics might include a favorite vacation, a book recommended for a younger child, the best kind of pet, or current events of interest. The topic itself is less important than the routine of speaking in front of others. We recommend creating a classroom job of Featured Speaker along with others like the Door Holder, Line Leader, and Materials Manager.

During independent learning, the featured speakers make notes about what they want to say, using many of the principles of accountable talk to prepare their talk. Students can write these on 3 × 5 cards. Later, they address the class by rereading their topic and speaking from their notes.

CONCLUSION

Like other aspects of literacy, oral language is a developmental process that is enhanced with intentional instruction. In the language arts workshop, this means that students have many opportunities to talk with each other, to use academic language to understand concepts, and to speak to groups on more formal topics. Oral language development is tied to reading and writing as well and is an integral part of the process of becoming literate.

ACTIVITIES AND QUESTIONS

Activities

1. Pair with one or more teachers (or prospective teachers) in your school (or class). Select a grade level to focus on. Examine CCSS in language to identify which skills are emphasized. Make a list of the skills that you think some or all of the students in the grade you selected still are in the process of acquiring (i.e., have not been mastered). Consider whether there are other skills that your students need that are not included in the CCSS. Make a plan for how these skills will be taught along with the four writing applications.

2. Create a professional development session for your colleagues. Use several of the instructional routines in this chapter to facilitate interactions between and among the adults in the session. Invite them to talk about their use of academic language and how this might be useful for students.

Questions

1. What interaction skills do students in your classroom or school use? Do they regularly use is accountable talk in their interactions? What can you do to increase the amount of student-to-student interaction in your classroom or school?

2. Discuss how the classroom instructional routines outlined in this chapter can be used to develop students' speaking and listening skills such that they master the CCSS. How can these routines be used in history and science to ensure that students have additional practice to develop their speaking and listening skills?

3. How can students be assessed for oral language development such that progress can be monitored and supplemental instruction provided? Record a conversation with two students with differing abilities in oral language, and discuss the kinds of instruction that would be useful for each child.

REFERENCES

Aronson, E. (1978). *The jigsaw classroom*. Beverly Hills, CA: Sage.

Ashton-Warner, S. (1963). *Teacher*. New York: Simon & Schuster.

Block, S. (2001). Ask me a question: How teachers use inquiry in a classroom. *American School Board Journal, 188*(5), 43–45.

Bloome, D., & Egan-Robertson, A. (1993). The social construction of intertextuality in classroom reading and writing lessons. *Reading Research Quarterly, 28*, 305–333.

Burgess, S. R. (2002). The influence of speech perception, oral language ability, the home literacy environment, and pre-reading knowledge on the growth of phonological sensitivity: A one-year longitudinal investigation. *Reading and Writing, 15*, 709–737.

Carr, E., & Ogle, D. (1987). K-W-L plus: A strategy for comprehension and summarization. *Journal of Reading, 30*, 626–631.

Cazden, C. B. (1988). *Classroom discourse: The language of teaching and learning*. Portsmouth, NH: Heinemann.

Cazden, C. B. (2001). *Classroom discourse: The language of teaching and learning* (2nd ed.). Portsmouth, NH: Heinemann.

Cooper, D. H., Roth, F. P., Speece, D. L., & Schatschneider, C. (2002). The contribution of oral language skills to the development of phonological awareness. *Applied Psycholinguistics, 23*, 399–416.

Cooper, P., & Morreale, S. (Eds.). (2003). *Creating competent communicators: Activities for teaching speaking, listening, and media literacy in K–6 classrooms*. Scottsdale, AZ: Holcomb Hathaway.

Daniels, H. (2002). *Literature circles: Voice and choice in book clubs and reading groups* (2nd ed.). York, ME: Stenhouse.

Devine, T. G. (1978). Listening: What do we know after fifty years of research and theorizing? *Journal of Reading, 21*, 269–304.

Education Department of Western Australia. (1994a). *Oral language developmental continuum.* Melbourne: Longman.

Education Department of Western Australia. (1994b). *Oral language resource book.* Melbourne: Longman.

Fisher, K. (2003). If we can talk about it, we can write about it; if we can write about it, we can read about it. *Michigan Reading Journal, 35*(2), 6–12.

Galda, L. (1984). Narrative competence: Play, storytelling, and story comprehension. In A. D. Pellegrini & T. Yawkey (Eds.), *The development of oral and written language is social contexts* (pp. 105–117). Norwood, NJ: Ablex.

Harste, J., & Short, K. G. (1988). *Creating classrooms for authors: The reading–writing connection.* Portsmouth, NH: Heinemann.

Hartman, D. K., & Allison, J. (1996). Promoting inquiry-oriented discussions using multiple texts. In L. B. Gambrell & J. F. Almasi (Eds.), *Lively discussions! Fostering engaged readings* (pp. 106–133). Newark, DE: International Reading Association.

Holden, C. (1993). Giving girls a chance: Patterns of talk in co-operative group work. *Gender and Education, 5,* 179–189.

Lyman, F. T. (1981). The responsive classroom discussion: The inclusion of all students. In A. Anderson (Ed.), *Mainstreaming digest* (pp. 109–113). College Park: University of Maryland Press.

Manzo, A. V. (1969). The ReQuest procedure. *Journal of Reading, 11,* 123–126.

McKenzie, M. G. (1985). Shared writing: Apprenticeship in writing. *Language Matters, 1–2,* 1–5.

Mehan, H. (1979). *Learning lessons.* Cambridge, MA: Harvard University Press.

National Center on Education and the Economy. (2001). *Speaking and listening for preschool through third grade.* Washington, DC: New Standards.

National Governors Association Center for Best Practices and Council of Chief State School Officers. (2010). *Common Core State Standards for English language arts & literacy in history/social studies, and technical subjects.* Washington, DC: Author.

Ogle, D. M. (1986). K-W-L: A teaching model that develops active reading of expository text. *The Reading Teacher, 39,* 564–570.

Pinnell, G. S., & Jaggar, A. M. (2003). Oral language: Speaking and listening in elementary classrooms. In J. Flood, D. Lapp, J. R. Squire, & J. M. Jensen (Eds.), *Handbook of research on teaching the English language arts* (2nd ed., pp. 881–913). Mahwah, NJ: Erlbaum.

Resnick, L. (1995). From aptitude to effort: A new foundation for our schools. *Daedalus, 124*(4), 55–62.

Ross, R. (1964). A look at listeners. *Elementary School Journal, 64,* 369–372.

Sadker, M., & Sadker, D. (1995). *Failing at fairness: How America's schools cheat girls.* New York: Scribner.

Spor, M. W., & Schneider, B. K. (1999). Content reading strategies: What teachers know, use, and want to learn. *Reading Research and Instruction, 38,* 221–231.

Vygotsky, L. S. (1986). *Thought and language* (A. Kozulin, Ed.). Cambridge, MA: MIT Press.

Wiencek, J., & O'Flahavan, J. F. (1994). From teacher-led to peer discussion groups about literature: Suggestions for making the shift. *Language Arts, 71,* 488–498.

Wood, K. D., & Jones, J. (1998). Flexible grouping and group retellings include struggling learners in classroom communities. *Preventing School Failure, 43,* 37–38.

CHILDREN'S BOOKS CITED

Berger, M. (2002). *Snap! A book about alligators and crocodiles.* New York: Cartwheel.

Berger, M. (2003). *Spinning spiders.* New York: HarperTrophy.

Bunting, E. (1992). *The wall.* New York: Clarion.

Chambers, C. E. (1998). *California Gold Rush.* New York: Troll.

Cole, J. (1995). *Spider's lunch: All about garden spiders.* New York: Grosset & Dunlap.

Corrigan, P. (2001). *Cougars: Our wild world.* Chanhassen, MN: NorthWord.

Gibbons, G. (1994). *Spiders.* New York: Holiday House.

Gibbons, G. (1995). *Wolves!* New York: Holiday House.

Glaser, L. (1999). *Spectacular spiders.* Riverside, NJ: Millbrook.

Golding, W. (1954). *Lord of the flies.* New York: Perigee.

Hodge, D. (1999). *Bears: Polar bears, black bears, and grizzly bears.* Tonawanda, NY: Kids Can Press.

Kalman, B. (1999). *The gold rush.* New York: Crabtree.

Krensky, S. (1996). *Strike it rich!* New York: Scott Foresman.

Quang, N. H. (1986). *The land I lost: A boy in Vietnam.* New York: HarperTrophy.

Reinhart, M. (2003). *Young naturalist's handbook: Insect-lo-pedia.* New York: Hyperion.

Robinson, F. (1996). *Hello spider!* New York: Scott Foresman.

Schanzer, R. (1999). *Gold fever!* Washington, DC: National Geographic.

Schlosser, E. (2002). *Fast food nation: The dark side of the all-American meal.* New York: HarperCollins.

Whelan, G. (1993). *Goodbye Vietnam.* New York: Yearling.

White, E. E. (2002). *The journal of Patrick Seamus Flaherty: U.S. Marine Corps, Khe Sanh, Vietnam, 1968.* New York: Scholastic.

Winer, Y. (1998). *Spiders spin webs.* Watertown, MA: Charlesbridge.

CHAPTER 7

Language Standards for Vocabulary

Camille L. Z. Blachowicz
James F. Baumann

In our work in schools, we have heard variants of the question, "Do new standards mean we have to start all over again?" In our responses, we emphasized that, just as any expert chef can use new tools and sharper knives, so teachers can use these new standards to sharpen their practice. When preparing this chapter on the Common Core State Standards (CCSS) (National Governors Association [NGA] Center for Best Practices and Council of Chief State School Officers [CCSSO], 2010), we considered the standards to be useful for informed teachers to focus and enhance their vocabulary curriculum and instruction. Our purpose in writing this chapter is to provide grade 3–5 elementary classroom teachers, reading teachers and specialists, literacy coaches and coordinators, and principals, along with fellow teacher educators, with a straightforward description of the language standards for vocabulary (anchor Standards 4, 5, and 6) and how they can be used to foster children's ability to understand and learn from narrative and informational text. Because of the limitations of space, and because of the centrality of vocabulary to the language standards and to all of the other CCSS, we are focusing on vocabulary. Language standards for conventions of standard English and knowledge of language are incorporated in some of the teaching examples but not discussed in detail.

We begin by describing the CCSS that address vocabulary and review the research and theory that support them. We then provide ideas on how teachers can use the vocabulary standards to design and guide their everyday classroom instruction. We then describe how teachers can efficiently embed the vocabulary standards into their language arts, social studies, and science curricula and assess students' performance. Finally, we present resources for teaching the vocabulary standards and some summative concluding remarks, followed by questions and activities related to the standards.

DEFINING THE STANDARDS FOR VOCABULARY INSTRUCTION

Analysis of the CCSS (see Appendix 7.1) suggests five major challenges for teachers of students in grades 3–5. Teachers must prepare students to:

1. Read and comprehend narrative text and to understand and learn from informational text;
2. Read texts that are increasingly more complex in substance, structure, and required background knowledge;
3. Use evidence from the text to construct meaning and arguments that can be developed and extended in writing and presentation;
4. Learn the meanings of more difficult words, including the academic vocabulary (Baumann & Graves, 2010) that is pervasive in informational texts, and be taught how to determine word meanings through word-learning strategies;
5. Develop the ability to read, analyze, write about, and learn from subject-matter texts across the curriculum.

These challenges ground the specific language arts CCSS, of which vocabulary is an essential component.

WHAT AND WHERE
ARE THE VOCABULARY STANDARDS?

None of the four domain strands in the CCSS specifically identifies vocabulary, but there are three standards within the language strand labeled Vocabulary Acquisition and Use. These standards are based on the college and career readiness (CRR) standards, which "anchor the document and define general, cross-disciplinary literacy expectations that must be met for students to be prepared to enter college and workforce training programs ready to succeed" (NGA and CCSSO, 2010, p. 4). In other words, the CRR "anchor" standards are the core abilities on which the individual K–12 grade-level standards were generated. The three Vocabulary Acquisition and Use CCR anchor standards for Language—numbered 4, 5, and 6—follow (p. 29): Nested under each of the three vocabulary anchor standards are substandards that provide elaboration and detail, which we reference in the classroom examples.

Although the majority of the CCSS related to vocabulary are embedded within the Vocabulary Acquisition and Use strand, it states in Appendix A of the standards that "the Standards take a hybrid approach to matters of conventions, knowledge of language, and vocabulary" and that these three strands "extend across reading, writing, speaking, and listening" (p. 28). The authors clarify further by stating that "the inclusion of Language standards in their own strand should not be taken as an indication that skills related to conventions, knowledge of language, and vocabulary are unimportant to reading, writing, speaking, and listening; indeed, they are inseparable from such contexts" (p. 28). In other words, there are additional vocabulary standards dispersed throughout the CCSS beyond those in the Vocabulary Acquisition and Use strand.

We combed the grade 3, 4, and 5 CCSS and identified all standards that address vocabulary in some fashion; these are assembled in Table 7.1. It is important to note that although the CCSS include a Speaking and Listening domain, it is not listed in Table 7.1 because we identified no explicit vocabulary-related standards in this domain.

TABLE 7.1. Vocabulary Standards in the Grade 3–5 CCSS (Codes Only)

Standard	Grade		
	3	4	5
Reading Standards			
Literature: Craft and Structure	RL.4 *WC*	RL.4 *WC*	RL.4 *WC*
Informational Text: Craft and Structure	RI.4 *TIW*	RI.4 *TIW*	RI.4 *TIW*
Reading Foundations: Phonics and Word Recognition	RF.3.a-b *WLS*	FR.3.a *WLS*	RF3.a *WLS*
Reading Foundations: Fluency	RF.4.c *WLS*	RF.4.c *WLS*	FR4.c *WLS*
Writing Standards			
Text Types and Purposes	—	W2.d *WC* W.3.d *WC*	W2.d *WC* W.3.d *WC*
Language Standards			
Conventions of Standard English	L.2.f *WLS*	—	—
Knowledge of Language	L.3.a *WC*	L.3.a *WC*	—
Vocabulary Acquisition and Use	L4.a-d *WLS* L.5.a-c *WC* L.6 *TIW*	L.4.a-c *WLS* L.5.a-c *WC* L.6 *TIW*	L.4.a-c *WLS* L.5.a-c *WC* L.6 *TIW*

Notes. The codes at the top of each cell correspond to CCSS as follows: domain (reading, writing, language), standard number within domains (e.g., 1, 2, 3), and substandard when they are present (e.g., a, b, c). The following abbreviations correspond to Graves's (2000, 2006) research-based categories: RVL, rich and varied language experiences; TIW, teach individual words; WLS, word-learning strategies; WC, word consciousness.

Additionally, only those domain strands that contain vocabulary standards are included in this table. Finally, codes in the table refer to domain (reading, writing, language), standard number within domains (e.g., 1, 2, 3), and substandard when they are present (e.g., a, b, c). For example, RF.4.c refers to reading fluency Standard 4, substandard c. There also are codes to identify four components of sound vocabulary instruction, which we discuss in the next section. Appendix A in this book contains a complete list of the standards, a useful resource for reference as you read this chapter.

WHAT RESEARCH AND THEORY SUPPORT THE VOCABULARY STANDARDS?

The CCSS states that the standards "are evidence-based" (Common Core State Standards Initiative, n.d.); additionally, the standards include a brief overview of vocabulary research (see CCSS Appendix A, Vocabulary, pp. 32–35). It does not, however, address the extensive research on vocabulary acquisition and instruction that supports the vocabulary standards (Baumann, Kame'enui, & Ash, 2003; Beck & McKeown, 1991; Blachowicz & Fisher, 2000; Nagy & Scott, 2000). Therefore, we provide a focused review of research findings that support key elements in the vocabulary CCSS. We do so according to Graves's (2000, 2006) four-component vocabulary instruction framework, which has been acknowledged several times in the literature (Baumann & Kame'enui, 2004; Nagy, 2005; Stahl & Nagy, 2006) as representing a balanced, comprehensive, multifaceted vocabulary instruction program (Baumann, Blachowicz, Manyak, Graves, & Olejnik, 2012; Baumann, Ware, & Edwards, 2007): "(1) providing rich and varied language experiences; (2) teaching individual words; (3) teaching word-learning strategies; and (4) fostering word consciousness" (Graves, 2006, p. 5). We elaborate on each component in following sections, acknowledging the research and theoretical literature relevant to the vocabulary standards.

Provide Rich and Varied Language Experiences (RVL)

The research is clear that children need to be immersed in a linguistically rich environment to develop aural and oral vocabulary (Hart & Risley, 1995). Likewise, children acquire words through the rich vocabulary in printed texts (Hayes & Ahrens, 1988)—both narrative and expository (Hiebert & Cervetti, 2012)—by listening to parents and teachers read aloud (Bus, van IJzendoorn, & Pellegrini, 1995; Elley, 1989). Vocabulary is also acquired through extensive independent reading (Cunningham, 2005; Cunningham & O'Donnell, 2012; Swanborn & de Glopper, 1999). There are no specific CCSS that address the linguistic immersion events and activities that fall under Graves's first component; hence, the RVL code does not appear in Table 7.1. The standards make clear, however, that "the importance of students acquiring a rich and varied vocabulary cannot be overstated" (CCSS Appendix A, p. 32), and that "new words and phrases are acquired . . . through reading and being read to" (CCSS Appendix A, p. 28). For example, speaking and listening Standard 2 implies RVL when stating that students must be able to "determine the main idea and supporting details" (grade 3), "paraphrase" (grade 4), or "summarize" (grade 5) a "text read aloud or information presented in diverse media and formats, including visually, quantitatively, and orally" (CCSS, p. 24). Thus, the CCSS support providing RVL experiences for children, be they oral conversation, reading aloud, or independent reading.

Teach Individual Words (TIW)

Extensive research evidence demonstrates that students can be taught the meanings of words directly through a variety of strategies and techniques (Beck & McKeown, 1991; Blachowicz & Fisher, 2010; Graves, 2009). We know that brief definitional word explanations provide students a limited "foot-in-the-door level of knowledge" (Baumann et al., 2003, p. 778) of words. More intensive instruction, however, that involves both definitional and contextual information, multiple exposures, and deep levels of processing are needed for students to acquire nuanced levels of word meaning (Mezynski, 1983; Graves, 1986; Nagy & Scott, 2000; Stahl & Fairbanks, 1986), particularly if one hopes for vocabulary instruction to enhance reading comprehension (Baumann, 2009; Elleman, Lindo, Morphy, & Compton, 2009). Standards that align with Graves's (2000,

2006) TIW component can be found for all grades in reading informational text: craft and structure and for all grades in language: vocabulary acquisition and use.

Teach Word-Learning Strategies (WLS)

Word-learning strategies are approaches for teaching students to infer the meanings of unknown or partially known words through the use of context clues and morphemic analysis (root words, prefixes, suffixes, and Latin and Greek word roots) and are directly called for in the CCSS. (L.4: determine or clarify the meaning of unknown and multiple-meaning word and phrases based on *grade* [3, 4, or 5] *reading and content*, choosing flexibly from a range of strategies" [CCSS, p. 29].) Several recent studies document the effectiveness of instruction in morphology to enhance students' independent word learning (Baumann, Edwards, Boland, Olejnik, & Kame'enui, 2003; Baumann et al., 2002, 2011; White, Sowell, & Yanagihara, 1989). Likewise, several meta-analyses support this same conclusion with respect to typically developing readers (Bowers, Kirby, & Deacon, 2010; Carlisle, McBride-Chang, Nagy, & Nunes, 2010) and to students who experience reading difficulties (Goodwin & Ahn, 2010; Reed, 2008). Additionally, there are individual studies (Baumann et al., 2002, 2007; Baumann, Edwards, et al., 2003; Buikema & Graves, 1993) as well as a meta-analysis by Fukkink and de Glopper (1998) that support the effectiveness of teaching students to infer word meanings. Thus, the many grade 3–5 CCSS identified as WLS in Table 7.1 have strong support in the research literature.

Foster Word Consciousness (WC)

"Word consciousness" is a term used to describe cognitive and metacognitive knowledge and behaviors with respect to vocabulary, including awareness of when a word's meaning is understood and when it is not; knowledge of the morphological, etymological, and interrelational aspects of words; appreciation of figurative language and language play; and recognition that interesting, colorful words can be used effectively in oral and written communication (Blachowicz, Fisher, Ogle, & Watts-Taffe, 2006; Graves & Watts-Taffe, 2002; Nagy, 2005; Scott, Miller, & Flinspach, 2012). This understanding of word relationships and how words work is also contained in the standards (e.g., "Demonstrate understanding of figurative language, word relationships, and nuances in word meanings," CCSS grade 3, 5a, p. 29).

The impact of WC instruction and environments on students' affective and cognitive growth in vocabulary has been thoroughly documented (Scott, Flinspach, Miller, Gage-Serio, & Vevea, 2009; Scott, Hoover, Flinspach, & Vevea, 2008; Scott, Vevea, & Flinspach, 2010), and several CCSS for grades 3–5 address WC, the fourth component of Graves's model (see Table 7.1 on page 133).

PUTTING THE VOCABULARY STANDARDS INTO PRACTICE

The classroom vignettes in this section illustrate how the standards can be used to plan and teach specific vocabulary lessons. The vignettes correspond to the three vocabulary acquisition and use anchor standards embedded in the language strand, which we presented and discussed earlier—Standards L.4, L.5, and L.6 in Table 7.1 and Appendix 7.1.

The vignettes are drawn from lessons taught by teachers in our federally funded vocabulary research project—Development of a Multi-Faceted, Comprehensive, Vocabulary Instructional Program for the Upper-Elementary Grades (Baumann et al., 2009–2012), or MCVIP. The lessons are either verbatim from our research records or close reconstructions of lessons actually taught by our teacher participants over the duration of our grant.

VOCABULARY STANDARDS IN ACTION: LEARNING ABOUT WORD RELATIONSHIPS THROUGH REAL-LIFE CONNECTIONS

Grade 3 Language Standard. 5 Demonstrate understanding of word relationships and nuances in word meanings.

  b. Identify real-life connections between words and their use (e.g., describe people who are *friendly* or *helpful*). (CCSS, p. 29)

Jenny and her colleagues were committed to helping their third-grade students comprehend the rich, nuanced, descriptive vocabulary found in narrative texts and to use such words in their speech and writing. This was especially important because two of the classrooms were two-way immersion (TWI) classes, in which instruction was delivered in both English and Spanish. Vocabulary instruction was a goal for all the classrooms, along with engaging students in rich language use. Helping students to identify real-life connections between words and their use (e.g., describe people who are *friendly* or *helpful*) was an important goal for understanding narrative text.

Jenny's team used a modified character trait analysis (CTA) (Manyak, 2007) instructional strategy to teach important character-related words as well as promote students' thoughtful text comprehension, understanding of word relationships, and engagement in rich dialogue about vocabulary. This strategy reflects the goals of CCSS grade 3 language goal 5b, which calls on students to be able to "demonstrate understanding of figurative language, word relationships, and nuances in word meanings." Because CTA's focus is on rich discussion, reading aloud, discussing quality children's books, and teaching character words, this strategy aligns with Graves's (2000, 2006) TIW vocabulary instruction and RVL components.

Here's how the team implemented one CTA unit. First, they selected engaging, age-appropriate books that contain interesting characters who embody some of the grade-level CTA words identified by Manyak (2007). They started with *The Recess Queen* in English (O'Neill, 2002), and then they added more books available in both English and in Spanish, including *La Historia de Ruby Bridges* (Coles, 1995), *Amazing Grace* (Hoffman, 1991), and *Crisantemo/Chrysanthemum* (Henkes, 1993). From Manyak's (2007) list the teachers identified several character trait words for study, some of which applied to characters in the selected books, although not all words applied to all characters. Figure 7.1 presents the selected words, including *brave, careful, confident,* and others drawn from Manyak's list.

To introduce the process and the words, Jenny and the other teachers read aloud or did a shared reading of each book without interruption so that the narrative flowed and students enjoyed the book. Afterward, the teachers engaged the students in a character

★ Character Traits ★
(Los rasgos de personajes diferentes)

* Put a ✓ next to the characteristics that the character in the story has!

Book title / Título del libro	Character's name / Nombre del personaje	brave / valiente	careful / cuidadoso	clever / listo	confident / seguro de sí mismo	considerate / considerado	honest / honesto	intelligent / inteligente	impatient / impaciente	irresponsible / irresponsable
The Recess Queen	Jean	✓			✓	✓			✓	✓
La historia de Ruby Bridges	Ruby Bridges	✓		✓	✓	✓	✓	✓		
Amazing Grace	Grace	✓		✓	✓			✓		
Crisantemo (Por Kevin Henkes)	Crisantemo	✓	✓	✓		✓	✓	✓		

FIGURE 7.1. Third-grade character trait analysis chart.

trait discussion in which they determined whether a particular character possessed or exhibited a given trait, and they completed a character matrix, as depicted in Figure 7.1. The students were required to provide evidence for their judgments as they constructed a character trait chart for the book.

After more than one book had been read and the students were familiar with the process, the individual CTA charts were combined on a team chart that included the central character from different books. Each class used a different-colored checkmark to represent their analyses of the characters (see Figure 7.1). Then the children were encouraged to begin to make between-book character comparisons. Interesting discussions ensued, as exemplified in the following dialogue between two students who shared their perspectives on the character trait word *bravery* as it applied to the character Ruby Bridges in *The Story of Ruby Bridges* and the character Cristenemo/Chrysanthemum in the book by the same name:

- Susan: I can see how Ruby was brave. See, on this page, how she went out there with all those people who didn't want her there and might hurt her? But why do you say Cristenemo was brave?
- Maria: She had to keep going to school even though all the kids teased her and she didn't change her name.
- Susan: Well, it's a different kind of brave, but it is a kind of being brave, not "body brave" but another kind.

This dialogue shows how the students had to identify real-life connections between words and their use in coming to a broader meaning for the word *brave.*

In addition to the discussion surrounding the charts, the teachers had students write character trait summaries using the new vocabulary. They use a Writer's Workshop approach to writing (Calkins & Mermelstein, 2003), within which they teach mini-lessons aligned to the language standards for conventions of standard English. In this unit, students were editing to apply Standard L1:

- d. Form and use regular and irregular verbs.
- e. Form and use the simple (e.g., *I walked*; *I walk*; *I will walk*) verb tenses.
- f. Ensure subject–verb and pronoun–antecedent agreement.

For overall assessment the teachers used the students' personal chart and written character descriptions to assess whether or not they understood meanings of new character trait words and could use them in their writing, demonstrating a command of the conventions of standard English grammar and usage.

The teachers also planned extensions of the CTA lessons to encourage more rich language use. For example, the third graders invited fourth and fifth graders in the school who were also working on character traits to examine the large chart (Figure 7.1) and direct questions to the third-grade Chart Masters. The older students asked questions like "How do you know Ruby Bridges was brave? Read to me from the book some proof" and "How was Crisantemo like Ruby Bridges? Where's your proof? Read to me what the author said that made you think that." Academic vocabulary like *evidence*, *proof*, *characteristics*, and *trait* were used often and correctly by the students of all grade levels as they continued to use CTA throughout the year.

VOCABULARY STANDARDS IN ACTION: USING CONTEXT CLUES TO CLARIFY MEANING

L.4 Determine or clarify the meaning of unknown and multiple-meaning word and phrases based on *grade 4 reading and content*, choosing flexibly from a range of strategies.

- a. Use context (e.g., definitions, examples, or restatements in text) as a clue to the meaning of a word or phrase.

Matthew's assessment revealed that his fourth-grade students had difficulty inferring the meanings of unknown words, which impaired their reading comprehending. He decided, therefore, to teach a series of lessons on understanding and using context clues. Matthew selected the grade 4 language Standard L.4.a, which aligns with Graves's (2000, 2006) WLS vocabulary instruction component.

After teaching an introductory lesson on general context clues, Matthew implemented his planned lesson on identifying and using definition context clues. Using an interactive white board, Matthew began by presenting and reviewing the definition of context clues. He wrote:

- Context clues are words or phrases that give readers hints or ideas about the meanings of other words.

Matthew then explains what a definition context clue is and provides an example on the white board using the word *brambles*:

- A definition context clue is when an author explains the meaning of a word right in the sentence or selection.

- Example: When Sara was hiking, she accidentally walked through a patch of *brambles*, which are *prickly vines and shrubs.*

After pairing up his students, Matthew supported the lesson with additional practice: "Look at these next sentences on the white board and see if you and your partner can find definition context clues for the words *gusty* and *quagmire.*"

- The wind was so *gusty*—very strong bursts of wind—that Sally's hat blew across the road.
- When we were walking by the pond, my dog Lady stepped in a *quagmire*, or soft, wet, mushy ground. I had to get my Mom to help pull her out.

After inviting several pairs of students to share their ideas on context clues for *gusty* ("very strong bursts of wind") and *quagmire* ("soft, wet, mushy ground"), Matthew asked, "Did anyone find punctuation marks in the sentences that helped you find the definitions?" Dianne responded that the dashes told her that the words in between were the definition for *gust*. Miguel added that the comma after the word *or* told him that the definition for *quagmire* followed. Matthew then asked, "Could anyone say the first sentence without using the word *gusty*?" to which Christina responded, "The wind was so strong that Sally's hat blew across the road."

For independent practice, Matthew asked his students to look for definition context clues when they are reading and come to a word they do not understand. He also reviewed definition context clues prior to his daily read-aloud periods. During his read-alouds, he stopped when he came across a clear example of a definition context clue and asked his students to identify it.

VOCABULARY STANDARDS IN ACTION: LEARNING ABOUT NUANCES IN WORD MEANINGS—CONNOTATIONS

L.5 Demonstrate understanding of figurative language, word relationships, and nuances in word meanings.

    c. Use the relationship between particular words (e.g., synonyms, antonyms, homographs) to better understand each of the words.

Nita, a fifth-grade teacher, was very concerned with her students' understanding of word connotations and other word relationships that depended on shades of meaning. This concern was a good match to CCSS grade 5 language Standard L5.c, which aligns with Graves's (2000, 2006) WC component.

To help her students develop their understanding of connotative meanings of words, Nita had her students work through a word-scaling activity (see Figure 7.2). This required students to arrange in order, using a thermometer chart—from positive to negative—synonymous adjectives such as *lazy*, *inactive*, and *relaxed*. Students first worked in teams to discuss the meanings of the words and their reasons for placing them on the positive or negative end of the continuum. The teams then participated in a class discussion, requiring them to give reasons for their placements. Disagreements arose and students had to defend their reasoning, as in this example:

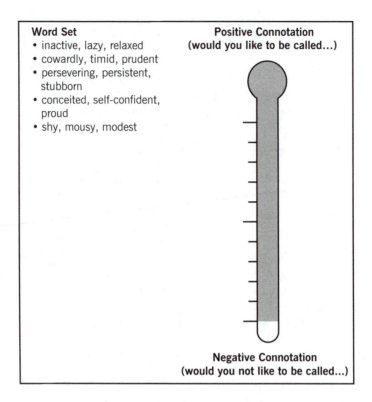

FIGURE 7.2. Fith-grade connotation scale.

TEAM 1: We think *relaxed* is a positive term. We'd like to be called "relaxed."

TEAM 2: Well, we think it could be negative. If there was a fire and you were just relaxed, you wouldn't be acting in a very positive way.

TEAM 3: If *relaxed* means *calm*, then being calm is a good thing to be in a crisis.

TEACHER: These are good points. It certainly depends on the situation. Let's all imagine the same situation . . .

TEAM 1: How about "at home for dinner"?

TEACHER: OK, what do you all think?

TEAM 1: Being at home for dinner and being relaxed is positive. Being inactive, you can't tell. Being lazy, you're not helping with anything.

TEAM 2: Well, OK for this one, but we still think "relaxed" is not good in a crisis.

TEAM 1: I don't know about that. Like in a crisis, they tell you to take a deep breath and relax so you can think clearly.

TEACHER: How about asking yourself which of these would you like to be called and which would you not like to be called in everyday life? That would be a positive connotation.

TEAM 2: OK, then *relaxed* is positive. (Other groups concur.) But we still think it could be different.

These discussions engaged students in recognizing and teasing out the shades of meanings of related words and participating in rich discussion while doing so. Teachers used the individual rating charts and student writing to assess their understanding of the new vocabulary words. They were also called on to "acquire and use accurately grade-appropriate general academic and domain-specific words and phrases, including those that signal precise actions, emotions, or states of being (L.6)," as seen in all of the examples in this section and the section to follow, which illustrates how teachers orchestrate the teaching of several standards at a time in content classes.

USING THE VOCABULARY STANDARDS THROUGHOUT THE SCHOOL DAY

As we noted earlier, one of the major themes of the standards is the concept of integrated instruction across the school day. Integration is important for vocabulary development, as students who read several texts on the same topic encounter vocabulary many times in both different and related contexts. In this section, we look at a classroom example of integrated instruction where standards for vocabulary are being met along with standards from literature, informational reading, speaking and listening, and other language standards.

Learning Science Vocabulary in Grade 3

Karen, a third-grade teacher in a TWI class, modified an instructional approach called Vocabulary Visits (Blachowicz & Obrochta, 2005, 2007) when teaching content units. Her goals for vocabulary address grade 3 CCSS for vocabulary in the language strand (L.4) as well as for non-vocabulary-specific standards in reading informational text (RI.4 and RI.5), writing (W.4), and speaking and listening (SL.1. and SL.2). Rather than block out the standards here, we intersperse them throughout the description.

For her science unit on sound, Karen first collected books at many reading levels on sound in both Spanish and in English. Because she used FOSS Science (2011), many books are provided for her, and she supplements these with other texts when necessary. For example, she added books from the series *A Creative, Hands-on Approach to Science* (Baker & Hasam, 1993a, 1993b, 1993c, 1993d), *Zounds: The Kids' Guide to Sound Making* (Newman, 1983), along with other texts that augment a "staircase of increasing text complexity" (CCSS, p. 8 [NGA and CCSSO, 2010]). Then she began her instructional sequence, focusing on using text features, using references to clarify meaning, and acquiring grade-appropriate content and academic vocabulary.

Before Reading

Karen introduced her unit by asking each student to brainstorm a list of words associated with the word *sound*. This First Write activity helped students activate their knowledge about sound. It also helped Karen preassess students' level of knowledge on the topic. On average, students generated fewer than five words each before this unit, and these tended to be general vocabulary, such as *loud*, *soft*, and *music*.

Then students selected informational books on sound from the classroom sets. Their assignment was to skim through their chosen book to locate three to five words they believed would be important to the unit and should be learned. They wrote these words on Post-it notes to bring to the large-group discussion. Karen prepared her students for this activity by teaching a mini-lesson on typographical clues and word frequency to help the students select appropriate words from the books. She also introduced them to the academic vocabulary *boldface* and *frequency*. She concluded her mini-lesson by stating, "You need to use text features to pick out important vocabulary. If a word is boldfaced and is frequent, or occurring many times, then it probably is an important word" (RI.3.5. Use text features and search tools [e.g., key words, sidebars, hyperlinks] to locate information relevant to a given topic efficiently.)

When the large group reconvened, one student began by placing a Post-it note on the chart, and then other students who had chosen the same word followed suit. In this way, the class constructed a chart of important terms (most frequent words on Post-it notes). This gave them experience in selecting critical academic vocabulary, a valuable study skill. Karen could also add words she believed were important if the students did not contribute them to the chart. Figure 7.3 presents a portion of the class chart that Karen's students constructed for their unit on sound.

During Reading

Karen had her students use a word log to record important words as they read, to write kid-friendly definitions, and to note any context clues that help them. They may also consult the glossary or conventional or electronic reference if needed (L.4c. Consult reference materials [e.g., dictionaries, glossaries, and thesauruses], both print and digital, to find the pronunciation and determine or clarify the precise meaning of key words and phrases.)

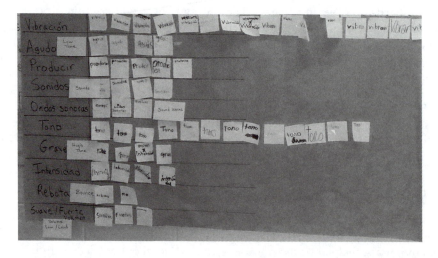

FIGURE 7.3. Vocabulary visits important word chart on sound—Spanish/English.

After Reading

Karen led small-group discussions in which the students shared words from their logs. For example, to understand the importance of vibration to sound, students had to explain the relationship of *movement*, *vibration*, *pitch*, and *intensity* of sound. Students also completed their FOSS lab sheets using the appropriate vocabulary (see Figure 7.4). Karen used the lab sheets that accompanied the units to assess learning. This textual use of the science words helped Karen assess learning.

At the end of the unit, each student also completed a Final Write, a timed brainstorming of all the words the student could connect to sound. Compared with the First Write, Karen's students wrote more words, and the words were more sophisticated and connected to the unit theme. From their use of the word on their lab sheets and their construction of a related set of sound words, Karen could determine whether they adequately demonstrated the ability to "acquire and use accurately grade-appropriate general academic and domain-specific words and phrases" (L.6). Karen and her colleagues were committed to integrating vocabulary instruction with content learning and saw this as part of the positive potential of the CCSS.

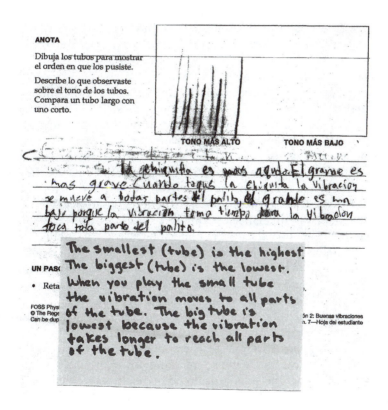

FIGURE 7.4. FOSS science lab sheet on sound—Spanish with translation.

CONCLUSION

We began this chapter by responding to the concerns of teachers faced with the important job of making theoretical and practical decisions about the use of the CCSS. As you read this chapter, we hope you could begin to envision instruction to help students develop their vocabularies and vocabulary learning skills and strategies in ways supported by the standards. To assist you in this work, we described the CCSS that relate to vocabulary as they appear in the Vocabulary Acquisition and Use domain of the language standards and charted for you the vocabulary-related standards that are embedded within and across the reading literature, reading informational text, reading foundation skills, and writing strands. We also matched the vocabulary standards to Graves's (2000, 2006) four-component vocabulary instructional framework, and sketched out the research and practice base for effective vocabulary instruction. To give life to these ideas, classroom vignettes illustrate ways teachers might put the vocabulary standards into practice in grades 3, 4, and 5. We also included an example of how the standards could be connected in integrated instruction throughout the school day.

We draw two conclusions from our analysis of vocabulary-related CCSS and how they may be used to guide instruction. First, we believe that the CCSS vocabulary standards are substantively sound, grounded in the literature, and useful for preparing practical, effective vocabulary lessons. The specificity of the CCSS enables teachers to examine their existing language arts curriculum and instructional materials and then to select or design lessons that help their students to acquire vocabulary knowledge and strategies.

At the same time, the standards are only a beginning. They are indeed a sensible framework for preparing and assessing vocabulary lessons, but they do not cover all the content of a sound vocabulary program (Baumann et al., 2009–2012, 2011; Graves, 2000, 2006). Therefore, we urge educators to rely on the many fine articles in journals (e.g., *The Reading Teacher, Journal of Adolescent & Adult Literacy*) and professional books on vocabulary (e.g., Beck, McKeown, & Kucan, 2002, 2008; Blachowicz & Fisher, 2010; Farstrup & Samuels, 2008; Graves, 2006, 2009; Hiebert & Kamil, 2005; Kame'enui & Baumann, 2012; Stahl & Nagy, 2006; Templeton, Bear, Johnston, & Invernizzi, 2010) to learn about specific instructional strategies and approaches that help structure research-based balanced vocabulary instruction.

Second, it is important for educators to understand that the vocabulary standards—or any educational standards for that matter—are limited in that they outline only what learners ought to know and be able to do. The CCSS vocabulary-related standards, therefore, are not curriculum and instruction and thus do not specify what teachers ought to do. For example, the CCSS vocabulary standards specify that students should be able to use context and word structure clues to infer a word's meaning, but they offer nothing about how to accomplish this. Additionally, because the standards emphasize the student, they may not address explicitly all that teachers must do to promote word learning. For example, the research is clear on the importance and power of a rich literate environment for vocabulary learning, but the standards do not explicitly state that teachers should be reading aloud quality fiction and nonfiction across the K–12 spectrum; providing ample time daily for independent, self-selected reading; scheduling time for daily student writing; and providing multiple opportunities for student-to-teacher and student-to-student dialogue about vocabulary.

RESOURCES TO SUPPORT STANDARDS-BASED INSTRUCTION

In all the chapter examples of how teachers used the CCSS, materials were important. Reading materials need to have engaging content and interesting vocabulary. The reading materials also need to be at an appropriate reading level for the student and increase in complexity.

Books

Manyak (2007) provides a list of suggested specific books of appropriate complexity and grade-level vocabulary for his character trait analysis lessons:

Cohen, C. L., & Begay, S. (1988). *The mud pony: A traditional Skidi Pawnee tale*. New York: Scholastic.

Farris, C. K., & Soentpiet, C. K. (2003). *My brother Martin: A sister remembers growing up with the Rev. Dr. Martin Luther King, Jr.* New York: Simon & Schuster Books for Children.

Kellogg, S. (1986). *Pecos Bill: A tall tale*. New York: William Morrow.

Lowry, L., & Ibatoulline, B. (2009). *Crow call*. New York: Scholastic Press.

Martin, R. (1992). *The rough-faced girl*. New York. Scholastic Press.

Stroud, B., Cornelious, V. W., & Hu, Y.-H. (2001). *Dance y'all*. New York: Marshall Cavendish.

Swain, G., & Conkle, N. (1994). *The black cowboy*. Santa Barbara, CA: Bellerophon Books.

Tunnell, M. O., & Rand, T. (1997). *Mailing May*. New York: Greenwillow Books.

Van, A. C. (1991). *The wretched stone*. Boston: Houghton Mifflin.

Wetterer, M. K., & Ritz, K. (1990). *Kate Shelley and the midnight express*. Minneapolis, MN: Carolrhoda Books.

Young, J., & Farnsworth, B. (2009). *Minnow and Rose: An Oregon trail story*. Chelsea, MI: Sleeping Bear Press.

Below are some children's books to stimulate interest in words and wordplay:

Adams, R. (1994). *The cowboy dictionary: The chin jaw words and whing-ding ways of the American West*. New York: Pedigree.

Asher, S. (1997). *Wild words and how to tame them*. New York: Walker.

Asimov, I. (1986). *Robot dreams*. New York: Berkley Books.

Bowler, P. (1994). *The superior person's second book of weird and wondrous words*. New York: Laurel.

Campbell, G. (1992). *Words: A potpourri of fascinating origins*. Santa Barbara, CA: Capra Press.

Cutler, C. (1994). *O brave new words: Native American loanwords in current English*. Norman: University of Oklahoma Press.

Dickson, P. (1992). *The Dickson's word treasury: A connoisseur's collection of old and new, weird and wonderful, useful and outlandish words*. New York: Wiley.

Dusseau, J. (1993). *Bugaboos, chimeras & Achilles' heels: 10,001 difficult words and how to use them*. Englewood Cliffs, NJ: Prentice Hall.

Flexner, S. (1993). *Wise words and wives' tales: The origins, meanings and time-honored wisdom of proverbs and folk sayings, olde and new*. New York: Avon.

Freeman, M. (1993). *Hue and cry and humble pie: The stories behind the words*. New York: Plume.

(cont.)

Gill, N. (1985). *Vocabulary boosters*. Belmont, CA: David S. Lake. (Grades 3–6)

Graham-Barber, L. (1993a). *Gobble! The complete book of Thanksgiving words*. New York: Avon.

Graham-Barber, L. (1993b). *Ho ho ho! The complete book of Christmas words*. New York: Bradbury.

Graham-Barber, L. (1993c). *Mushy: The complete book of Valentine words*. New York: Bradbury.

Gwynne, F. (1988). *The king who rained*. New York: Aladdin.

Gwynne, F. (2005). *Chocolate moose for dinner*. New York: Aladdin.

Hendrickson, R. (1994). *Grand slams, hat tricks, and alley-oops: A sports fan's book of words*. New York: Prentice Hall.

Hill, E. (1989). *Spot's big book of words*. New York: Putnam. (PreK–Grade 1)

Jeans, P. (1993). *Ship to shore: A dictionary of everyday words and phrases derived from the sea*. Santa Barbara, CA: ABC-C40.

Linfield, J. (1993). *Word traps: A dictionary of the 7,000 most confusing sound-alike and look-alike words*. New York: Collier.

Michaels, A. (1993). *Suffix obsession*. Jefferson, NC: McFarland.

Moncure, J. (1993). *Butterfly express*. Elgin, IL: Children's Press. (Grades 1–3)

Rovin, J. (1994). *What's the difference?: A compendium of commonly confused and misused words*. New York: Ballantine.

Sarnoff, J. (1981). *Words: A book about the origins of everyday words and phrases*. New York: Scribner.

Schwartz, L. (1978). *The usage sleuth*. Santa Barbara, CA: Learning Works.

Supraner, R. (1977a). *I can read about homonyms*. Mahwah, NJ: Troll.

Supraner, R. (1977b). *I can read about synonyms & antonyms*. Mahwah, NJ: Troll.

Terban, M. (1989). *Superdupers: Really funny real words*. New York: Clarion.

In addition, the *Readwritethink* website (*www.readwritethink.org*) is an excellent resource to use for recommendations of books that are rich, complex, and grade appropriate.

References for Students

Students also need excellent and usable references in order to develop and demonstrate the abilities required by the language convention standards (L.2). We find the Longman Learner Dictionaries (published by Pearson) useful in all grade 3–5 classrooms because they introduce the concept of definition in a learner-friendly way and deal with complex vocabulary in a manner accessible to upper elementary students.

Games and Puzzles

Building word interest and consciousness is aided by having good word games in the classroom. We suggest *Bananagrams* (Workman) and *Apples to Apples* (Mattel) to stimulate interest in words for upper elementary-grade students and allow them to "demonstrate their command of the conventions of standard English spelling (L.1)." Crossword Creator (Read, Write, Think, 2012) has turned many students into crossword devotees. Students love to make puzzles for one another, and the online puzzle maker is easy and fun to use.

(cont.)

Technology

In each of the preceding teaching examples, teachers made flexible use of technology, and found engaging ways for students to develop and demonstrate their command of the conventions of language and understanding of meaning. Here are just a few ideas and examples:

- The *Readwritethink* website, sponsored by the National Council of Teachers of English and the International Reading Association, is the source for the puzzle maker and has many interactive options for classroom use.
- Youtube (*www.youtube.com*) is a great resource for teachers. One can find audio versions of many books, so they can be accessible to all readers. For example, *Chrysanthemum* (Henkes, 1991) has a video read-aloud at *www.youtube.com/watch?v=kxMlxbgYvLI*.
- Computer and phone applications. There are many applications for vocabulary, such as a word a day (*www.superkids.com/aweb/tools/words/wod.shtml*).
- A good dictionary online for grades 3–5 is *www.merriam-webster.com*.

We began this chapter with an analogy about a cook's need for good tools. Yet we all understand that good tools do not make good cooks—or good meals. These come about by connecting the tools to "the cook's" deeper knowledge and experiences. Similarly, we believe that the CCSS are helpful tools to inform instruction. They provide a clearly articulated set of grade-level goals for student learning, which can form the basis for educator discussion, teacher study groups, and curriculum team deliberations. When used thoughtfully, we believe that the CCSS can be useful tools for administrators, supervisors, and teachers, who have the responsibility for implementing pedagogically sound, differentiated curriculum, and instruction for their students.

ACTIVITIES AND QUESTIONS

Activities

1. Design an activity for one grade to address anchor Standard 4 using vocabulary from your curriculum materials. Be sure to include differentiated examples of performance outcomes so both advanced and struggling readers meet the standard.

2. For anchor Standard 5, find grade-appropriate words to construct a word scale such as the one in Figure 7.3. Try it out with your students and evaluate how it worked.

3. Evaluate your own teaching of vocabulary for anchor Standard 6. After you have completed teaching a narrative selection, ask your students to write a summary using the vocabulary you presented. Give them 2 points for every word they use correctly both semantically and syntactically, 1 point for any word that is used correctly either semantically or syntactically, and 0 points for words not used correctly. How did they do? How did *you* do?

Questions

1. Looking at language anchor Standards 4, 5, and 6 for grades 3–5, which will be new additions to your curriculum? What ideas from this chapter might help you in integrating them into your existing curriculum?

2. How do you/would you help students use word learning strategies other than context? Give specific examples.

3. What technology tools could help you meet these standards? Give specific examples and references.

ACKNOWLEDGMENTS

The preparation of this chapter was supported in part by the Institute of Education Sciences, U.S. Department of Education, through Grant No. R305A090163 to the University of Missouri–Columbia, University of Wyoming, and National Louis University. The opinions expressed are those of the authors and do not represent views of the Institute or the U.S. Department of Education.

REFERENCES

Baumann, J. F. (2009). Vocabulary and reading comprehension: The nexus of meaning. In S. E. Israel & G. G. Duffy (Eds.), *Handbook of research on reading comprehension* (pp. 323–346). New York: Routledge.

Baumann, J. F., Blachowicz, C. L. Z., Manyak, P. C., Graves, M. F., & Olejnik, S. (2009–2012). *Development of a multi-faceted, comprehensive, vocabulary instructional program for the upper-elementary grades* [R305A090163]. Washington, DC: U.S. Department of Education, Institute of Education Sciences, National Center for Education Research.

Baumann, J. F., Edwards, E. C., Boland, E., Olejnik, S., & Kame'enui, E. W. (2003). Vocabulary tricks: Effects of instruction in morphology and context on fifth-grade students' ability to derive and infer word meanings. *American Educational Research Journal, 40*, 447–494.

Baumann, J. F., Edwards, E. C., Font, G., Tereshinski, C. A., Kame'enui, E. J., & Olejnik, S. (2002). Teaching morphemic and contextual analysis to fifth-grade students. *Reading Research Quarterly, 37*, 150–176.

Baumann, J. F., & Graves, M. F. (2010). What is academic vocabulary? *Journal of Adolescent and Adult Literacy, 54*, 4–12.

Baumann, J. F., & Kame'enui, E. J. (Eds.). (2004). *Vocabulary instruction: Research to practice.* New York: Guilford Press.

Baumann, J. F., Kame'enui, E. J., & Ash, G. (2003). Research on vocabulary instruction: Voltaire redux. In J. Flood, D. Lapp, J. R. Squire, & J. Jensen (Eds.), *Handbook of research on teaching the English language arts* (2nd ed., pp. 752–785). Mahwah, NJ: Erlbaum.

Baumann, J. F., Manyak, P. C., Peterson, H., Blachowicz, C. L. Z., Cieply, C., Bates, A., et al. (2011, December). *Windows on formative/design-based research on vocabulary instruction: Findings and methodological challenges.* Symposium at the annual meeting of the Literacy Research Association, Jacksonville, FL.

Baumann, J. F., Ware, D., & Edwards, E. C. (2007). "Bumping into spicy, tasty words that catch your tongue": A formative experiment on vocabulary instruction. *The Reading Teacher, 62*, 108–122.

Beck, I. L., & McKeown, M. G. (1991). Conditions of vocabulary acquisition. In R. Barr, M.

Kamil, P. Mosenthal, & P. D. Pearson (Eds.), *Handbook of reading research* (Vol. II, pp. 789–814). New York: Longman.

Beck, I. L., McKeown, M. G., & Kucan, L. (2002). *Bringing words to life: Robust vocabulary instruction.* New York: Guilford Press.

Beck, I. L., McKeown, M. G., & Kucan, L. (2008). *Creating robust vocabulary: Frequently asked questions and extended examples.* New York: Guilford Press.

Blachowicz, C. L. Z., & Fisher, P. (2000). Vocabulary instruction. In M. L. Kamil, P. B. Mosenthal, P. D. Pearson, & R. Barr (Eds.), *Handbook of reading research* (Vol. III, pp. 503–523). Mahwah, NJ: Erlbaum.

Blachowicz, C. L. Z., & Fisher, P. (2010). *Teaching vocabulary in all classrooms* (4th ed.). Englewood Cliffs, NJ: Merrill/Prentice Hall.

Blachowicz, C. L. Z., Fisher, P. J. L., Ogle, D., & Watts-Taffe, S. (2006). Vocabulary: Questions from the classroom. *Reading Research Quarterly, 41,* 524–539.

Blachowicz, C. L. Z., & Obrochta, C. (2005). Vocabulary visits: Developing content vocabulary in the primary grades. *Reading Teacher, 59,* 262–269.

Blachowicz, C. L. Z., & Obrochta, C. (2007). "Tweaking practice": Modifying read-alouds to enhance content vocabulary learning in Grade 1. In *56th annual yearbook of the National Reading Conference* (pp. 111–121). Oak Creek, WI: National Reading Conference.

Bowers, P. N., Kirby, J. R., & Deacon, S. H. (2010). The effects of morphological instruction on literacy skills: A systematic review of the literature. *Review of Educational Research, 80,* 144–179.

Buikema, J. L., & Graves, M. F. (1993). Teaching students to use context cues to infer word meanings. *Journal of Reading, 36,* 450–457.

Bus, A. G., van IJzendoorn, M. H., & Pellegrini, A. D. (1995). Join book reading makes for success in learning to read: A meta-analysis on intergenerational transmission of literacy. *Review of Educational Research, 65,* 1–21.

Calkins, L., & Mermelstein, L. (2003). *Launching the writing workshop.* Portsmouth, NH: Heinemann.

Carlisle, J. F., McBride-Chang, C., Nagy, W., & Nunes, T. (2010). Effects of instruction in morphological awareness on literacy achievement: An integrative review. *Reading Research Quarterly, 45*(4), 464–487.

Common Core State Standards Initiative. (n.d.). About the standards. Retrieved from *www.corestandards.org/about-the-standards.*

Cunningham, A. E. (2005). Vocabulary growth through independent reading and reading aloud to children. In E. H. Hiebert & M. L. Kamil (Eds.), *Teaching and learning vocabulary: Bringing research to practice* (pp. 45–68). Mahwah, NJ: Erlbaum.

Cunningham, A. E., & O'Donnell, C. R. (2012). Reading and vocabulary growth. In E. J. Kame'enui & J. F. Baumann (Eds.), *Vocabulary instruction: Research to practice* (2nd ed., pp. 256–279). New York: Guilford Press.

Elleman, A. M., Lindo, E. J., Morphy, P., & Compton, D. L. (2009). The impact of vocabulary instruction on passage-level comprehension of school-age children: A meta-analysis. *Journal of Research on Educational Effectiveness, 2,* 1–44.

Elley, W. (1989). Vocabulary acquisition from listening to stories. *Reading Research Quarterly, 24,* 174–187.

Farstrup, A. E., & Samuels, S. J. (Eds.). (2008). *What research has to say about vocabulary instruction.* Newark, DE: International Reading Association.

FOSS. (2011). Full option science system. Retrieved from *http://lhsfoss.org.*

Fukkink, R. G., & de Glopper, K. (1998). Effects of instruction in deriving word meaning from context: A meta-analysis. *Review of Educational Research, 68,* 450–469.

Goodwin, A. P., & Ahn, S. (2010). A meta-analysis of morphological interventions: Effects on literacy achievement of children with literacy difficulties. *Annals of Dyslexia, 60,* 183–208.

Graves, M. F. (1986). Vocabulary learning and instruction. In E. Z. Rothkopf (Ed.), *Review of research in education* (Vol. 13, pp. 49–89). Washington, DC: American Educational Research Association.

Graves, M. F. (2000). A vocabulary program to complement and bolster a middle-grade comprehension program. In B. M. Taylor, M. F. Graves, & P. van den Broek (Eds.), *Reading for meaning: Fostering comprehension in the middle grades* (pp. 116–135). Newark, DE: International Reading Association.

Graves, M. F. (2006). *The vocabulary book: Learning and instruction.* New York: Teachers College Press.

Graves, M. F. (2009). *Teaching individual words: One size does not fit all.* New York: Teachers College Press.

Graves, M. F., & Watts-Taffe, S. M. (2002). The place of word consciousness in a research-based vocabulary program. In S. J. Samuels & A. E. Farstrup (Eds.), *What research has to say about reading instruction* (3rd ed., pp. 140–165). Newark, DE: International Reading Association.

Hart, B., & Risley, T. R. (1995). *Meaningful differences in the everyday experience of young American children.* Baltimore: Brookes.

Hayes, D. P., & Ahrens, M. G. (1988). Vocabulary simplification for children: A special case of "motherese." *Journal of Child Language, 15,* 395–410.

Hiebert, E. H., & Cervetti, G. N. (2012). What differences in narrative and informational texts mean for the learning and instruction of vocabulary. In E. J. Kame'enui & J. F. Baumann (Eds.), *Vocabulary instruction: Research to practice* (2nd ed., pp. 322–344). New York: Guilford Press.

Hiebert, E. H., & Kamil, M. L. (Eds.). (2005). *Teaching and learning vocabulary: Bringing research to practice.* Mahwah, NJ: Erlbaum.

Kame'enui, E. J., & Baumann, J. F. (Eds.). (2012). *Vocabulary instruction: Research to practice* (2nd ed.). New York: Guilford Press.

Manyak, P. (2007, March). Character trait vocabulary: A schoolwide approach. *The Reading Teacher, 60,* 574–577.

Mezynski, K. (1983). Issues concerning the acquisition of knowledge: Effects of vocabulary training on reading comprehension. *Review of Educational Research, 53,* 253–279.

Nagy, W. E. (2005). Why vocabulary instruction needs to be long-term and comprehensive. In E. H. Hiebert & M. L. Kamil (Eds.), *Teaching and learning vocabulary: Bringing research to practice* (pp. 27–44). Mahwah, NJ: Erlbaum.

Nagy, W. E., & Scott, J. A. (2000). Vocabulary processes. In M. L. Kamil, P. B. Mosenthal, P. D. Pearson, & R. Barr (Eds.), *Handbook of reading research* (Vol. III, pp. 269–284). Mahwah, NJ: Erlbaum.

National Governors Association Center for Best Practices and Council of Chief State School Officers. (2010). Common Core State Standards for English language arts & literacy in history/social studies, science, and technical subjects. Washington, DC: Author. Retrieved from *www.corestandards.org/assets/CCSSI_ELA%20Standards.pdf.*

Read, Write, Think. (2012). Read, write, think. Retrieved from *www.readwritethink.org.*

Reed, D. K. (2008). A synthesis of morphology interventions and effects on reading outcomes for students in grades K–12. *Learning Disabilities Research and Practice, 23*(1), 36–49.

Scott, J. A., Flinspach, S., Miller, T., Gage-Serio, O., & Vevea, J. (2009). An analysis of reclassified English learners, English learners and native English fourth graders on assessments of receptive and productive vocabulary. In Y. Kim, V. Risko, D. Compton, D. Dickinson, M. Hundley, R. Jimenez, et al. (Eds.), *58th annual yearbook of the National Reading Conference* (pp. 312–329). Oak Creek, WI: National Reading Conference.

Scott, J. A., Hoover, M., Flinspach, S. L., & Vevea, J. L. (2008). A multiple-level vocabulary assessment tool: Measuring word knowledge based on grade-level materials. In Y. Kim, V. Risko, D. Compton, D. Dickinson, M. Hundley, R. Jimenez, et al. (Eds.), *57th annual yearbook of the National Reading Conference* (pp. 325–340). Oak Creek, WI: National Reading Conference.

Scott, J. A., Miller, T. F., & Flinspach, S. L. (2012). Developing word consciousness: Lessons from highly diverse fourth-grade classrooms. In E. J. Kame'enui & J. F. Baumann (Eds.), *Vocabulary instruction: Research to practice* (2nd ed., pp. 169–188). New York: Guilford Press.

Scott, J. A., Nagy, W. E., & Flinspach, S. L. (2008). More than merely words: Redefining vocabulary learning in a culturally and linguistically diverse society. In A. E. Farstrup & S. J. Samuels (Eds.), *What research has to say about vocabulary instruction* (pp. 182–210). Newark, DE: International Reading Association.

Scott, J. A., Vevea, J., & Flinspach, S. (2010, December). Vocabulary growth in fourth grade classrooms: A quantitative analysis. In K. Moloney (Chair), *The VINE Project: A three-year study of word consciousness in fourth-grade classrooms.* Symposium conducted at the annual meeting of the National Reading Conference/Literacy Research Association, Fort Worth, TX.

Stahl, S. A., & Fairbanks, M. M. (1986). The effects of vocabulary instruction: A model-based meta-analysis. *Review of Educational Research, 56,* 72–110.

Stahl, S. A., & Nagy, W. E. (2006). *Teaching word meanings.* Mahwah, NJ: Erlbaum.

Swanborn, M. S. L., & de Glopper, K. (1999). Incidental word learning while reading: A meta-analysis. *Review of Educational Research, 69,* 261–285.

Templeton, S., Bear, D. R., Johnston, F., & Invernizzi, M. (2010). *Vocabulary their way: Word study with middle and secondary students.* Boston: Pearson.

White, T. G., Sowell, J., & Yanagihara, A. (1989). Teaching elementary students to use word-part clues. *The Reading Teacher, 42,* 302–308.

CHILDREN'S BOOKS CITED

Baker, W., & Hasam, A. (1993a). *Earth: A creative, hands-on approach to science.* New York: Aladdin Books.

Baker, W., & Hasam, A. (1993b). *Electricity: A creative, hands-on approach to science.* New York: Aladdin Books.

Baker, W., & Hasam, A. (1993c). *Plants: A creative, hands-on approach to science.* New York: Aladdin Books.

Baker, W., & Hasam, A. (1993d). *Sound: A creative, hands-on approach to science.* New York: Aladdin Books.

Coles, R. (1995). *La historia de Ruby Bridges.* New York: Scholastic.

Henkes, K. (1993). *Crisantemo.* Madrid: Everest.

Hoffman, M. (1991). *Amazing grace.* New York: Dial Books for Young Readers.

Newman, F. R. (1983). *ZOUNDS! The kids' guide to sound making.* New York: Random House Books for Young Readers.

O'Neill, A. (2002). *The recess queen.* New York: Scholastic.

Roop, P., Roop, C., & Hanson, P. E. (1985). *Keep the light burning, Abbie.* Minneapolis, MN: Carolrhoda Books.

APPENDIX 7.1. Language Standards: Vocabulary Acquisition and Use

Grade 3 students	Grade 4 students	Grade 5 students
4. Determine or clarify the meaning of unknown and multiple-meaning word and phrases based on *grade 3 reading and content*, choosing flexibly from a range of strategies.	4. Determine or clarify the meaning of unknown and multiple-meaning words and phrases based on *grade 4 reading and content*, choosing flexibly from a range of strategies.	4. Determine or clarify the meaning of unknown and multiple-meaning words and phrases based on *grade 5 reading and content*, choosing flexibly from a range of strategies.
a. Use sentence-level context as a clue to the meaning of a word or phrase.	a. Use context (e.g., definitions, examples, or restatements in text) as a clue to the meaning of a word or phrase.	a. Use context (e.g., cause/effect relationships and comparisons in text) as a clue to the meaning of a word or phrase.
b. Determine the meaning of the new word formed when a known affix is added to a known word (e.g., *agreeable/ disagreeable, comfortable/ uncomfortable, care/ careless, heat/preheat*).	b. Use common, grade-appropriate Greek and Latin affixes and roots as clues to the meaning of a word (e.g., *telegraph, photograph, autograph*).	b. Use common, grade-appropriate Greek and Latin affixes and roots as clues to the meaning of a word (e.g., *photograph, photosynthesis*).
c. Use a known root word as a clue to the meaning of an unknown word with the same root (e.g., *company, companion*).	c. Consult reference materials (e.g., dictionaries, glossaries, thesauruses), both print and digital, to find the pronunciation and determine or clarify the precise meaning of key words and phrases.	c. Consult reference materials (e.g., dictionaries, glossaries, thesauruses), both print and digital, to find the pronunciation and determine or clarify the precise meaning of key words and phrases.
d. Use glossaries or beginning dictionaries, both print and digital, to determine or clarify the precise meaning of key words and phrases.		
5. Demonstrate understanding of figurative language, word relationships, and nuances in word meanings.	5. Demonstrate understanding of figurative language, word relationships, and nuances in word meanings.	5. Demonstrate understanding of word relationships and nuances in word meanings.
a. Explain the meaning of simple similes and metaphors (e.g., *as pretty as a picture*) in context.	a. Interpret figurative language, including similes and metaphors, in context.	a. Distinguish the literal and nonliteral meanings of words and phrases in context (e.g., *take steps*).
b. Recognize and explain the meaning of common idioms, adages, and proverbs.	b. Recognize and explain the meaning of common idioms, adages, and proverbs.	b. Identify real-life connections between words and their use (e.g., describe people who are *friendly* or *helpful*).
c. Demonstrate understanding of words by relating them to their opposites (antonyms) and to words with similar but not identical meanings (synonyms).	c. Use the relationship between particular words (e.g., synonyms, antonyms, homographs) to better understand each of the words.	c. Distinguish shades of meaning among related words that describe states of mind or degrees of certainty (e.g., *knew, believed, suspected, heard, wondered*).

(cont.)

APPENDIX 7.1. *(cont.)*

Grade 3 students	Grade 4 students	Grade 5 students
6. Acquire and use accurately grade-appropriate general academic and domain-specific words and phrases, including those that signal precise actions, emotions, or states of being (e.g., *quizzed, whined, stammered*) and that are basic to a particular topic (e.g., *wildlife, conservation,* and *endangered* when discussing animal preservation).	6. Acquire and use accurately grade-appropriate general academic and domain-specific words and phrases, including those that signal contrast, addition, and other logical relationships (e.g., *however, although, nevertheless, similarly, moreover, in addition*).	6. Acquire and use accurately grade-appropriate conversational, general academic, and domain-specific words and phrases, including those that signal spatial and temporal relationships (e.g., *After dinner that night we went looking for them*).

Note. From CCSS (2010, p. 29).

CHAPTER 8

Technology and the Common Core Standards

Erica C. Boling
Christina Spiezio

In today's information-rich digital society, being literate involves much more than simply being able to read and write the written language (Burkhardt et al., 2003; Lemke, 2006). As important as effective reading and writing are, it is "no longer realistic to talk about 'reading' or 'writing' as discrete skills needed for the future workplace" (Walsh, 2008, p. 101). Reading and writing rarely occur in isolation for today's students, "whose environment is filled with visual, electronic and digital texts that offer facilities for reading, writing, viewing, listening and responding simultaneously" (Walsh, 2008, p. 101). In essence, technology is "changing the face of modern life" (Lefever-Davis & Pearman, 2005, p. 446). Without preparing students' for the literacy needs of a digital age society, students are "being prepared to succeed in yesterday's world—not tomorrow's" (Burkhardt et al., 2003, p. 2). It is vital—now more than ever—that students are provided with opportunities "to use technology and acquire digital literacy skills during their school years" (Lefever-Davis & Pearman, 2005, p. 446). The purpose of this chapter is to introduce the role of technology and digital literacy skills throughout the Common Core State Standards (CCSS), to illustrate the integration of technology in practice, and to provide additional resources to teachers who seek to improve students' digital literacy skills throughout the third- through fifth-grade curriculum.

Although there remains "a profound gap between the knowledge and skills most students learn in school and the knowledge and skills they need in typical 21st century communities and workplaces," the CCSS attempt to close this gap through their integration of technology, the use of multimedia, and acknowledgment of digital literacies as being embedded and integrated throughout the standards (Partnership for 21st Century Skills, 2008, p. 3). In today's "wired, networked society, it is imperative that students learn to communicate effectively using a range of media, technology, and environments" (Burkhardt et al., 2003, p. 56).

Based on the Common Core standards, a portrait of a literate student in the 21st century includes a self-directed learner who effectively seeks out and uses resources for assistance, including teachers, peers, and print and digital reference materials. These are learners who are able to "strategically and capably" use technology and digital media (National Governors Association [NGA] Center for Best Practices and Council of Chief State School Officers [CCSSO], 2010, p. 7):

> They use technology and digital media strategically and capably. Students employ technology thoughtfully to enhance their reading, writing, speaking, listening, and language use. They tailor their searches online to acquire useful information efficiently, and they integrate what they learn using technology with what they learn offline. They are familiar with the strengths and limitations of various technological tools and mediums and can select and use those best suited to their communication goals. (NGA and CCSSO, 2010, p. 7)

Honey, Culp, and Spielvogel (2005) describe differences between learning both "from" and "with" computers. When technology is being used to essentially serve as a tutor, serving to increase basic skills and knowledge, its use illustrates how students can learn "from" the technology. Learning "with" technology includes using tools that "can be applied to a variety of goals in the learning process and can serve as a resource to help develop higher-order thinking, creativity and research skills" (Honey et al., 2005; Reeves, 1998; Ringstaff & Kelley, 2002). It is this view—of learning "with" technology—that is best reflected and embraced by the Common Core standards.

> Research and media skills blended into the Standards as a whole. To be ready for college, workforce training, and life in a technological society, students need the ability to gather, comprehend, evaluate, synthesize, and report on information and ideas, to conduct original research in order to answer questions or solve problems, and to analyze and create a high volume and extensive range of print and nonprint texts in media forms old and new. The need to conduct research and to produce and consume media is embedded into every aspect of today's curriculum. In like fashion, research and media skills and understandings are embedded throughout the Standards rather than treated in a separate section. (NGA and CCSSO, 2010, p. 4)

In the area of digital literacies and 21st-century technologies, the Common Core standards call for students to be able to critically analyze and produce various types of media. In addition, critical analysis and production of media are integrated throughout components of the standards, blended into the standards as a whole. Technology, research, and media skills are embedded throughout the standards rather than treated in their own sections.

In the English language arts standards and the area of writing instruction, for example, students are expected to use technology and multimedia to create informative and explanatory texts and to aid comprehension of text (NGA and CCSSO, 2010). They are also expected to use technology "to produce and publish writing and to interact and collaborate with others" (p. 18). In addition to learning basic keyboarding skills, students are expected to be able to use technology to conduct research, "draw on information from digital sources" (p. 14), gather "relevant information from multiple print and digital sources," and use technology and various forms of multimedia to build and present knowledge (p. 41). In the area of reading, the standards illustrate how students are expected to "interpret animations and interactive elements on Web pages and explain how information contributes to an understanding of the text in which it appears" (p. 14). Additionally, when considering education around language, teachers are expected to integrate technology into vocabulary acquisition as students are expected to be able to consult and use digital reference materials such as digital dictionaries, glossaries, and thesauruses to find the meanings and pronunciations of words.

Learning "with" technology is also reflected throughout the speaking and listening standards, where students at all levels are expected to "integrate and evaluate information presented in diverse media, [and] strategically use digital media to express information and enhance understanding of presentations" (NGA and CCSSO, 2010, p. 22). Students are expected to paraphrase and summarize "information presented in diverse media and formats" (p. 24). In addition, they should be able to use technology and multimedia for the "presentation of knowledge and ideas, thereby using today's technologies to create audio recordings and visual displays when appropriate to enhance development of main ideas, themes" (p. 24).

According to Partnership for 21st Century Skills (2008), current education systems are failing to adequately prepare all students and workers with the essential 21st-century skills that are necessary for success in today's global economy. The Common Core standards acknowledge the role of the teacher and the human factor that are essential to learning. Experts point out "that the most sophisticated technology is meaningless without teachers and students who know how to make good use of it" (Robelen, 1999). By integrating technology throughout the standards and acknowledging the role of various types of multimedia that are available to teachers and students, the Common Core standards provide a framework that educators can use as they help students acquire the 21st-century skills that are necessary for success in today's global economy (Partnership for 21st Century Skills, 2008).

PUTTING THE STANDARDS INTO PRACTICE BY INTEGRATING TECHNOLOGY

In this section, we present various teaching vignettes to illustrate how technology can be integrated throughout the literacy curriculum to support the Common Core standards. Through these examples, we hope to illustrate just how naturally technology can be woven throughout the standards in ways that enhance literacy learning. Each of the following examples illustrates how teachers can use technology to enhance student literacy learning in ways that would not be possible through more traditional instructional approaches. To organize the content for this section, we begin by listing relevant Common Core standards for various grade levels, followed by a discussion of how technology can be woven throughout these standards. We then provide a teaching vignette to illustrate how technology can be integrated throughout each listed standard. Last, we make brief comments about how each vignette satisfies the specific expectations of grade-level use of technology.

The following vignette illustrates how students can use technology for presentation of knowledge and ideas, thereby using today's technologies to create audio recordings and visual displays when appropriate to enhance development of main ideas and themes. At the same time, technology supports the development of listening and speaking skills

---

Reading Standards for Informational Text: Key Ideas and Details

Grade 4 Anchor Standard 1: Refer to details and examples in a text when explaining what the text says explicitly and when drawing inferences from the text.

Grade 4 Anchor Standard 2: Determine the main idea of a text and explain how it is supported by key details; summarize the text.

Grade 4 Anchor Standard 3: Explain events, procedures, ideas, or concepts in a historical, scientific, or technical text, including what happened and why, based on specific information in the text.

Reading Standards for Informational Text: Integration of Knowledge and Ideas

Grade 4 Anchor Standards 7: Interpret information presented visually, orally, or quantitatively (e.g., in charts, graphs, diagrams, time lines, animations, or interactive elements on Web pages) and explain how the information contributes to an understanding of the text in which it appears.

---

use to share their knowledge of the reading skill they had been practicing that week. With a program like *VoiceThread*, students were able to use audio and still images to retell the major events of their independent reading books using multiple mediums. Recording their VoiceThreads provided them with opportunities to practice oral speaking skills and reading fluency. Listening to and watching each other's VoiceThread digital stories also provided emphasis on listening skills. While selecting images for their stories, students had to determine which parts of the story to highlight. This, in turn, supported them in meeting the literature Common Core standards category of Key Ideas and Details. As students progress in grade level, the Common Core standards require fourth-grade students to integrate video and audio into their multimedia presentations. In fifth grade, they are expected to integrate even more multimedia components into their presentations, using such elements as graphics, sound, and visual displays when appropriate.

In the following vignette, students interpret, summarize, and use information presented in various formats to create multimedia presentations. As seen in the CCSS (NGA and CCSSO, 2010), students are expected to paraphrase and summarize "information presented in diverse media and formats" (p. 24). The following vignette presents Mrs. Hughes's fourth-grade class as they finish their biography unit and complete a final multimedia project using *Glogster* (*www.glogster.com*), a Web-based program for creating online, interactive posters. Having been properly prepared by their teacher, elementary-school students can use the Internet as a tool for finding more information about something they are reading in their independent books. By incorporating Web tools such as Glogster into the reading curriculum, students are able to use multimedia to present and share learned information and new knowledge with others. While working on the nonfiction unit, Mrs. Hughes's students use multiple online sources to gather information about topics of interest, thereby increasing student knowledge by creating a more complex understanding of the issue being researched.

develop a deeper understanding of the content being studied. In this section, we provide classroom vignettes for integrating technology and the Common Core standards into science and social studies lessons. These examples help provide a better understanding of how technology can be used to enhance students' comprehension of a certain topic. To organize the content for this section, we begin by listing relevant Common Core standards for various grade levels, followed by a discussion of how technology can be weaved throughout these standards. We then provide a teaching vignette to illustrate how this looks in practice. Last, we make brief comments about how each vignette satisfies the specific expectations of grade-level use of technology.

For some social studies lessons, a teacher's dream would be for students to be able to actually experience the concepts being taught—an unrealistic ideal, especially when studying other cultures, locations, and even climate in a third-grade classroom! The next best option comes from Google Earth (*www.google.com/earth*), an interactive satellite globe that makes this dream a closer, albeit virtual, reality by bringing the world to students' fingertips. Teachers can take students on virtual field trips, projecting images of the area being studied and having students explore the region together. In the following vignette, Mrs. Castles's third-grade class takes virtual field trips across the globe in order to better understand how a region's climate and geographical features influence the culture of its inhabitants.

VIGNETTE: INTEGRATING TECHNOLOGY IN GRADE 3

Mrs. Castles's third-grade class is studying culture and climate in social studies. Although her students were developing a basic understanding of the concept, she wanted to give them a unique experience that would solidify what they were learning in class.

Before class, Mrs. Castles downloads Google Earth to her school computer and identifies three different regions she wants to explore with her students—the Sahara Desert, the Arctic Circle, and the Amazon jungle—and saves files of each. When students arrive to class, she has them sit on the carpet at the front of the room. She tells them they are taking a virtual field trip today, and while they are exploring the new areas together, she wants students to share ideas about the geographical features they are seeing. The class first travels to the Sahara Desert. An image of this vast desert region appears, and the students stir with excitement. "Boys and girls," Mrs. Castles begins, "What kinds of things do you see in the desert?" The students volunteer answers; Mrs. Castles records each. The students ask Mrs. Castles to move the picture left, then right, and to zoom in and out of the screen, each time revealing more geographical features of the desert.

Reading Standards for Informational Text: Integration of Knowledge and Ideas

Grade 3 Anchor Standard 7: Use information gained from illustrations (e.g., maps, photographs) and the words in a text to demonstrate understanding of the text (e.g., where, when, why, and how key events occur).

Grade 3 Anchor Standard 9: Compare and contrast the most important points and key details presented in two texts on the same topic.

After several minutes of exploring, Mrs. Castles asks her students to think about the climate of a desert; students share their responses and the teacher notes them. Mrs. Castles uses the next 15 minutes to explore the Arctic Circle and then the Amazon jungle, asking her class the same questions for each. When they finish their virtual field trip, Mrs. Castles asks her students to recall three things they learned about the different regions.

The next day, she pulls up a chart on the computer that shows the students' responses. She also performs an online search so that she can show charts illustrating the average monthly temperatures for each location they visited using Google Earth. As a class, Mrs. Castles reviews the information on the charts and asks students to recall information they learned the previous day.

Dividing the class into thirds, Mrs. Castles assigns each group to a different region. Each group is given a printout of their region's geographical features and climate, along with a blank sheet. Mrs. Castles asks each group to create a drawing of a person who lives in that region. She asks the students to think about what the person might wear, what tools the person would need, and how he or she moves around the area. Students work together to create their drawing. Upon completion, the groups share their pictures and explanations with the class, and other students share their comments on the drawings. After all students have shared, Mrs. Castles displays photos of the regions' indigenous people for students to see. For the remainder of the week, Mrs. Castles teaches her students about various social studies concepts, frequently referring back to their virtual field trip.

Using Google Earth created an authentic experience for the students in Mrs. Castles's class that would not have been possible otherwise. By incorporating Google Earth into the lesson, students were able to explore the region with their classmates in order to develop a deeper understanding of social studies concepts. This program encouraged the students to discover more about the geographical features of each region, made the concepts come to life, and created similar background knowledge about the topic for all students. At the same time, the Google Earth activities supported Common Core reading standards for informational text in the Integration of Knowledge and Ideas category. Students learned about concepts and better understood various texts after discussing and interpreting the different maps, illustrations, and graphs that were introduced to them in class. They compared and contrasted key points of information while comparing data from different locations around the world.

Science concepts can be difficult for students to understand. Through the use of experiments, however, teachers can help students visualize the idea being taught, thereby developing a stronger understanding of the material. Technology can help teachers capture these experiments forever, and allow them to create resources for students to access at any time in order to further their understanding of a given topic. With integration of technology throughout the curriculum, students will have opportunities to improve their

---

Reading Standards for Informational Text: Key Ideas and Details

Grade 4 Anchor Standard 3: Explain events, procedures, ideas, or concepts in a historical, scientific, or technical text, including what happened and why, based on specific information in the text.

digital literacy skills. The following vignette illustrates how fourth-grade teacher Ms. Patel used video to engage her students in classroom science experiments, all while creating an online database of videos for students of any age to watch and learn about science topics at the elementary level.

VIGNETTE: INTEGRATING TECHNOLOGY IN GRADE 4

For the first 5 months of the school year, Ms. Patel videorecords every science experiment she conducts with fourth graders. She carefully follows the same format with each experiment—introducing the topic, telling what the experiment will show, explaining the procedures she will follow, and reviewing postexperiment conclusions—so that her students will have had plenty of "experience" not only with the in-class routine but also with navigating through the class website to where the experiment videos are posted.

By January, her students are well prepared to begin creating their own videos of the weekly class experiments. From now on, after an experiment is completed in class, a group of students is chosen to replicate the experiment for the video website. After being briefed on the rules of filming, and following Ms. Patel's modeling of the process, the students create a script for the experiment and practice until it is perfected. The students arrive to Ms. Patel's class before school and film their experiment using the class Flip camera.

Throughout their video, not only are students responsible for following the procedures, but they must also explain what is being done, what the video is showing, and what conclusions can be made from the experiment. In addition, the group's script is collected and graded.

After the group has completed their video, Ms. Patel makes any minor necessary edits using Windows Movie Maker, and then she uploads the video onto the class website. The link for this website is shared not only with the students in her class but with all fourth-grade students and teachers. Other teachers in the school also use Ms. Patel's videos to aid in explaining science concepts to students.

At the end of the year, Ms. Patel has a video resource library that holds each experiment completed in her class.

By incorporating the use of video into her classroom, Ms. Patel accomplishes many important things. First, students have a visual representation of the material being learned in class, which can be accessed from home as well as at school. Second, because students take part in filming their own videos, they take ownership of the science concepts, which motivates them to understand the material even more. Finally, by making her class videos public, other teachers in the school are able to incorporate multimedia into their classrooms, keeping consistency with the material being taught in each classroom.

CONCLUSION

The role of technology in the English language arts (ELA) Common Core State Standards (CCSS) is unique. Rather than having a separate section and separate standards that focus solely on technology, media and digital literacy skills are blended throughout the standards as a whole. The standards reflect how a successful 21st-century learner must be

RESOURCES FOR INTEGRATING TECHNOLOGY WITH THE STANDARDS

Glogster EDU

http://edu.glogster.com

- Create a Gloster account for your class. Get a teacher account, student accounts, and teacher-level management. Have students create dynamic, online multimodal "posters" when doing projects across content areas.

Glogster EDU Inspiration

www.scoop.it/t/glogster-edu-inspiration

- Visit Glogster EDU Inspiration for sample lesson plans, teaching ideas, and projects using Glogster.

Detailed Tutorial on Glogster EDU

www.youtube.com/watch?v=8ONISdsoouE

- This video tutorial provides information and directions for creating a glog and using Glogster EDU.

Google Earth

www.google.com/earth

- Download Google Earth for free and use it with your class. (Note: Download onto the computer that you will be using with your students!)

Google Earth Lessons

http://gelessons.com/lessons

- Visit this site to get tons of Google Earth resources, from how-to tutorials to sample lessons.

Google Earth Virtual Field Trips

www.bridge.edu.au/verve/_resources/GoogleEarthHowToVFT.pdf

- This resource provides great step-by-step information in the form of a pdf packet for creating your own Google Earth virtual field trip. Screenshots and help guides are included.

Flip Videos and Video Library

www.freetech4teachers.com/2010/03/20-ways-to-use-flip-cameras-in.html

- Learn 20+ ways for using Flip cameras in the classroom. Ideas for using student/teacher-created videos are provided.

(cont.)

Flip Video How-Tos

www.youtube.com/watch?v=abZjFCjp99w

- This video provides a tutorial for using Flip cameras.

EdVoiceThread

http://ed.voicethread.com

- Create a VoiceThread account for teachers.

Introduction to Using VoiceThread

www.youtube.com/watch?v=-U1wlRrKyyk

- This is a VoiceThread video tutorial.

VoiceThread 4 Education

http://voicethread4education.wikispaces.com

- This site provides sample VoiceThreads, professional development, educational resources, and teacher-submitted ideas.

Voki

www.voki.com

- Create free, cartoon, speaking avatars. The program can convert text to speech, or upload your own audio file.

Voki Lesson Plans

www.voki.com/lesson_plans.php

- This site provides ideas for how to incorporate Vokis into any lesson at any grade level.

Wikispaces for Educators

www.wikispaces.com/content/for/teachers

- Sign up for your free Wiki for Educators here.

Examples of Educational Wikis

http://educationalwikis.wikispaces.com/Examples+of+educational+wikis

- Samples of educational wikis from around the world labeled by teacher, grade level, and country.

50 Ways to Use Wikis

www.smartteaching.org/blog/2008/08/50-ways-to-use-wikis-for-a-more-collaborative-and-interactive-classroom

- Extensive list of ideas for using wikis in any classroom divided into categories of "resources creation," "student participation," "group projects," "student interaction," "for the classroom," "community," and "other."

able to use technology and digital media strategically and capably. They need to be famil-iar with "various technological tools and mediums" and should know how to "select and use those best suited to their communication goals" (NGA and CCSSO, 2010, p. 7). The purpose of this chapter was to introduce teachers to these technology skills and describe them in relation to the ELA. Additionally, through the various teaching vignettes that are provided, this chapter helps teachers consider ways that technology can be thoughtfully used to enhance students' reading, writing, speaking, listening, and language use.

Six teaching vignettes illustrated the use of technology in grade 3–5 classrooms. Four vignettes illustrated the use of technology to support the ELA, and two demon-strated the integration of technology throughout the day in other content areas. In the first ELA vignette, we introduced a third-grade teacher's use of VoiceThread to create digital stories based on books the class was reading, supporting the reading standards for integrating technology in literature, foundational skills, and listening and speaking. In the second vignette, we introduced a fourth-grade teacher's use of *Glogster* for stu-dents to create interactive posters. These projects reflected the research that students were conducting while reading biographies and learning about famous people. In the third vignette, a fifth-grade teacher used Wikispaces to support writing instruction in her Writer's Workshop groups. Students shared their writings using Wikispaces so that they could easily give feedback to and receive feedback from their classmates. For the fourth vignette, we introduced another fourth-grade classroom and how students used Vokis during their explanatory writing projects. This project required students to create audio-recorded podcasts, thereby supporting a number of ELA skills, including oral fluency.

The final two vignettes show how technology skills can be supported throughout the school day in different content areas: one third-grade teacher used Google Earth to create virtual field trips in a social studies class, and a fifth-grade teacher used teacher- and student-created videos to record, post, and share the science experiments they were conducting. In these examples, technology was being embedded throughout the reading standards for informational text as students learned how to use, compare, contrast, and explain different types of information they compiled from a variety of media. As one can see through these examples and from the resources included at the end of this chapter, teachers can seamlessly weave technology throughout the curriculum in ways that both support and enhance the ELA Common Core standards. Although there are no specific standards dedicated solely to technology and media skills, this does not mean that they are not important. On the contrary, embedding these skills throughout the entire set of Common Core standards reflects just how important and necessary they are to today's learners.

QUESTIONS AND ACTIVITIES

Questions

1. According to the Common Core State Standards for English language arts, why should technology be integrated throughout the curriculum?

2. How will integrating technology throughout the curriculum help better prepare students for the literacy demands of today's 21st-century society?

3. What special demands and challenges might teachers confront when integrat-ing technology into their classrooms? How can they deal with these challenges

in order to successfully use technology in support of the Common Core State Standards?

4. How can online communication and collaboration tools, such as Wikispaces and VoiceThread, be used to support the development of students' reading, writing, speaking, listening, and language skills?

5. What needs to be communicated to parents/guardians if teachers want to use online tools like Glogster, Wikispaces, and Voki with elementary students? What concerns might parents have, and how might teachers help alleviate these concerns?

6. After reflecting upon the example teaching vignettes provided in this chapter, what does it mean to learn "with" computers versus learning "from" computers? Give examples.

Activities

1. *CCS Reading Standards for Foundational Skills: Fluency Category.* After reading a text together, create a Voicethread to share with all of your students. Assign each student a section of the text to summarize and a slide on the class Voicethread. During computer time, students will go to their slide and record their summary for that part of the text. When all of the students have recorded, watch the Voicethread as a class as a review.

   Challenge! Have students watch the Voicethread on their own and leave comments to their classmates of their reactions to certain parts in the text.

2. *CCS Reading Standards for Informational Text: Key Ideas and Details Category.* Prior to reading a historical fiction text, assign groups of students different passages about the time period to read. Ask students to pull out the main idea of the text, as well as supporting details. Using Glogster, students will work with their partners to design a Glog that includes information from the passage and images from the time period to share with the class.

   Challenge! Embed student glogs onto a class Web page to be shared with other classes in the grade.

3. *CCS Writing: Production and Distribution of Writing Category.* Following a poetry study, create a page on a class wiki for each of your students using Wikispaces. Have students create poems using the different strategies learned in the poetry unit. Students then publish their poems onto their individual page previously created by the teacher. Students will read and comment on each other's poems using the discussion tab on each page.

   Challenge! Ask students to embed at least one image, video, or music file on their wiki page.

4. *CCS Speaking and Listening: Presentation of Knowledge and Ideas Category.* Have students select a main character from a book they are reading for a character study. For the activity, students will identify traits to describe the character and an example from the text to support this idea. To present their information, ask students to create a voki. Vokis should look like the main

character of the book and provide the audience with the information required in the assignment.

Challenge! Embed all student vokis to a class Web page for all to view.

REFERENCES

Burkhardt, G., Monsour, M., Valdez, G., Gunn, C., Dawson, M., Lemke, C., et al. (2003). *enGauge 21st century skills: Literacy in the digital age.* Los Angeles: North Central Regional Educational Laboratory and the Metiri Group.

DiCamillo, K. (2000). *Because of Winn-Dixie.* Somerville, MA: Candlewick Press.

Honey, M., Culp, K. M., & Spielvogel, R. (2005). *Critical issue: Using technology to improve student achievement.* Los Angeles: North Central Regional Educational Laboratory. Retrieved from *www.ncrel.org/sdrs/areas/issues/methods/technlgy/te800.htm.*

Lefever-Davis, S., & Pearman, C. (2005). Early readers and electronic texts: CD-ROM storybook features that influence reading behaviors. *The Reading Teacher, 58*(5), 446–454.

Lemke, J. L. (2006). Towards critical multimedia literacy: Technology, research, and politics. In M. McKenna, D. Reinking, L. Labbo, & R. Kieffer (Eds.), *International handbook of literacy and technology* (Vol. 2, pp. 3–14). Mahwah, NJ: Erlbaum.

National Governors Association Center for Best Practices and Council of Chief State School Officers. (2010). Common Core State Standards for English language arts & literacy in history/social studies, science, and technical subjects. Washington, DC: Author. Retrieved from *www.corestandards.org.*

Partnership for 21st Century Skills. (2008). *Learning for the 21st century: A report and mile guide for 21st century skills.* Washington, DC: Author.

Reeves, T. C. (1998). *The impact of media and technology in schools.* Unpublished manuscript.

Ringstaff, C., & Kelley, L. (2002). *The learning return on our educational technology investment.* San Francisco: WestEd. Retrieved from *www.wested.org/cs/we/view/rs/619.*

Robelen, E. W. (1999). Info brief: The promise and the pitfalls. *Technology in Schools, 16.* Retrieved from *www.ascd.org/publications/newsletters/policy-priorities/mar99/num16/toc.aspx.*

Walsh, M. (2008). Worlds have collided and modes have merged: Classroom evidence of changed literacy practices. *Literacy, 42*(2), 101–108.

CHAPTER 9

Assessment and
the Common Core Standards

Peter Afflerbach

A fourth grader sits at his desk, reading and answering questions about a social studies text, his high school graduation far in the distance. Across the next 8 years, and following the developmental trajectory that underlies the Common Core State Standards (CCSS; National Governors Association Center for Best Practices and Council of Chief State School Officers, 2010), it is expected that this fourth grader will develop as an engaged and accomplished reader. He will read broadly and deeply in content-area subjects and use reading as a powerful tool in analysis, critique, and application of what is learned. At this moment, the student is answering literal and inferential questions, demonstrating his ongoing reading development. The teacher notes his responses, recording successes and challenges, and updates her understanding of his reading development. In the here and now of the fourth grader further developing as a reader, the teacher gathers valuable assessment information.

How can we connect this fourth-grade student's reading of the social studies text and answering comprehension questions with the increasing complexities of text and task that the CCSS will demand in later grades? How can we effectively conduct the increasingly complex assessment of higher-order thinking strategies (e.g., analyzing and critiquing) in reading? What must happen from this day in fourth grade through to graduation day in high school for the student to realize his potential? What is the role of assessment in this student's evolution toward superior reading performance?

In this chapter, I examine the requisites of a successful elementary reading assessment program that is aligned with the CCSS. The chapter is based on seven premises— that reading assessment must:

- Reflect the most recent and comprehensive understanding of reading.
- Describe in detail the ongoing development of elementary-school readers in relation to both near (daily learning) and far (year-end and school–career CCSS) goals.

- Combine formative and summative assessments in a symbiotic relationship.
- Report, support, and teach in relation to student learning.
- Focus on both the cognitive and affective aspects of students' reading development.
- Be developed with clear understanding of the specific roles and responsibilities the CCSS create for teachers and students.
- Help all students meet the CCSS "raised bar" of achievement, even as some students struggle to meet basic reading levels.

READING ASSESSMENT MUST REFLECT THE MOST RECENT AND COMPREHENSIVE UNDERSTANDING OF READING

Theory, research, and practice continually contribute information that updates our understanding of reading. They provide the opportunity to reflect on how we regard reading and to determine whether our instructional goals, learning benchmarks, and related assessments are suitable representatives of this evolving knowledge. The CCSS offer an opportunity to examine curriculum and assessment concurrently and to conceptualize them as important partners in the development of effective instructional programs. There are numerous definitions of reading. For this chapter, I focus on one that has much in common with how the CCSS represent reading. The National Assessment of Educational Progress (National Assessment Governing Board, 2008) defines reading as:

an active and complex process that involves:

- Understanding written text
- Developing and interpreting meaning
- Using meaning as appropriate to type of text, purpose, and situation.

According to this definition, constructing meaning from text is no longer the end point of reading: Reading involves the reader's use of that which is understood. This theory of use is a profound shift, one that should effect change in both reading instruction and reading assessment. Many CCSS reflect the fact that applying, analyzing, critiquing, or synthesizing what is understood is an essential part of reading. In addition, the CCSS focus on increasing text and task complexity as students matriculate, developing higher-order thinking that will prepare them for success after high school. Under the CCSS, students are expected to make increasingly detailed critique of increasingly complex texts. They are expected to conduct accurate syntheses of multiple texts with related but differing viewpoints.

To illustrate how reading becomes more complex across the grades, consider this fourth-grade reading standard for literature, under the category of Key Ideas and Details:

Determine a theme of a story, drama, or poem from details in the text; summarize the text. (CCSS, p. 12)

Over the ensuing years, and aided by effective instruction and assessment, the student should develop the ability to perform more complex tasks, with more complex texts, as exemplified in the grade 11–12 reading standard for literature, also in the category of Key Ideas and Details:

Analyze the impact of the author's choices regarding how to develop and relate elements of a story or drama (e.g., where the story is set, how the action is ordered, how the characters are introduced and developed). (CCSS, p. 38)

The fourth grader sitting at his desk is probably not imagining what lies ahead in terms of reading, learning, and assessment. Our careful attention to assessment within the CCSS will help him realize a productive future from the challenging present.

All CCSS-related assessment must have construct validity, and a successful reading assessment program is informed by our most recent and comprehensive understanding of reading. Specifically, valid reading assessment maps onto the construct of reading, focusing on those things that are known to operate in successful reading. While differing perspectives on reading may be characterized more by contention than consensus, the following points are relatively unassailable:

- Reading is a constructive act that combines information from text with information from the reader's prior knowledge.
- Reading varies in the complexity of texts and tasks.
- Reading requires both strategies and skills.
- Reading is influenced by both cognitive and affective factors.

These points help describe the construct of reading, which should inform both the CCSS and the development of related curriculum and assessment.

Figure 9.1 portrays the alignment of four related aspects of the education enterprise: construct, CCSS and benchmarks, curriculum and instruction, and reading assessment. We can check on an assessment's validity by comparing the construct (Level 1) with an assessment (Level 4). All that is assessed should be part of the construct of reading. The

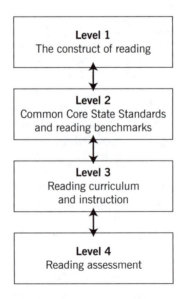

FIGURE 9.1. Necessary alignments for reading assessment.

CCSS derive from consensus understanding of what reading and literacy "are:" the construct of reading (Level 1). It follows that the CCSS and related benchmark performances (Level 2) derive from this construct. CCSS are aligned with cognitive understanding of reading: They acknowledge the role of reading strategies and skills and the importance of students' prior knowledge, and they include a focus on higher-order thinking. The next alignment involves Levels 2 and 3: the CCSS and classroom curriculum and instruction (Level 3). What is taught and learned in classrooms directly relates to both the CCSS and the construct of reading. The final alignment involves curriculum and instruction and assessment (Levels 3 and 4). We want to assess the important learning and development that are the outcomes of CCSS-related instruction. In a well-functioning assessment system, all four components are aligned; one can examine an assessment and perceive its connection to all other components.

Reading assessment in grades 3–5 in relation to the CCSS involves a series of challenges and opportunities. Although the CCSS are most often considered in relation to preparation for college and employment, they involve student learning and achievement in the elementary grades. Becoming an accomplished reader, and assessing reading well both have roots in these grades. Effective assessment helps us to consider students' current strengths and needs and to anticipate the future demands that increasingly complex reading texts and tasks will place on our students.

The assessments used in conjunction with CCSS must reflect what we know about reading. Assessment must also follow readers' developmental trajectories. It must follow them as fourth graders, discussing and answering questions in relation to content-area chapters and stories, through high school, where readers describe how the author's craft contributes to a short story and evaluate the value of information provided in a social studies text.

READING ASSESSMENT MUST DESCRIBE IN DETAIL THE ONGOING DEVELOPMENT OF ELEMENTARY SCHOOL READERS IN RELATION TO BOTH NEAR (DAILY LEARNING) AND FAR (YEAR-END AND SCHOOL–CAREER CCSS) GOALS

Many assessments of reading in grades 3–5 have partial construct validity: They focus on important but limited aspects of reading. For example, many commercial reading materials in the content areas focus assessment on literal and inferential comprehension questions. While important, these are only part of the cognitive strategy and skill repertoire that students need to succeed as they move toward the complex demands of the CCSS. We must have assessments that inform our understanding of elementary-school readers' development across the broad base of reading. We cannot focus only on comprehension strategies, because this misses the obvious links to students' strategic use of what they learn from reading. In addition, we must use assessments that describe the unstated standards and competencies that undergird grade 4 students' success at the CCSS: the ability to decode, read fluently, and identify and use vocabulary. While grade 4 students are expected to possess those skills and strategies, we know that considerable numbers of students in grades 3 to 5 struggle to read successfully.

Take, for example, the reading standards for informational text, grade 4, Craft and Structure:

Compare and contrast a firsthand and secondhand account of the same event or topic; describe the differences in focus and the information provided. (CCSS, p. 14)

This standard comes with the assumption that all "basic" reading skills, strategies, and knowledge are in place and operating successfully. Although the standard will be challenging for some students, it will be impossible for those who lack the basics.

The standards do not address in detail the prerequisite strategies and skills that are expected of our elementary-grade students so that they read, comprehend, and use what is understood from reading. Related to foundational skills, the standards state that:

These standards are directed toward fostering students' understanding and working knowledge of concepts of print, the alphabetic principle, and other basic conventions of the English writing system. These foundational skills are not an end in and of themselves; rather, they are necessary and important components of an effective, comprehensive reading program designed to develop proficient readers with the capacity to comprehend texts across a range of types and disciplines. (CCSS, p. 15)

Thus, curriculum and assessment that focus on phonemic awareness, phonics, and fluency *may* be essential for some students in grades 3–5, when indicated by individual student needs. The CCSS help us focus on a broader array of what is "basic" in reading development. This should be reflected in both our instruction and assessment. Thus, CCSS-related assessment in elementary grades must attend to two priorities: describing students in relation to the prerequisite skills, strategies, and knowledge they need to approach CCSS texts and tasks, and describing students' progression through these texts and tasks. When assessment acts as a complement to curriculum, teaching, and learning (and not as a constraint), it can be assigned a passing grade.

In close affiliation with the CCSS, reading assessment must provide detailed accounts of what students can do when they arrive at school and of their weekly, monthly, and yearly progress in elementary school experience. Such assessment must be comprehensive—describing the cognitive components of reading development as well as the affective factors that impact development. This assessment is also regular, conducted frequently to provide continual updates of our understanding of individual students. Just as readers update their mental model of the text as they gather information through reading, teachers must update their mental models of students with information from assessment. Using this formative assessment, teachers address the immediate needs of students in relation to the array of cognitive skills and strategies and affective factors that impact reading development. Such assessment is occurring within a curriculum that fosters student growth toward CCSS attainment, and student growth moves them closer to success with text and tasks of increasing complexity.

READING ASSESSMENT MUST COMBINE FORMATIVE AND SUMMATIVE ASSESSMENTS IN A SYMBIOTIC MANNER

Students' reading development in relation to the CCSS will be enhanced by the strategic combination of formative and summative assessments. Formative assessment provides information for understanding individual students and their immediate needs, determining teachable moments during the school day, and creating scaffolded approaches to instruction (Afflerbach, 2012). In contrast, summative assessment provides information about students' literacy products in relation to CCSS benchmarks and performances. A well-functioning assessment program is marked by formative and summative assessment working together toward common goals. However, in many schools, the two types of assessment compete for time and resources.

I noted earlier that as assessments associated with the CCSS prove construct valid, they will better represent the complexity of reading. This complexity demands the increased use of formative assessment to inform us of how students are progressing in their ability to do well on summative performance assessments. Consider what is required of our grade 4 students by the following grade 4 standard for informational text—Integration of Knowledge and Ideas:

> Interpret information presented visually, orally, or quantitatively (e.g., in charts, graphs, diagrams, time lines, animations, or interactive elements on Web pages) and explain how the information contributes to an understanding of the text in which it appears. (CCSS, p. 14)

A cursory task analysis indicates that a fourth grader who meets this standard engages in complex thinking. To demonstrate achievement in the related performance assessment, the student must:

- Construct meaning from the text.
- Comprehend related charts, graphs, diagrams, time lines, animations, or interactive elements on Web pages.
- Compare the two related understandings.
- Analyze the two for their separate and joint contributions to understanding.
- Explain (through writing or speaking) how the two comprehended parts of the text relate to one another.
- Describe how the charts, graphs, diagrams, time lines, animations, or interactive elements on Web pages help comprehension.

We should also assume the student's metacognitive ability to coordinate these skills and strategies and to guide the entire reading process. For the fourth grader, each of these seven facets of the standard represents significant learning and achievement. Each is a necessary focus of instruction and assessment, as is the student's strategic combination of them to meet the standard.

It is difficult to imagine a fourth-grade reader undertaking and succeeding at a related, complex summative assessment task without the prior benefits of ongoing formative assessment and related teacher feedback and instruction. For the struggling reader, the need for formative assessment may be more acute. Detailed assessment information is necessary for each of the facets of performance (as well as the coordination of these facets) for students to succeed at the summative performance. Formative assessment related to the CCSS just presented helps the classroom teacher identify students' zones of proximal development (Vygotsky, 1978) and related teachable moments. Thus, formative assessment must inform us about how students are faring in the aspects of the performance listed, and how they are combining these aspects in a complex and successful performance. Formative assessment informs the teacher's choice of timely, suitable instruction.

Without formative assessment, the opportunity to understand how students are progressing toward a complex performance is lost, as is the opportunity to influence the process. Without formative assessment, that certain students cannot construct meaning from text (which is an entry point, not an end point, in many CCSS) may be missed. Accordingly, the stakes could not be higher for either formative or summative assessment. Should our formative assessment be wanting, we will have little idea of students' development in relation to an upcoming complex performance assessment. We will have diminished ability to determine, through examination of the performance assessment, what was and what wasn't learned in terms of the parts that make the whole.

Assessment that is aligned with CCSS and related complex texts and tasks must reflect text and task complexity. Such complexity demands that formative and summative assessment work together. Over students' K–12 school experience, there should be continuing progress toward the long-term goals of CCSS; the standards are so structured. Assessment must follow this lead, gauging students' progression toward long-term goals that the summative assessment represents, while providing fine-grained information about their near-term work and accomplishments with formative assessment.

READING ASSESSMENT MUST BE USED TO REPORT, SUPPORT, AND TEACH IN RELATION TO STUDENT LEARNING

Reading assessment can realize an expanded role and influence as students and teachers work toward attainment of the CCSS. Consider the following reading standard for literature, Key Ideas and Details. Fourth graders will:

> Determine a theme of a story, drama, or poem from details in the text; summarize the text. (CCSS, p. 12)

Reading assessment in the elementary grades typically focuses on diagnosis and reporting of students' strategies and skills, fluency, vocabulary, and construction of meaning. Assessment information reports the state of student learning and is useful for teachers, parents, and the students themselves. In relation to the prior standard, diagnostic assessment can help to identify key aspects of students' cognitive strategy and skill development, including but not restricted to literal comprehension, summarization, and determining theme. A CCSS-related assessment should help us further determine how (and if) fourth graders take their understanding of a story and use it to discern a theme, moral, or lesson. The results of such diagnostic assessment are used to inform instruction, helping teachers determine what students need and how students are developing in relation to standards.

A second important use of assessment is teaching. In the long view, we hope that students in a CCSS curriculum are on a path to independent and successful reading. Along that path, students must assume increasing responsibility for assessing their own reading. As students become accomplished readers, they must also become independent and accurate assessors of their own work (Afflerbach, 2012; Black & Wiliam, 1998). The CCSS expect complex student performance across texts and tasks of increasing difficulty and duration. For example, with the CCSS for fourth-grade literature under the domain of Integration of Knowledge and Ideas, students are expected to:

Compare and contrast the treatment of similar themes and topics (e.g., opposition of good and evil) and patterns of events (e.g., the quest) in stories, myths, and traditional literature from different cultures. (CCSS, p. 12)

In relation to this and other CCSS, students must develop the ability to manage and assess their reading in the midst of complexity. Thus, a comprehensive assessment program will feature the teaching of reading assessment. Assessment must help set a foundation on which students can build an understanding of the ways and means of assessment. Rarely a focus on classroom discussion, assessment is worthy of our attention, and discussions about assessment with students help them better understand its value and how it works. As students develop across the elementary-school years, we should assist them in cultivating the ability to set goals, to plan, to work on increasingly complex tasks, to monitor progress, to note and fix problems, and eventually to gain independence for assessing their own reading.

Formative assessment, conducted regularly by the teacher, can help us teach assessment. For example, as teachers ask questions related to the prior CCSS (comparing and contrasting important points in two texts), they can describe the relationship of the question to the goals of the lesson: "Questions I like to ask myself when I am comparing the important points in two texts are, What is different about these two texts, and what do the two texts have in common?" As students respond to questions, teachers can describe what they are looking for in student responses and how they are evaluating those responses. For example, "I like that you are paying attention to the questions to help guide your thinking. Your answer is correct. Both of these texts, one from Asia and one from Africa, focus on the value of doing good for others. Now, what about a difference? Again, good work! One is realistic, and the other is fantasy. As we continue to read, let's remember that good answers depend on us paying careful attention to the questions that are asked."

Assessment checklists provided to students can serve as one foundation of self-assessment. In addition to questions that directly address CCSS content, we can provide questions that focus on general, powerful self-assessment routines. Fourth graders vary in their knowledge of self-assessment, but regularly answering the following questions provides introductory experience on which students can build complex self-assessment strategies:

- Why am I reading?
- Does this make sense?
- Is there a problem?
- What is the problem?
- Can I fix it?
- Can I get back on track?

Over time, these questions can become internalized and used as part of fourth-grade students' independent monitoring routines for increasingly complex reading. With teacher explanation, modeling, and thinking aloud, it is possible to transfer assessment knowledge and strategies from teacher to student, much in the manner of the reciprocal teaching of reading comprehension strategies.

A third important purpose of reading assessment is the support of student learning. Meeting a particular CCSS is arduous work. Our assessment feedback can provide students with guidance, encouragement, and scaffolded instruction that serve to support this work. Support for students can be provided by assessment in two ways. First, our assessment feedback can direct students to immediate areas of concern, focusing attention and preparing them for teachable moments. Assessment feedback helps students make the link between their work and the outcomes of reading. Second, assessment feedback should focus on student effort—building self-efficacy as students realize that their effort can lead to successful reading (Johnston, 2004). We must be aware of how reading assessment information is received and understood by our students. How might a struggling student interpret teacher feedback or a test result? Our continuing work to have students focus on their effort can be influenced by what we say in relation to assessment. Handing back a graded assignment without speaking is different than returning it while saying, "I know you worked hard on the written assignment to compare and constrast these texts, and your hard work shows." We can also connect effort with specific outcomes: "You included lots of information from each of the two texts on doing good deeds—that is interesting to the reader. I know that your attention to comparing and contrasting the texts, combined with the effort you put into the drafts of your report, made a difference." Furthermore, self-efficacy matters greatly as students move through grades. Without self-efficacy, it is difficult for students to imagine themselves succeeding at complex tasks. Thus, we should use every opportunity to take our reading assessment information and use it in ways that are supportive of students' growth.

READING ASSESSMENT MUST FOCUS ON BOTH THE COGNITIVE AND AFFECTIVE ASPECTS OF STUDENTS' READING DEVELOPMENT

Reading assessment dwells on students' cognitive strategy and skill development and the ability to learn content from text. In the elementary grades, much assessment focuses on the mechanics of reading. There is clear need to chart each student's development through phonemic awareness, sound–symbol correspondences, and fluency, but these aspects of becoming a successful reader are only a part of what we need to assess. By grade 4, students must also develop large vocabularies and the ability to construct literal, inferential, and critical understanding of text. From grades K–6, there is a decreasing emphasis on mechanics and increasing focus on reading comprehension and vocabulary. The good news is that many schools' reading assessment programs reflect this dynamic; the bad news is that there is a cognitive monopoly in reading assessment (Afflerbach, Pearson, & Paris, 2008).

We need to ask whether reading strategy and skill, and their use to construct meaning, are the only things that matter in students' reading development. Consider this stated goal of the CCSS:

> Students will learn in school in a manner that prepares them for success in college, and in life . . .

Elementary-school students must traverse considerable ground to reach this goal. The CCSS demand ever-increasing sophistication and coordination of reading skill and strategy. Throughout their school careers, students will be asked to demonstrate higher-order thinking. Despite the importance of gaining in cognitive skill and strategy, we must establish a focus on the noncognitive aspects of school and learning that support student development and represent legitimate outcomes of schooling in their own right (Afflerbach, Cho, Kim, & Crassas, 2011). We must assess student development in areas that are related to school success, but are "other" than skill and strategy. Three areas critical to students' reading development and success include metacognition, motivation and engagement, and self-efficacy. As assessments better reflect the full construct of reading, attending to aspects of reading development that have been heretofore neglected, they can support student growth in all areas relevant to reading development.

Underlying students' success with increasingly complex texts and tasks is metacognition. Effective reading requires metacognition (Baker & Brown, 1984), and metacognition supports academic learning (Paris & Winograd, 1990). In relation to CCSS, metacognition allows students to set goals, monitor both near and far progress toward those goals, identify problems, fix the problems, and stay "on track." (Zimmerman, 2008). Higher-order thinking in reading is a strong thread that runs through all of the CCSS, and we can infer the success of metacognition as students successfully complete complex performance tasks. However, less than competent performance may indicate the lack of appropriate metacognitive strategies. Text complexity gets much attention in CCSS and it is accompanied by task complexity, reminding us of the need to monitor both the construction of meaning from reading and then how that meaning is used in higher-order thinking. If our CCSS-related assessment program does not provide information on how all students are developing a reflective mindset, or on the establishment of key metacognitive questions (e.g., "Why am I reading? How am I doing? Do I understand? Is there a problem?"), then we construct only a partial picture of our developing readers. Examples of questions that can help students focus on metacognition were provided earlier in the section on teaching self-assessment.

The CCSS also acknowledge that motivation and engagement are central to reading development and reading achievement. Consider the following:

> Students who meet the *Standards* . . . actively seek the wide, deep, and thoughtful engagement with high-quality literary and informational texts that builds knowledge, enlarges experience, and broadens worldviews. (CCSS, p. 3)

When engagement and motivation are strong, reading instruction improves students' reading comprehension (Guthrie, Wigfield, & You, 2012). Engaged students possess enthusiasm for learning, and motivation is integral to students' participation in school (Skinner, Kindermann, & Furrer, 2009). In contrast, students who lack engagement and motivation often struggle with reading. As motivation supports students' learning of strategies, skills, and content-domain knowledge, assessment must include it as a focus. Consider the earlier example of the fourth grader who must "interpret information presented visually, orally, or quantitatively (e.g., in charts, graphs, diagrams, time lines, animations, or interactive elements on Web pages) and explain how the information contributes to an understanding of the text in which it appears" (CCSS, p. 14). Can we imagine all of our students persevering as they undertake this complex task without adequate motivation? How will fourth graders succeed if they are not engaged?

Self-efficacy is a third area worthy of assessment attention. The CCSS demand that students undertake increasingly complex tasks. As they read difficult texts and engage in CCSS tasks, students must believe that they can be successful, and this belief is directly tied to student self-efficacy. Self-efficacy influences reading success (Schunk & Zimmerman, 2007), and unless students believe they can produce desired effects by their actions, they have little incentive to act (Bandura, 2006). Consider the different reactions that a successful, self-assured reader and a struggling reader would have to the following assessment task:

> Explain major differences between poems, drama, and prose, and refer to the structural elements of poems (e.g., verse, rhythm, meter) and drama (e.g., casts of characters, settings, descriptions, dialogue, stage directions) when writing or speaking about a text. (CCSS, p. 12)

The student who sees herself as up to the challenge likely will approach the task with confidence and positive motivation, while a student with diminished self-efficacy cannot see himself succeeding.

Including metacognition, motivation and engagement, and self-efficacy as foci within a CCSS assessment program requires that we use appropriate assessments. We are fortunate to have assessment materials and procedures that help us better understand these aspects of students' development, related to motivation for reading (Gambrell, Palmer, Codling, & Mazzoni, 1996), students' attitudes toward reading (McKenna & Kear, 1990), and student readers' self-concepts (Chapman & Tunmer, 1995). Each of these assessments might be adapted and used in relation to our elementary-grade students. In addition, the affective side of students' reading development will benefit from both formative and summative assessment. For example, formative assessment allows us to keep track of students' self-efficacy—whether it improves or declines in relation to ongoing reading challenges and successes. With this information, we can adjust instruction and reading tasks accordingly. Formative assessment also helps us understand the development of students' metacognition and engagement and motivation. When affective factors are taken seriously, we will see summative assessments that describe engaged and motivated readers, readers who are self-efficacious, and readers who effectively manage complex acts of reading.

READING ASSESSMENT MUST BE DEVELOPED WITH CLEAR UNDERSTANDING OF THE SPECIFIC ROLES AND RESPONSIBILITIES THE CCSS CREATE FOR TEACHERS AND STUDENTS

The CCSS require substantial changes in reading instruction and reading assessment, and these changes create new responsibilities for teachers and students. An assessment program that focuses on detailed, formative assessment demands teacher expertise. Consider the following scenario: Reba is a fourth-grade teacher who regularly uses checklists to help assess her students' growing repertoire of reading strategies and reading knowledge. She has spent hundreds of hours honing her ability to analyze the information they yield and to use the information to tailor reading instruction to student needs. The advent of CCSS creates new demands related to assessment, and Reba is preparing for the challenge of meeting them. She regularly visits the websites of the Partnership for Assessment of Readiness for College and Careers (PARCC), and the Smarter Balanced Assessment Consortium (SBAC), searching for information and examples of the performance assessments that are to be developed.

In particular, Reba is interested in using rubrics and related performance assessments. Her school district has decided to implement simple performance assessments in the early elementary grades in part to introduce students to the idea of performance assessments and in part to use in the measure of students' comprehension of narrative and informational texts. There are only very limited examples of the assessments that PARCC (2012) and SBAC (2012) are creating on their respective websites, but Reba is encouraged by her school and district to develop and use checklists that will be tied to the rubrics, so that students can begin to develop independent assessment routines. Reba needs detailed assessment information to inform instructional decision making, in the midst of lessons and while planning future instruction. With her focus on formative assessment, Reba must be expert in understanding and using the assessment, interpreting assessment results, taking that assessment information to modify her understanding of individual students, shaping instruction in relation to her knowledge of curriculum and teaching, using a rubric to scaffold student learning, and then evaluating each student's performance. As the performance assessments from PARCC and SBAC are developed and released, Reba and her colleagues will be prepared to conduct a careful linking of their performance checklists with performance assessment rubrics.

Students must also adapt to the new assessments. Many fourth-grade students have limited roles and responsibilities with reading assessment. Assessment is done to or for them, and their assessment activity is marked by preparing for and taking quizzes and tests. The complexity and detail of CCSS-related assessments demand that students become more active participants in assessment as opposed to passive contributors. Students need to learn forms of assessment that are new to the classroom and to their way of thinking about assessment. Students can learn the ways and means of performance assessment and use related illustrative scoring rubrics and checklists, as demonstrated by the previous example. These student-centered assessment strategies are introduced early in school and practiced in anticipation of students' reading independence. As their reading develops, students must also become increasingly responsible for assessing their reading. Metacognition, self-regulated learning, and independence all have roots in students' increased role in assessment.

Students' acclimation to the role of assessment user can be enhanced through the use of vertical and horizontal alignment of assessments. The CCSS represent instruction and learning that is connected across the school years and between school subjects. When our assessment programs are aligned across grades and across school subjects, we can enhance students' learning and use of assessment materials and procedures. For example, a district plan to vertically align assessment from kindergarten through grade 12 introduces kindergartners to simple performance assessments, checklists, and rubrics early in their school careers. Ensuing years and related assessments build on this knowledge, encouraging students to build on their foundation of assessment knowledge.

Helping students develop the ability to use assessment is also accomplished by horizontal alignment of assessment. Across content areas, there can be commonalities in assessment forms and uses. For example, students in science, social studies, math, and English become increasingly familiar with performance assessments as they are used throughout the school year in all content areas. The CCSS position reading as an important tool in learning across the curriculum, and the opportunity to develop understanding of the uses and benefits of performance assessment is provided across the school day, leading to competence and then expertise in students' assessment routines.

READING ASSESSMENT MUST HELP ALL STUDENTS MEET THE CCSS "RAISED BAR" OF ACHIEVEMENT, EVEN AS SOME STUDENTS STRUGGLE TO MEET BASIC READING LEVELS

The CCSS raise the bar in terms of student work and learning outcomes. Students are required to read increasingly complex tasks and to engage in increasingly complex tasks. The CCSS link this raising of the bar to the goal of students being best prepared to realize their potential during and upon completion of school. This approach comes with risk— there are currently millions of U.S. students who do not reach "basic" levels in reading and writing (National Assessment Governing Board, 2008). Creating the CCSS and teaching to them does not guarantee that all students will meet them. Students who struggle daily to construct literal understanding of texts will likely be overwhelmed by a task that asks them to comment on the author's craft or to compare and contrast content with another text.

How can students who do not meet basic levels of reading achievement hope to attain the more difficult reading characterized by the CCSS? What are their chances of succeeding at the CCSS, which are arguably more challenging than many extant state reading standards? There are several implications for assessment. We must continue to use assessments that are detailed in the diagnostic information they provide to help teachers identify and teach to readers' basic needs. This diagnostic assessment must be available as our elementary-school students work through their school reading development. We must have assessments that help us understand both the cognitive strategy and the skill profiles of all readers as well as their affective development. We must be able to identify those students who are struggling to develop phonemic awareness, who have imprecise understandings of sound–symbol correspondences, and who are challenged to read fluently and with comprehension. Using the appropriate assessment, we can help students create a foundation from which they can progress toward the attainment of increasingly challenging CCSS.

CONCLUSION

Impetus for change in reading assessment is related to CCSS, but the reading assessment encountered in many districts, schools, and classrooms has been in need of change for some time. The development and maintenance of exemplary reading assessment programs can be in reference to CCSS and informed by the evolving understanding of the nature of reading and of effective assessment. Successful reading assessment programs are developed in concert with curriculum and instruction. They are not added on, after the fact of curriculum development.

A programmatic approach to reading assessment development and use related to the CCSS will have several features. There will be attention to alignments between construct, standards, curriculum and instruction, and reading assessment. In grades 3–5, assessments must measure a broadened concept of basic skills in reading, while anticipating the array of higher-order thinking that is at the core of CCSS in later years. The CCSS also require strategic combinations of formative and summative assessment that help teachers and students chart progress across increasingly complex texts and tasks. These assessments help us simultaneously focus on near and far reading goals.

Furthermore, the development of assessment in relation to CCSS should focus on reporting student progress as well as teaching and supporting students. Teaching assessment is critical as students embark on the path toward independent reading marked by increasingly complex texts and tasks. Assessment must also support students in their cognitive and affective growth. Relatedly, our assessments must change to include focus on powerful factors that include motivation, engagement, and self-efficacy. Instructional programs that increase reading achievement and create positive affect should be documented. New assessments create new roles and responsibilities for teachers and students. With the CCSS, assessment programs must be accompanied by a full accounting of this change. What must teachers do as they regularly collect detailed formative assessment information? How do students become active participants in assessing their reading? Finally, assessment must help all students meet the CCSS "raised bar" of achievement: those students who struggle to meet basic reading level, and those for whom the CCSS represent an array of doable challenges.

REFERENCES

Afflerbach, P. (2012). *Understanding and using reading assessment, K–12* (2nd ed.). Newark, DE: International Reading Association.

Afflerbach, P., Cho, B., Kim, J., & Crassas, M. (2011). Best practices in literacy assessment. In L. M. Morrow & L. B. Gambrell (Eds.), *Best practices in literacy instruction* (4th ed., pp. 264–282). New York: Guilford Press.

Afflerbach, P., Pearson, P. D., & Paris, S. (2008). Clarifying differences between reading skills and reading strategies. *The Reading Teacher, 61*, 364–373.

Baker, L., & Brown, A. L. (1984). Metacognitive skills and reading. In P. D. Pearson, R. Barr, M. L. Kamil, & P. Mosenthal (Eds.), *Handbook of reading research* (Vol. 1, pp. 353–394). New York: Longman.

Bandura, A. (2006). Toward a psychology of human agency. *Perspectives on Physiological Science, 1*, 164–180.

Black, P., & William, D. (1998). Assessment and classroom learning. *Educational Assessment: Principles, Policy and Practice, 5*, 7–74.

Chapman, J. W., & Tunmer, W. E. (1995). Development of young children's reading self-concepts: An examination of emerging subcomponents and their relationship with reading achievement. *Journal of Educational Psychology, 87*, 154–167.

Gambrell, L., Palmer, B., Codling, R., & Mazzoni, S. (1996). Assessing motivation to read. *The Reading Teacher, 49*, 518–533.

Guthrie, J. T., Wigfield, A., & You, W. (2012). Instructional contexts for engagement and achievement in reading. In S. Christensen, A. Reschly, & C. Wylie (Eds.), *Handbook of research on student engagement* (pp. 601–634). New York: Springer Science.

Johnston, P. (2004). *Choice words: How our language affects children's learning*. Portland, ME: Stenhouse.

McKenna, M., & Kear, D. (1990). Measuring attitude towards reading: A new tool for teachers. *The Reading Teacher, 43*, 626–639.

National Assessment Governing Board. (2008). *Reading framework for the 2009 National Assessment of Educational Progress*. Washington, DC: American Institutes for Research.

National Governors Association Center for Best Practices and Council of Chief State School Officers. (2010). Common Core State Standards for English language arts & literacy in history/social studies, science, and technical subjects. Washington, DC: Author. Retrieved from *www.corestandards.org/assets/CCSSI_ELA%20Standards.pdf*.

Partnership for Assessment of Readiness for College and Careers. (2012). PARCCPlace. Retrieved from *http://parcconline.org/sites/parcc/files/March2012PARCCPlaceNewsletter.pdf*.

Paris, S., & Winograd, P. (1990). How metacognition can promote academic learning and instruction. In B. J. Jones & L. Idol (Eds.), *Dimensions of thinking and cognitive instruction* (pp. 15–51). Hillsdale, NJ: Erlbaum.

Schunk, D., & Zimmerman, B. (2007). Influencing children's self-efficacy and self-regulation of reading and writing through modeling. *Reading and Writing Quarterly, 23,* 7–25.

Skinner, E., Kindermann, T., & Furrer, C. (2009). A motivational perspective on engagement and disaffection: Conceptualization and assessment of children's behavioral and emotional participation in academic activities in the classroom. *Educational and Psychological Measurement, 69,* 493–525.

Smarter Balanced Assessment Consortium. (2012). The Smarter Balanced assessment system. Retrieved from *www.smarterbalanced.org/k-12-education/teachers.*

Vygotsky, L. (1978). *Mind in society: The development of higher psychological processes.* Cambridge, MA: Harvard University Press.

Zimmerman, B. (2008). Investigating self-regulation and motivation: Historical background, methodological developments, and future prospects. *American Educational Research Journal, 45,* 166–183.

CHAPTER 10

In Conclusion

On Implementing the Common Core Standards Successfully in Grades 3–5

Karen K. Wixson

The purpose of this book is to assist grade 3–5 teachers and specialists in the implementation of the Common Core State Standards (CCSS) for English language arts (ELA). Several themes emerge from the chapters in this volume, which serve as the basis for this concluding chapter and bring the information in this book full circle from the ideas presented in the introduction. Dominant themes across chapters include increased emphasis on higher-order knowledge and skills, informational text, complex text, reading and writing across texts and within subject-area instruction, and using evidence from text to construct arguments that can be developed and extended in oral and written language. Uniting these themes is attention to the need for integrated curriculum and instruction, which is the focus of this chapter.

The chapter begins with a discussion about an integrated perspective on English language arts as reflected in the CCSS-ELA. It then moves to an examination of the advantages and potential pitfalls of thematic instruction as a means to accomplish integration and many of the higher-order knowledge and skills described in the preceding chapters. Within the context of thematic curriculum and instruction, it addresses the need to balance attention to content and process in curriculum and instruction. The balance between content and process is also addressed in relation to the concept of text complexity put forward in the CCSS-ELA.

As noted in the introductory chapter and throughout this volume, the title of the CCSS-ELA, Standards for English Language Arts and Literacy in History/Social Studies, Science, and Technical Subjects, implies an integrated perspective on English language arts. This is stated clearly as one of the "key design considerations" in the opening sections of the CCSS-ELA, which calls for "an integrated model of literacy."

Benefits of Thematic Instruction

Coherence and Connections

A thematic approach can provide coherence in curriculum and instruction for both teachers and students. Strong themes can give the work of the classroom a focus and provide guidance for making decisions about what and how to teach. The focus provided by themes can also make it easier for students to understand why they are engaged in particular instructional activities rather than struggling to make connections among fragmented activities.

Because thematic instruction brings the language arts together around authentic purposes rather than separating them into distinct lessons, new skills and strategies are learned together and in ways that serve real purposes (e.g., gather information, research a question, solve a problem). Similarly, the relationship between content and process is likely to be much clearer to students, because they will be acquiring knowledge and skill in ELA processes as a means of learning specific content (discussed further later). This, in turn, helps students see broader connections to the world, and learn to use knowledge and skills flexibly to transfer what they have learned to new situations.

Students who cannot see meaningful connections across content or skills are less likely to be able to use their knowledge and skills to solve problems or make decisions about issues raised in the curriculum. Several decades of research have demonstrated that cognitive abilities can be domain specific and that becoming knowledgeable in a specific area requires acquiring both the content and the ways of knowing of a discipline (cf. Lee & Spratley, 2010). By examining a theme from many different perspectives, a thematic approach can promote the acquisition of an integrated knowledge base, which generally results in faster retrieval of information, more flexible problem solving, and better concept transfer across domains.

Depth and Breadth

A compelling reason for adopting a thematic approach as a means of implementing the CCSS-ELA is the potential for more meaningful, in-depth student learning, which is fostered as students study powerful ideas and concepts. By focusing student learning on conceptual knowledge, flexible, higher-order thinking is privileged (Alleman & Brophy, 1993; Bransford et al., 2000; Case, 1991; Spiro et al., 1987). Students use complex psychological tools such as analyzing and synthesizing information, asking questions, identifying and solving problems, weighing and gathering various perspectives, using multiple sources, taking a critical stance, and transferring knowledge and skills to new situations. They gain insights about complex phenomenon and inquire and construct knowledge rather than simply gather it.

Thematic curriculum and instruction also permits both teachers and students to sample a variety of genre, authors, and topics. This breadth of learning is difficult to accomplish when teachers and students read from a single source or write on discrete topics. When students read, write, and speak on thematically related texts, they can gain a deeper knowledge of particular concepts and genres, enhancing their background knowledge in significant ways, which, in turn, enables them to engage with increasingly complex ideas. The accumulation of knowledge and skills in ways that enable increased learning and application to new situations is an essential feature of the CCSS-ELA.

Engagement

Another reason commonly given for using a thematic approach is that it promotes student engagement. Thematic instruction is considered by many to be more "authentic" than other approaches, because it is more consistent with the way people learn (e.g., Hughes, 1991). Many argue that more authentic instruction is related to student engagement because ELA knowledge and skills are acquired and refined within the context of real-world applications, which creates a motivation to learn. Student engagement may also be enhanced by the increase in choices and options provided by thematic instruction, allowing for personal interests. Research has demonstrated that students learn more and persist longer when reading and studying information that is interesting to them (e.g., Guthrie et al., 2006). Although not addressed directly by the CCSS-ELA, student engagement is an essential piece of the instructional puzzle that will need to be solved if implementation of the new Standards is to be successful.

Time

Another strong argument for thematic curriculum and instruction is that it has the potential for greater efficiency than traditional forms of instruction because it folds together aspects of the curriculum that are typically treated separately. By combining several separate curricular areas and reducing redundancy in the process, teachers and students should not only have more time but better-quality time, time that is less fragmented. Gaining control over time may also mean that more of it might be available for students to make choices and engage in personally interesting and relevant literacy activities, which, as noted previously, is essential for improving student engagement.

It seems clear that thematic instruction has the potential to address many of the goals of the CCSS-ELA. However, it is also important to recognize that quality thematic instruction is difficult to accomplish, and that there are a number of issues that educators need to be aware of when they move in this direction. More specifically, Valencia and Lipson (1998) caution that thematic curriculum and instruction do not always demonstrate curricular relevance and that in some instances it has been observed to constrain learning, lack attention to needed explicit instruction, and require more, rather than less time.

Challenges of Thematic Instruction

Curriculum Relevance

Although thematic curriculum and instruction has the potential to guide students toward important and meaningful learning, the realization of this potential depends on the quality of the instructional goals and the learning experiences and instruction. Time is better spent teaching substantive curricular goals that are not organized thematically than teaching less important curricular goals that are "thematically" linked. Thematic teaching has been known to result in "themes of convenience" (Lipson et al., 1993), which superficially join together activities. Routman (1994) refers to this as correlation rather than integration. Although some of the activities associated with themes may be fun and engaging for students, they may not advance powerful ideas or promote meaningful connections. Thematic curriculum and instruction must be used to fulfill substantive curricular purposes, not just to stimulate student interest or cut across subject-matter lines (Alleman & Brophy, 1993; Parker, 2012).

Constrained Learning

Thematic instruction that integrates ELA with subject areas is often designed around central ideas from science and social studies curricula. However, subject-matter experts caution that this can lead to attention to superficial content that appears to be related to the theme at the expense of more important content (Alleman & Brophy, 1993). Just as subject-matter experts worry that their content will be marginalized, others fear that thematic instruction will lead to an overreliance on nonfiction and a narrowing of the range of texts and purposes for which students read. Further, the aesthetic and efferent responses to literature and literary understanding may be lost if texts are selected only on the basis of how well they serve a particular subject matter (Pearson, 1994).

Explicit Instruction

Although well-planned thematic projects and activities can provide important learning experiences for students, this is sometimes done at the expense of explicit teaching. It may be assumed that through thematic instruction students are meaningfully using and integrating their language arts skills as they work on unit projects. However, it is not enough to provide instructions about how to carry out specific theme activities. Rather, explicit teaching is often necessary to help students develop new skills, strategies, and subject-matter knowledge, and needs to be integral to thematic instruction. If students are not provided with the necessary explicit instruction, especially at the early stages of literacy development, it is likely that those who bring "rich" literacy abilities to thematic instruction will continue to get "richer" and those who do not will simply get "poorer."

Time

Thematic instruction requires a different view of ELA curriculum and instruction with different organizational structures. Teachers need to see opportunities to combine goals that have traditionally been taught separately if thematic instruction is to result in time savings. Developing meaningful thematic units takes a substantial amount of time, knowledge, and experience (Routman, 1994). It is challenging to understand all the facets of strong thematic instruction, time consuming to develop the units and find the resources, and difficult to orchestrate its implementation in the classroom. Even when teachers take the time to develop and implement thematic instruction, it is not likely to save time if it is simply added to what is already in place rather than serving as a new way of organizing curriculum and instruction.

Teaching with themes does not automatically ensure that more time will be available, that learning will be meaningful, that tasks and activities will be authentic, or that children will acquire an integrated knowledge base. Given the ambitious goals, potential advantages, serious cautions, and lack of direction in the professional literature, it is no surprise that thematic instruction has often fallen short of expectations. Evidence from the past indicates that many of the themes used by teachers and publishers are inadequate to accomplish the goals discussed previously; even when they are more substantive, the activities are often loosely related to the content and are not likely to help students see connections either among the language arts or between the language arts and other subject areas. What is needed is more instruction that balances an emphasis on content with that on process, which is the topic of the next section.

CONTENT AND PROCESS IN INTEGRATED CURRICULUM AND INSTRUCTION

The implementation of an integrated view of ELA such as the one proposed by the CCSS-ELA requires attention to both content and process in ELA curriculum and instruction, whether in the context of a thematic approach or through some other means. Attention to content is apparent throughout the CCSS-ELA, as exemplified by the "portrait" of students who meet the standards, which specifies "They Build Strong Content Knowledge":

> Students establish a base of knowledge across a wide range of subject matter by engaging with works of quality and substance. They become proficient in new areas through research and study. They read purposefully and listen attentively to gain both general knowledge and discipline-specific expertise. They refine and share their knowledge through writing and speaking. (p. 7)

Similar to the integrated view of ELA presented in the CCSS, Peters and Wixson (1998, 2003) describe a content–process view of English language arts curriculum and instruction as composed of both the processes of reading, writing, listening, and speaking and the content of the texts that promote connections with other disciplines as well as the world outside the classroom. Content refers to what is to be processed, specifically the ideas to which skills and strategies will be applied (Suhor, 1988). This view of content differs from many traditional views in that it acknowledges a wide range of text and includes nonprint media as well as students' stores of personal experience. Ideas are the content of the English language arts—not skills, processes, or specific texts.

The processes involved in reading, writing, listening, and speaking are the tools that support students as they explore language, construct meaning, experiment with voice, conduct research and inquiry, examine diverse perspectives, craft a response, and critique ideas. The process focus in the curriculum provides the tools that foster a deeper understanding of the ideas and issues that define the content. Insights from the significant ideas and concepts, cultural perspectives, ethical and moral questions in all types of texts help us shape our personal vision, understand our own cultural, linguistic, and literary heritages, and value the diversity and commonalties of local, state, national, and world communities.

At issue here is the appropriate balance and/or relations between content and process in English language arts curriculum and instruction. Over the years, there has been every possible configuration from almost exclusive attention to content to almost exclusive attention to process. The pendulum has swung back and forth between these emphases over the years, especially at the elementary level. At the risk of overgeneralizing, we are currently experiencing a situation where English language arts at the elementary level is driven by a skills/strategies (process) curriculum and the CCSS-ELA is moving us back toward a greater emphasis on content. By comparison, ELA at the secondary level has for many years and continues to be "content" driven, and the CCSS-ELA is focusing more attention on process. This is true for secondary English language arts instruction, which often focuses on the content of particular literary works, as well as for subject-area instruction, which is driven by the content in the text/curriculum.

As Peters and Wixson noted in 1998, a skills-driven view implies that skills are static and generalizable across all interactions with text; however, skills simply do not operate the same way under all conditions. That is why students' performance often varies across instructional and assessment contexts. Differences in text type, length, coherence, familiarity, and task requirements often account for differences in performance across contexts. For example, when one talks about understanding main ideas, inferring an implicit idea from a short story is not the same thing as understanding an explicitly stated idea from an unfamiliar expository text. Similarly, picking the best title from a list of possibilities does not require the same skill set as generating a written summary.

Conversely, a content-driven approach implies that there is nothing students need to know or be able to do to help them process text more fully or deeply. Years of comprehension research have demonstrated repeatedly that students can be taught skills and strategies that enhance their comprehension and transfer to other, similar reading situations. Given that the CCSS-ELA call for students to engage with more complex texts than is currently the norm, it will be increasingly important to provide instruction in strategies that have been demonstrated to improve comprehension. However, this should be in the service of understanding and learning content, not as the sole goal for engaging with text.

CONTENT AND PROCESS IN THEMATIC INSTRUCTION

When content is an important part of the English language arts curriculum, planning for instruction begins by identifying the powerful ideas that are important for students to know. These powerful ideas are the basis for the "theme" in thematic instruction. However, powerful ideas or concepts by themselves tend to be too abstract and broad, so we need to transform them into a statement or question that focuses on meaningful and worthwhile learning experiences connected to the world outside the classroom.

Thematic statements or enduring questions must establish a clear purpose for learning, connect powerful ideas to authentic learning situations, and be oriented toward issues that have relevance for the people of a diverse society in many aspects of their lives, both in and out of school. This means there are no predetermined answers or solutions, nor can the issues or questions be adequately addressed with single words or short phrases. Overly broad topics often become repositories for large quantities of fragmented information. Units driven by thematic statements/enduring questions derived from powerful ideas encourage teachers to move from the role of knowledge transmitter to that of inquiry facilitator.

Thematic statements express a relationship between two or more big ideas from the curriculum rather than broad topics or limited concepts. Examples of such thematic statements might include "living in a diverse society requires respect, cooperation, and negotiation" or "human interactions with the environment have intended and unintended consequences." Such thematic statements reflect relations among concepts that are powerful, complex, and far reaching. Valencia and Lipson (1998) point out that not all statements or generalizations meet these criteria. For example, statements such as "recycling is good for the planet" or "people took different sides during the Civil Rights Movement" are more narrowly defined, less transferable to other situations, and less likely to engage students in higher level thinking and learning.

Similarly, enduring questions must center on significant curricular goals, engage students in rigorous learning and higher-order thinking, and have long-lasting application to students' lives. The difference is that thematic questions ask students to use the information and skills they are developing in the unit to take a position on an issue, suggest a solution to a problem, or answer a critical question. Strong questions push students to learn and think about complex ideas as well as the relation among ideas (e.g., "How do different communities adjust to, adapt to, or resist the diversity of their members?"). Weak questions are often too specific, simple, or fact oriented to be considered strong thematic questions (e.g., "How are people the same and different?).

Certainly it is possible to transform broad topics, limited statements, and specific questions into more substantive themes. Teachers should ask themselves, "What do I want my students to learn about (a topic or idea)? How can this theme reflect substantive curricular goal(s) that require deep, rigorous thinking? How can this theme help students build knowledge and skills that will transfer to other parts of their lives? How can this theme help students develop ways of thinking—habits of mind?" Such questions can lead teachers to form statements or develop questions. It is also possible to use thematic statements in combination with questions in a given thematic unit.

In identifying themes, teachers need to ask themselves, "What will be integrated?" and "What connections will be emphasized?" (Lipson et al., 1993). As suggested previously, distinctions are often made between themes that integrate the areas of the ELA and those that make connections between ELA and subject areas. Themes within ELA often focus on understanding humanity (ourselves and others) by exploring our various experiences, values, and cultural practices, although they may also focus on the big ideas reflected in the work of a particular author or genre. The content here is literary understanding, and the materials are drawn heavily from literature. Units of this type might focus on a theme such as "Personal change often involves interpersonal and intrapersonal conflict" or a question such as "How can humans reconcile personal integrity and group norms?"

Themes that integrate the English language arts with subject areas tend to focus more heavily on disciplinary content than on issues related to the human condition found in literature. Examples of thematic statements/questions that include curricular content/goals from social studies or science include "People have a responsibility to consider the rights of others when making community change" or "How do cultural beliefs and survival needs influence humans' relation with their environment?" It is not always obvious from the thematic statement/question which themes might be focused more on English language arts and which might be more interdisciplinary. The difference becomes clear only once the specific learning outcomes have been identified and instantiated within a performance assessment.

Once a thematic statement and/or enduring question has been identified, Peters and Wixson (1998) suggest that the next step in developing a thematic unit is to create the performance assessment for the unit. Developing the performance assessment involves an examination of the standards to determine which aspects of English language arts "processes" (i.e., reading, writing, speaking, listening and language knowledge and skills) are needed to address the statement/enduring question. This then becomes the basis for identifying the process goals for the unit that are most likely to result in the achievement of the content outcomes embodied by the thematic statement/question. Only then does it make sense to develop the instructional activities and experiences appropriate for achieving both the content and process outcomes for the unit of instruction.

CONTENT AND PROCESS IN RELATION TO TEXT COMPLEXITY

The relation between content and process is also important for thinking about how to implement reading Standard 10 of the CCSS-ELA—range of reading and level of text complexity—whether in the context of thematic instruction or not. Standard 10 specifies that students should be able to "read and comprehend complex literary and informational texts independently and proficiently" (p. 10). As outlined by Malloy and Gambrell (Chapter 2, this volume), the CCSS-ELA model for describing and measuring text complexity consists of three equally important parts: quantitative measures, qualitative measures, and reader and task considerations. These are to be used together with grade-specific standards that require increasing sophistication in students' reading comprehension ability (reading Standards 1–9).

Text Analysis

Although the three-part model does not deal directly with text content, it is clear from other parts of the CCSS-ELA documents that text content is an important consideration in identifying appropriately complex texts for the purpose of meeting reading Standard 10. For example, a description of the key features of the reading standards states, "The Reading standards place equal emphasis on the sophistication of *what* students read and the skill with which they read" (p. 8, emphasis added). Similarly, the criterion used for the quality of the exemplar texts provided in CCSS Appendix B is described as follows: "While it is possible to have high-complexity texts of low inherent quality, the work group solicited only texts of recognized value. From the pool of submissions gathered from outside contributors, the work group selected classic or historically significant texts as well as contemporary works of comparable literary merit, cultural significance, and rich content" (p. 2).

The CCSS-ELA emphasis on text content means that text complexity analyses need to go beyond just ensuring that texts are sufficiently complex for a particular grade-band level, as defined by the three-part model for measuring text complexity in Appendix A. It means ensuring that the content of the texts (and by implication the accompanying instruction) is adequate to build knowledge in ways that make it possible for students to comprehend increasingly substantive texts as they move up from grade to grade. Increased attention to content also provides a logical tie among measuring text complexity, developing instructional goals/plans, and building teacher capacity to implement the CCSS-ELA in ways that improve teaching and learning.

As noted in the introductory chapter of this volume, the standards will not be achieved simply by asking students to engage in more challenging tasks with more challenging texts. Rather, the success of the standards is dependent on building teacher capacity to understand and implement the core vision and intent. If establishing the grade/grade-band level of the texts students are reading is the sole or primary purpose of measuring text complexity, then what is likely to happen is that publishers, test developers, and/or districts will do mass analyses of texts to locate them as best they can at the appropriate grade/grade-level band—without the immediate involvement of the classroom teachers most likely to use the texts. This will mean a missed opportunity to help teachers learn how to identify the appropriate purpose(s) for engaging with a particular text in relation to different text–task–reader combinations, which make units of instruction more or less difficult for particular readers.

Teachers will need to understand more about the relations among reader, texts, and tasks and how to help their students become independent and strategic in their ability to engage successfully with different texts in different contexts for different purposes. Directly involving teachers in conducting text complexity analyses as part of instructional planning has the potential to help build capacity for improved teaching and learning consistent with the vision of the CCSS-ELA.

Instructional Goals

Attention to measuring text complexity as defined by the three-part model in the CCSS-ELA might simply result in the use of different (more complex) texts for instruction, with no discernible effect on improving the quality of instruction. Alternatively, text complexity analyses in the context of developing instructional goals/plans, possibly thematic units, could be the basis for professional development, which has the potential to improve teaching and learning. Such professional development would be aimed at helping teachers identify instructional goals/plans based on an understanding of the relations among text content, characteristics, and the skills needed to learn from text. This understanding is essential to the development of instructional goals/plans that can help students become independent in their use of a variety of texts for a variety of purposes, thereby building the knowledge and skills they need to understand increasingly complex texts.

For text complexity analyses to help improve teaching and learning, they must be tied to instructional planning, starting with instructional goals. This may seem fairly obvious and easily accomplished. However, professional educators with years of experience working with preservice and inservice teachers are constantly surprised at how difficult it is for many prospective and practicing teachers to grasp the importance of taking time, before initiating instruction, to examine the texts they are asking students to read and consider the most appropriate instructional goals for a given text or set of texts and the best means of accomplishing those goals.

As noted previously, English language arts curriculum and instruction tend to be driven either by process (skills/strategies) or by content outcomes. Because reading is a dynamic, interactive process, reading instruction needs to be driven by the predicted interaction among reader factors such as knowledge, skill, experience, and motivation; text factors such as the type and organization of the material; and contextual factors such as the purposes, tasks, and settings for the reading. Skills then become a means of achieving the goal of successfully comprehending a variety of texts under a variety of different reading conditions for a variety of purposes rather than an end themselves. Similarly, the goal is not simply to teach the content of the reading but to develop an understanding of how to read particular types of texts under various reading conditions. This suggests that texts should be taught both for their content and as a vehicle for learning how to read a particular type of text for particular purposes, and that reading instruction must have both content and process goals that serve each other.

Lipson and Wixson (2009), among others, have long noted that sound instruction must contain provisions for each of the following types of objectives:

- *Attitude objectives:* Students need to develop the motivation and desire to read for a variety of purposes.
- *Content objectives:* Students need to understand and learn the ideas they are reading about.
- *Process objectives:* Students need to acquire knowledge and skill in using reading processes.

Effective reading instruction must achieve the delicate balance between focusing on understanding content and developing the ability to process different types of materials for different purposes. Students must acquire the skills and strategies that will enable them to comprehend and learn on their own, and teachers need to think carefully about how they address these important process objectives. What needs to be avoided is instruction that emphasizes process objectives at the expense of content objectives or vice versa. What is needed is a balance among attitude, content, and process objectives.

Attitude objectives are important, legitimate concerns for all teachers and are often neglected in instructional planning. The relationship between positive attitudes and achievement suggests that students' expectations and values have a significant effect on both their effort and their achievement. To become effective readers and writers, students must demonstrate both skill and will (Paris, Lipson, & Wixson, 1994). If they are not willing to engage in independent reading, students will not have sufficient opportunity to practice acquired skills, nor will they develop the facility to read flexibly for their own purposes. Attention to attitude objects will be more important than ever before with the CCSS-ELA mandate for independent reading of specific types of challenging texts.

The point here is that text complexity analyses should be tied to the development of instructional goals and planning that emphasize content, process, and motivation. Without this tie, text complexity analyses are likely to become an exercise in labeling texts according to grade band without any increased understanding of the factors that make a text more or less challenging and how those factors can be addressed through instruction.

CONCLUSION

As mentioned early in this chapter, dominant themes across the other chapters in this volume regarding the implementation of the CCSS-ELA include increased emphasis on higher-order knowledge and skills, informational text, complex text, reading and writing across texts and within subject-area instruction, and using evidence from text to construct arguments that can be developed and extended in oral and written language. The ambitious goals of the CCSS-ELA, as reflected in these themes, call for integrated approaches to organizing curriculum and instruction: "While the Standards delineate specific expectations in reading, writing, speaking, listening, and language, each standard need not be a separate focus for instruction and assessment. Often, several standards can be addressed by a single rich task" (p. 5).

A thematic approach, as described in this chapter, is certainly one way of accomplishing the integration called for by the CCSS-ELA. However, no one should underestimate the challenges of developing and implementing substantive thematic curriculum and instruction. A key component of quality thematic instruction is understanding the relationship between content and process in developing units of instruction. This understanding is essential for the development of substantive curriculum and instruction, whether it is organized thematically or not. It can also serve as the link between curriculum and instruction and the emphasis on complex texts in the CCSS-ELA.

The bottom line is that successful implementation of the CCSS-ELA will require long-term, ongoing professional development to build the teacher and administrator capacity necessary to fulfill the vision put forward by the standards. As president of the International Reading Association (IRA) at the time the CCSS-ELA were published, Kathy Au summed this up by saying: "While a good start has been made, we know from over two decades of work with standards that this first component is the easiest of the three to put in place. The heavy lifting comes when we address the other two components: assessment and professional development. It's the expertise of the classroom teacher that will allow standards to elevate the achievement of each and every student in the classroom. Let's keep in mind that standards don't teach—teachers teach" (IRA, 2010).

REFERENCES

Alleman, J., & Brophy, J. (1993). Is curriculum integration a boon or a threat to social studies? *Social Education, 57*, 287–291.

Bransford, J. D., Brown, A. L., & Cocking, R. R. (2000). *How people learn.* Washington, DC: National Academy Press.

Brophy, J., & Alleman, J. (1991). A caveat: Curriculum integration isn't always a good idea. *Educational Leadership, 49*, 61–65.

Bruner, J. (1960). *The process of education.* Cambridge, MA: Harvard University Press.

Case, R. (1991). *The anatomy of curricular integration* (Tri-University Integration Project 5). Unpublished manuscript, Simon Fraser University, Burnaby, BC, Canada.

Dewey, J. (1933). *How we think* (rev. ed.). Boston: Heath.

Gavelek, J. R., Raphael, T. E., Biondo, S. M., & Wang, D. (2000). Integrated literacy instruction. In M. L. Kamil, P. B. Mosenthal, P. D. Pearson, & R. Barr (Eds.), *Handbook of reading research* (Vol. III, pp. 587–608). Mahwah, NJ: Erlbaum.

Guthrie, J. T., Wigfield, A., Humenick, N. M., Perencevich, K. C., Taboada, A., & Barbosa, P. (2006). Influences of stimulating tasks on reading and motivation and comprehension. *Journal of Educational Research, 99*, 232–245.

Hughes, M. (1991). *Curriculum integration in the primary grades: A framework for excellence.* Alexandria, VA: Association of Supervision and Curriculum Development.

International Reading Association. (2010). IRA calls for three-part initiative to raise literacy achievement through Common Core State Standards. Newark, DE: Author. Retrieved from *http://reading.org/Libraries/Press/pr_Common_Core_Standards.sflb.ashx.*

Lee, C. D., & Spratley, A. (2010). *Reading in the disciplines: The challenges of adolescent literacy.* New York: Carnegie.

Lipson, M. Y., Valencia, S. W., Wixson, K. K., & Peters, C. W. (1993). Integration and thematic teaching. *Language Arts, 70*, 252–263.

Lipson, M. Y., & Wixson, K. K. (2009). *Assessment and instruction of reading and writing difficulty* (4th ed.). New York: Allyn & Bacon.

National Governors Association Center for Best Practices and Council of Chief State School Officers. (2010). Common Core State Standards for English language arts & literacy in history/social studies, science, and technical subjects. Washington, DC: Author. Retrieved from *www.corestandards.org.*

Paris, S. G., Lipson, M. Y., & Wixson, K. K. (1994). Becoming a strategic reader. In R. B. Ruddell, M. R. Ruddell, & H. Singer (Eds.), *Theoretical models and processes of reading* (4th ed., pp. 788–810). Newark, DE: International Reading Association.

Parker, W. C. (2012). *Social studies in elementary education* (14th ed.). Boston: Pearson.

Pearson, P. D. (1994). Integrated language arts: Sources of controversy and seeds of consensus. In L. M. Morrow, J. K. Smith, & L. C. Wilkinson (Eds.), *Integrated language arts: Controversy to consensus* (pp. 11–31). Needham Heights, MA: Allyn & Bacon.

Peters, C. W., & Wixson, K. K. (1998). Aligning curriculum, instruction and assessment in literature-based approaches. In T. Raphael & K. Au (Eds.), *Literature-based instruction: Reshaping the curriculum* (pp. 261–284). Norwood, MA: Christopher-Gordon.

Peters, C. W., & Wixson, K. K. (2003). Unifying the domain of K–12 English language arts curriculum. In D. Lapp & J. Flood (Eds.), *Handbook of English language arts* (2nd ed., pp. 573–589). Mahwah, NJ: Erlbaum.

Routman, R. (1994). *Invitations: Changing as teachers and learners K–12.* Portsmouth, NH: Heinemann.

Shanahan, T., & Shanahan, C. (2008). Teaching disciplinary literacy to adolescents: Rethinking content-area literacy. *Harvard Educational Review, 78,* 40–59.

Spiro, R. J., Vispoel, W., Schmitz, J., Samarapungavin, A., & Boerger, A. (1987). Knowledge acquisition for application: Cognitive acquisition for application: Cognitive flexibility and transfer in complex content domains. In B. Britton & S. Glynn (Eds.), *Executive control processes in reading* (pp. 177–199). Hillsdale, NJ: Erlbaum.

Suhor, C. (1988). Content and process in the English curriculum. In R. S. Brandt (Ed.), *Content of the curriculum* (pp. 31–52). Alexandria, VA: Association for Supervision and Curriculum Development.

Valencia, S. W., & Lipson, M. Y. (1998). Thematic instruction: A quest for challenging ideas and meaningful learning. In T. Raphael & K. Au (Eds.), *Literature-based instruction: Reshaping the curriculum* (pp. 95–123). Norwood, MA: Christopher-Gordon.

Vars, G. F. (1991). Integrated curriculum inhistorical perspective. *Educational Leadership, 49,* 14–15.

Walmsley, S., & Walp, T. (1990). Toward an integrated language arts curriculum in elementary school: Philosophy, practice, and implications. *Elementary School Journal, 90,* 251–274.

APPENDIX A

Common Core State Standards for English Language Arts, Grades 3–5

ENGLISH LANGUAGE ARTS STANDARDS FOR GRADE 3

Reading: Literature » Grade 3

Key Ideas and Details

- RL.3.1. Ask and answer questions to demonstrate understanding of a text, referring explicitly to the text as the basis for the answers.
- RL.3.2. Recount stories, including fables, folktales, and myths from diverse cultures; determine the central message, lesson, or moral and explain how it is conveyed through key details in the text.
- RL.3.3. Describe characters in a story (e.g., their traits, motivations, or feelings) and explain how their actions contribute to the sequence of events.

Craft and Structure

- RL.3.4. Determine the meaning of words and phrases as they are used in a text, distinguishing literal from nonliteral language.
- RL.3.5. Refer to parts of stories, dramas, and poems when writing or speaking about a text, using terms such as chapter, scene, and stanza; describe how each successive part builds on earlier sections.
- RL.3.6. Distinguish their own point of view from that of the narrator or those of the characters.

Integration of Knowledge and Ideas

- RL.3.7. Explain how specific aspects of a text's illustrations contribute to what is conveyed by the words in a story (e.g., create mood, emphasize aspects of a character or setting).
- RL.3.8. (Not applicable to literature)
- RL.3.9. Compare and contrast the themes, settings, and plots of stories written by the same author about the same or similar characters (e.g., in books from a series).

Range of Reading and Complexity of Text

- RL.3.10. By the end of the year, read and comprehend literature, including stories, dramas, and poetry, at the high end of the grades 2–3 text complexity band independently and proficiently.

Reading: Informational Text » Grade 3

Key Ideas and Details

- RI.3.1. Ask and answer questions to demonstrate understanding of a text, referring explicitly to the text as the basis for the answers.
- RI.3.2. Determine the main idea of a text; recount the key details and explain how they support the main idea.
- RI.3.3. Describe the relationship between a series of historical events, scientific ideas or concepts, or steps in technical procedures in a text, using language that pertains to time, sequence, and cause/effect.

Craft and Structure

- RI.3.4. Determine the meaning of general academic and domain-specific words and phrases in a text relevant to a *grade 3 topic or subject area.*
- RI.3.5. Use text features and search tools (e.g., key words, sidebars, hyperlinks) to locate information relevant to a given topic efficiently.
- RI.3.6. Distinguish their own point of view from that of the author of a text.

Integration of Knowledge and Ideas

- RI.3.7. Use information gained from illustrations (e.g., maps, photographs) and the words in a text to demonstrate understanding of the text (e.g., where, when, why, and how key events occur).
- RI.3.8. Describe the logical connection between particular sentences and paragraphs in a text (e.g., comparison, cause/effect, first/second/third in a sequence).
- RI.3.9. Compare and contrast the most important points and key details presented in two texts on the same topic.

Range of Reading and Level of Text Complexity

- RI.3.10. By the end of the year, read and comprehend informational texts, including history/social studies, science, and technical texts, at the high end of the grades 2–3 text complexity band independently and proficiently.

Reading: Foundational Skills » Grade 3

Phonics and Word Recognition

- RF.3.3. Know and apply grade-level phonics and word analysis skills in decoding words.
  - o Identify and know the meaning of the most common prefixes and derivational suffixes.
  - o Decode words with common Latin suffixes.
  - o Decode multisyllable words.
  - o Read grade-appropriate irregularly spelled words.

Fluency

- RF.3.4. Read with sufficient accuracy and fluency to support comprehension.
  - Read grade-level text with purpose and understanding.
  - Read grade-level prose and poetry orally with accuracy, appropriate rate, and expression.
  - Use context to confirm or self-correct word recognition and understanding, rereading as necessary.

Writing 》 **Grade 3**

Text Types and Purposes

- W.3.1. Write opinion pieces on topics or texts, supporting a point of view with reasons.
  - Introduce the topic or text they are writing about, state an opinion, and create an organizational structure that lists reasons.
  - Provide reasons that support the opinion.
  - Use linking words and phrases (e.g., *because, therefore, since, for example*) to connect opinion and reasons.
  - Provide a concluding statement or section.

- W.3.2. Write informative/explanatory texts to examine a topic and convey ideas and information clearly.
  - Introduce a topic and group related information together; include illustrations when useful to aiding comprehension.
  - Develop the topic with facts, definitions, and details.
  - Use linking words and phrases (e.g., *also, another, and, more, but*) to connect ideas within categories of information.
  - Provide a concluding statement or section.

- W.3.3. Write narratives to develop real or imagined experiences or events using effective technique, descriptive details, and clear event sequences.
  - Establish a situation and introduce a narrator and/or characters; organize an event sequence that unfolds naturally.
  - Use dialogue and descriptions of actions, thoughts, and feelings to develop experiences and events or show the response of characters to situations.
  - Use temporal words and phrases to signal event order.
  - Provide a sense of closure.

Production and Distribution of Writing

- W.3.4. With guidance and support from adults, produce writing in which the development and organization are appropriate to task and purpose. (Grade-specific expectations for writing types are defined in standards 1–3 above.)
- W.3.5. With guidance and support from peers and adults, develop and strengthen writing as needed by planning, revising, and editing.
- W.3.6. With guidance and support from adults, use technology to produce and publish writing (using keyboarding skills) as well as to interact and collaborate with others.

Research to Build and Present Knowledge

- W.3.7. Conduct short research projects that build knowledge about a topic.
- W.3.8. Recall information from experiences or gather information from print and digital sources; take brief notes on sources and sort evidence into provided categories.
- W.3.9. (Begins in grade 4)

Range of Writing

- W.3.10. Write routinely over extended time frames (time for research, reflection, and revision) and shorter time frames (a single sitting or a day or two) for a range of discipline-specific tasks, purposes, and audiences.

Speaking and Listening 》 Grade 3

Comprehension and Collaboration

- SL.3.1. Engage effectively in a range of collaborative discussions (one-on-one, in groups, and teacher-led) with diverse partners on *grade 3 topics and texts*, building on others' ideas and expressing their own clearly.
  - o Come to discussions prepared, having read or studied required material; explicitly draw on that preparation and other information known about the topic to explore ideas under discussion.
  - o Follow agreed-upon rules for discussions (e.g., gaining the floor in respectful ways, listening to others with care, speaking one at a time about the topics and texts under discussion).
  - o Ask questions to check understanding of information presented, stay on topic, and link their comments to the remarks of others.
  - o Explain their own ideas and understanding in light of the discussion.
- SL.3.2. Determine the main ideas and supporting details of a text read aloud or information presented in diverse media and formats, including visually, quantitatively, and orally.
- SL.3.3. Ask and answer questions about information from a speaker, offering appropriate elaboration and detail.

Presentation of Knowledge and Ideas

- SL.3.4. Report on a topic or text, tell a story, or recount an experience with appropriate facts and relevant, descriptive details, speaking clearly at an understandable pace.
- SL.3.5. Create engaging audio recordings of stories or poems that demonstrate fluid reading at an understandable pace; add visual displays when appropriate to emphasize or enhance certain facts or details.
- SL.3.6. Speak in complete sentences when appropriate to task and situation in order to provide requested detail or clarification.

Language 》 Grade 3

Conventions of Standard English

- L.3.1. Demonstrate command of the conventions of standard English grammar and usage when writing or speaking.
  - o Explain the function of nouns, pronouns, verbs, adjectives, and adverbs in general and their functions in particular sentences.
  - o Form and use regular and irregular plural nouns.

- o Use abstract nouns (e.g., *childhood*).
- o Form and use regular and irregular verbs.
- o Form and use the simple (e.g., *I walked*; *I walk*; *I will walk*) verb tenses.
- o Ensure subject-verb and pronoun-antecedent agreement.
- o Form and use comparative and superlative adjectives and adverbs, and choose between them depending on what is to be modified.
- o Use coordinating and subordinating conjunctions.
- o Produce simple, compound, and complex sentences.

- L.3.2. Demonstrate command of the conventions of standard English capitalization, punctuation, and spelling when writing.

  - o Capitalize appropriate words in titles.
  - o Use commas in addresses.
  - o Use commas and quotation marks in dialogue.
  - o Form and use possessives.
  - o Use conventional spelling for high-frequency and other studied words and for adding suffixes to base words (e.g., *sitting*, *smiled*, *cries*, *happiness*).
  - o Use spelling patterns and generalizations (e.g., *word families, position-based spellings, syllable patterns, ending rules, meaningful word parts*) in writing words.
  - o Consult reference materials, including beginning dictionaries, as needed to check and correct spellings.

Knowledge of Language

- L.3.3. Use knowledge of language and its conventions when writing, speaking, reading, or listening.

  - o Choose words and phrases for effect.
  - o Recognize and observe differences between the conventions of spoken and written standard English.

Vocabulary Acquisition and Use

- L.3.4. Determine or clarify the meaning of unknown and multiple-meaning words and phrases based on grade 3 reading and content, choosing flexibly from a range of strategies.

  - o Use sentence-level context as a clue to the meaning of a word or phrase.
  - o Determine the meaning of the new word formed when a known affix is added to a known word (e.g., *agreeable/disagreeable, comfortable/uncomfortable, care/careless, heat/preheat*).
  - o Use a known root word as a clue to the meaning of an unknown word with the same root (e.g., *company, companion*).
  - o Use glossaries or beginning dictionaries, both print and digital, to determine or clarify the precise meaning of key words and phrases.

- L.3.5. Demonstrate understanding of word relationships and nuances in word meanings.

  - o Distinguish the literal and nonliteral meanings of words and phrases in context (e.g., *take steps*).
  - o Identify real-life connections between words and their use (e.g., describe people who are *friendly* or *helpful*).
  - o Distinguish shades of meaning among related words that describe states of mind or degrees of certainty (e.g., *knew, believed, suspected, heard, wondered*).

- L.3.6. Acquire and use accurately grade-appropriate conversational, general academic, and domain-specific words and phrases, including those that signal spatial and temporal relationships (e.g., *After dinner that night we went looking for them*).

ENGLISH LANGUAGE ARTS STANDARDS FOR GRADE 4

Reading: Literature 》 Grade 4

Key Ideas and Details

- RL.4.1. Refer to details and examples in a text when explaining what the text says explicitly and when drawing inferences from the text.
- RL.4.2. Determine a theme of a story, drama, or poem from details in the text; summarize the text.
- RL.4.3. Describe in depth a character, setting, or event in a story or drama, drawing on specific details in the text (e.g., a character's thoughts, words, or actions).

Craft and Structure

- RL.4.4. Determine the meaning of words and phrases as they are used in a text, including those that allude to significant characters found in mythology (e.g., Herculean).
- RL.4.5. Explain major differences between poems, drama, and prose, and refer to the structural elements of poems (e.g., verse, rhythm, meter) and drama (e.g., casts of characters, settings, descriptions, dialogue, stage directions) when writing or speaking about a text.
- RL.4.6. Compare and contrast the point of view from which different stories are narrated, including the difference between first- and third-person narrations.

Integration of Knowledge and Ideas

- RL.4.7. Make connections between the text of a story or drama and a visual or oral presentation of the text, identifying where each version reflects specific descriptions and directions in the text.
- RL.4.8. (Not applicable to literature)
- RL.4.9. Compare and contrast the treatment of similar themes and topics (e.g., opposition of good and evil) and patterns of events (e.g., the quest) in stories, myths, and traditional literature from different cultures.

Range of Reading and Complexity of Text

- RL.4.10. By the end of the year, read and comprehend literature, including stories, dramas, and poetry, in the grades 4–5 text complexity band proficiently, with scaffolding as needed at the high end of the range.

Reading: Informational Text 》 Grade 4

Key Ideas and Details

- RI.4.1. Refer to details and examples in a text when explaining what the text says explicitly and when drawing inferences from the text.
- RI.4.2. Determine the main idea of a text and explain how it is supported by key details; summarize the text.
- RI.4.3. Explain events, procedures, ideas, or concepts in a historical, scientific, or technical text, including what happened and why, based on specific information in the text.

Craft and Structure

- RI.4.4. Determine the meaning of general academic and domain-specific words or phrases in a text relevant to a *grade 4 topic or subject area.*

- RI.4.5. Describe the overall structure (e.g., chronology, comparison, cause/effect, problem/solution) of events, ideas, concepts, or information in a text or part of a text.

- RI.4.6. Compare and contrast a firsthand and secondhand account of the same event or topic; describe the differences in focus and the information provided.

Integration of Knowledge and Ideas

- RI.4.7. Interpret information presented visually, orally, or quantitatively (e.g., in charts, graphs, diagrams, time lines, animations, or interactive elements on Web pages) and explain how the information contributes to an understanding of the text in which it appears.

- RI.4.8. Explain how an author uses reasons and evidence to support particular points in a text.

- RI.4.9. Integrate information from two texts on the same topic in order to write or speak about the subject knowledgeably.

Range of Reading and Level of Text Complexity

- RI.4.10. By the end of year, read and comprehend informational texts, including history/social studies, science, and technical texts, in the grades 4–5 text complexity band proficiently, with scaffolding as needed at the high end of the range.

Reading: Foundational Skills 》 Grade 4

Phonics and Word Recognition

- RF.4.3. Know and apply grade-level phonics and word analysis skills in decoding words.
    - Use combined knowledge of all letter-sound correspondences, syllabication patterns, and morphology (e.g., roots and affixes) to read accurately unfamiliar multisyllabic words in context and out of context.

Fluency

- RF.4.4. Read with sufficient accuracy and fluency to support comprehension.
    - Read grade-level text with purpose and understanding.
    - Read grade-level prose and poetry orally with accuracy, appropriate rate, and expression.
    - Use context to confirm or self-correct word recognition and understanding, rereading as necessary.

Writing 》 Grade 4

Text Types and Purposes

- W.4.1. Write opinion pieces on topics or texts, supporting a point of view with reasons and information.
    - Introduce a topic or text clearly, state an opinion, and create an organizational structure in which related ideas are grouped to support the writer's purpose.
    - Provide reasons that are supported by facts and details.
    - Link opinion and reasons using words and phrases (e.g., *for instance, in order to, in addition*).
    - Provide a concluding statement or section related to the opinion presented.

- W.4.2. Write informative/explanatory texts to examine a topic and convey ideas and information clearly.
  - o Introduce a topic clearly and group related information in paragraphs and sections; include formatting (e.g., headings), illustrations, and multimedia when useful to aiding comprehension.
  - o Develop the topic with facts, definitions, concrete details, quotations, or other information and examples related to the topic.
  - o Link ideas within categories of information using words and phrases (e.g., *another, for example, also, because*).
  - o Use precise language and domain-specific vocabulary to inform about or explain the topic.
  - o Provide a concluding statement or section related to the information or explanation presented.
- W.4.3. Write narratives to develop real or imagined experiences or events using effective technique, descriptive details, and clear event sequences.
  - o Orient the reader by establishing a situation and introducing a narrator and/or characters; organize an event sequence that unfolds naturally.
  - o Use dialogue and description to develop experiences and events or show the responses of characters to situations.
  - o Use a variety of transitional words and phrases to manage the sequence of events.
  - o Use concrete words and phrases and sensory details to convey experiences and events precisely.
  - o Provide a conclusion that follows from the narrated experiences or events.

Production and Distribution of Writing

- W.4.4. Produce clear and coherent writing in which the development and organization are appropriate to task, purpose, and audience. (Grade-specific expectations for writing types are defined in standards 1–3 above.)
- W.4.5. With guidance and support from peers and adults, develop and strengthen writing as needed by planning, revising, and editing.
- W.4.6. With some guidance and support from adults, use technology, including the Internet, to produce and publish writing as well as to interact and collaborate with others; demonstrate sufficient command of keyboarding skills to type a minimum of one page in a single sitting.

Research to Build and Present Knowledge

- W.4.7. Conduct short research projects that build knowledge through investigation of different aspects of a topic.
- W.4.8. Recall relevant information from experiences or gather relevant information from print and digital sources; take notes and categorize information, and provide a list of sources.
- W.4.9. Draw evidence from literary or informational texts to support analysis, reflection, and research.
  - o Apply *grade 4 Reading standards* to literature (e.g., "Describe in depth a character, setting, or event in a story or drama, drawing on specific details in the text [e.g., a character's thoughts, words, or actions].").
  - o Apply *grade 4 Reading standards* to informational texts (e.g., "Explain how an author uses reasons and evidence to support particular points in a text").

Range of Writing

- W.4.10. Write routinely over extended time frames (time for research, reflection, and revision) and shorter time frames (a single sitting or a day or two) for a range of discipline-specific tasks, purposes, and audiences.

Speaking and Listening 》 Grade 4

Comprehension and Collaboration

- SL.4.1. Engage effectively in a range of collaborative discussions (one-on-one, in groups, and teacher-led) with diverse partners on *grade 4 topics and texts*, building on others' ideas and expressing their own clearly.
  - Come to discussions prepared, having read or studied required material; explicitly draw on that preparation and other information known about the topic to explore ideas under discussion.
  - Follow agreed-upon rules for discussions and carry out assigned roles.
  - Pose and respond to specific questions to clarify or follow up on information, and make comments that contribute to the discussion and link to the remarks of others.
  - Review the key ideas expressed and explain their own ideas and understanding in light of the discussion.

- SL.4.2. Paraphrase portions of a text read aloud or information presented in diverse media and formats, including visually, quantitatively, and orally.

- SL.4.3. Identify the reasons and evidence a speaker provides to support particular points.

Presentation of Knowledge and Ideas

- SL.4.4. Report on a topic or text, tell a story, or recount an experience in an organized manner, using appropriate facts and relevant, descriptive details to support main ideas or themes; speak clearly at an understandable pace.

- SL.4.5. Add audio recordings and visual displays to presentations when appropriate to enhance the development of main ideas or themes.

- SL.4.6. Differentiate between contexts that call for formal English (e.g., presenting ideas) and situations where informal discourse is appropriate (e.g., small-group discussion); use formal English when appropriate to task and situation.

Language 》 Grade 4

Conventions of Standard English

- L.4.1. Demonstrate command of the conventions of standard English grammar and usage when writing or speaking.
  - Use relative pronouns (*who, whose, whom, which, that*) and relative adverbs (*where, when, why*).
  - Form and use the progressive (e.g., *I was walking; I am walking; I will be walking*) verb tenses.
  - Use modal auxiliaries (e.g., *can, may, must*) to convey various conditions.
  - Order adjectives within sentences according to conventional patterns (e.g., *a small red bag* rather than *a red small bag*).
  - Form and use prepositional phrases.
  - Produce complete sentences, recognizing and correcting inappropriate fragments and run-ons.
  - Correctly use frequently confused words (e.g., *to, too, two; there, their*).

APPENDIX B

Thematic Units for Grades 3–5, with Common Core State Standards Embedded

Erin Kramer
Mary Rodgers
Kelly Lovejoy
Jessica Sullivan
Rutgers University

COMMUNITY—GRADE 3

Desired results: Literacy	Desired results: Social Studies
Established Goals • Common Core State Standards for English language arts grade 3 (articulated in the learning plan that follows).	**Established Goals** • Compare and contrast characteristics of regions in the United States based on culture, economics, politics, and physical environment to understand the concept of regionalism. • Describe how landforms, climate and weather, and availability of resources have impacted where and how people live and work in different regions of both their own state and the United States. (N.J. Department of Education, 2010)
Enduring Understandings • Knowledge can be acquired by reading, listening to, and viewing diverse print, digital, and oral texts. • Writing is for communicating ideas and recording thoughts/questions.	**Enduring Understandings** • Each community is unique. • Many influences impact the type of community that develops. • Where people live helps shape who they are.

Essential Questions	Essential Questions
• How can I further my knowledge of a topic? • What is the purpose of writing? • How can I collaborate effectively?	• How are communities alike and different? • How are communities formed and shaped? • How does my community impact me?
Knowledge Students will know: • Learners ask and answer questions in order to assist their comprehension and further their understanding. • A variety of print and digital sources can be used to further understanding of a topic.	**Knowledge** Students will know: • Regions form and change as a result of unique physical/ecological conditions, economies, and cultures. • Places are jointly characterized by their physical and human properties. (N.J. Department of Education, 2010)
Skills Students will be able to: • Conduct research to learn about a topic. • Ask and answer questions to clarify understanding and demonstrate knowledge. • Participate in collaborative projects and discussions. • Use images, print, and digital text features to identify information and further knowledge of a topic. • Write for a variety of purposes and audiences. • Use a variety of digital tools and texts to further knowledge and publish work.	**Skills** Students will be able to: • Identify characteristics of urban, suburban, and rural communities and classify communities using those labels. • Evaluate which type of community fits their wants/needs the best. • Demonstrate an appreciation for their own and other communities. • Identify landforms and natural resources. • Identify goods that are created from resources. • Describe the factors that impact the community that develops.

Assessment Evidence

Performance Task
- **My Community Wiki Project**
  - Goal and Role: As a citizen of (town), you are to make a contribution to a class Web page about your community.
  - Audience: Members of your collaborative wiki site, which includes other communities across the country and around the world.
  - Situation: The challenge involves contributing something unique that will further an outsider's understanding of our (urban, suburban, or rural) community by either highlighting features/characteristics of our community or important landforms and natural resources that helped shape it.
  - Product: Photographs with captions, video clips, or written work that describes your community.
  - Standards: All writing and audio recordings must demonstrate command of all grade-appropriate standard English conventions, including grammar and usage, capitalization, punctuation, and spelling. Your contribution must be different from your classmates.

Other Evidence
- Community test

LEARNING PLAN

Routines and Morning Meeting

CCSS in English Language Arts: RF.3.4, W.3.4, W.3.6, W.3.10, SL.3.1, SL.3.3, SL.3.4, SL.3.5, SL.3.6, L.3.5, L3.6

Objectives: Students will be able to:
- Read fluently.
- Speak audibly.
- Create recordings of reading.
- Use and connect community vocabulary with real-life situations.

Activities:
- Greeting: Secret class handshake
- Share: *My favorite place to visit . . .*
- Share: *Which do you prefer: urban, suburban, or rural?*
- Activity: Students write an acrostic poem together for the community. They read it multiple times for fluency practice and record it for a class podcast.
- Activity: Students write to friends and relatives from different communities asking them to fill out a questionnaire about their community and send along pictures, brochures, and items that represent important parts of their community. When the packages arrive, allow students to share them with the class.
- K-W-L Chart: After Lesson 1, post chart in the classroom and add to it throughout the unit.
- ePals: Participate in "We Are ePals" activities on *www.epals.com*.
- Social Studies Word Wall: Keep a running list of social studies vocabulary words throughout the unit.

Lesson Assessment: Take anecdotal notes on students' vocabulary use and speech. Audio recording can be student work sample.

LESSON 1: INTRODUCTION TO COMMUNITIES USING DIGITAL TEXTS

CCSS in English Language Arts: RI.3.1, RI.3.7, W.3.4, SL.3.1, SL.3.3

Objectives: Students will be able to:
- Write what they know and want to find out about communities in an organized chart.
- Identify the three types of communities: urban, suburban, and rural.
- Ask and answer questions to demonstrate understanding of an interactive map.
- Participate in collaborative conversations, asking and answering questions to clarify and develop understanding.

Activities:

- Begin by asking the class what they know about communities. Provide each student with a K-W-L chart. Display the same chart on the board. Allow students about 5 minutes to independently complete the What I Know (K) and What I Want to Find Out (W) sections.
- Create a class K-W-L chart. Have students share what they included on their individual charts. Explain that they will continue to add to their charts and the class chart throughout the unit. Their charts should remain in their designated folders.
- Show the students the clip below to help them identify what a community is: *www.nextvista. org/moriches-shirley-mastic-and-mastic-beach/.*
- After watching the clip, update the class K-W-L chart and begin the What I Learned (L) section.
- Explain that there are three types of communities: rural, urban, and suburban. Display the following interactive map on the board: *www.eduplace.com/kids/socsci/books/applications/ imaps/maps/g3_u1/index.html.*
- Explore the different features that make up each of the communities. Ask questions pertaining to the map displayed. Have the students discuss the differences and similarities that they recognize. They should be encouraged to ask and answer questions about the information presented.

Lesson Assessment: K-W-L charts will be assessed for content and organization.

LESSON 2: INFORMATIONAL TEXT PROFILING THREE COMMUNITIES

CCSS in English Language Arts: RI.3.3, RI.3.5, RI.3.8, RI.3.10, W.3.10, SL.3.1, SL.3.2, SL.3.4

Objectives: Students will be able to:

- Identify characteristics of urban, suburban, and rural communities and classify communities using those labels.
- Use a graphic organizer to determine the overall structure of a text.
- Use text features to locate relevant information.
- Participate in small-group collaborative conversations and present information to the whole class.

Activities:

- Independent Reading: *Hometowns*, by Carolyn Jackson
  - Set purpose: *This is an informational text that provides an example of each of the three types of communities. Read to find out what makes each community unique. As you read, think about the structure of the text.*
  - During: Students are to read independently. Struggling readers can read along with the tape recording.
  - After: Students look back in the text using the table of contents to complete a graphic organizer, filling out the sentence stem that matches with each book section:
    - Description: A(n) _____ is a kind of _____ that _____.
    - Compare–Contrast: X and Y are similar in that they both _____, but X, whereas Y.
    - Sequence: _____ begins with _____ continues with _____ and ends with _____.
    - Problem–Solution: _____ wanted _____ but _____ so _____.
    - Cause–Effect: _____ happens because _____.

(Morrow, 2012)

- Students discuss their graphic organizers in small groups and classify each community as urban, suburban, or rural. The group finds evidence in the text to support their analysis. Each group presents their thoughts.

Lesson Assessment: Teacher will check graphic organizer.

LESSON 3: EXPLORING RURAL, URBAN, AND SUBURBAN COMMUNITIES WITH LITERATURE

CCSS in English Language Arts: RL.3.1, RL.3.5, RL.3.7, RL.3.10, W.3.2, W.3.4, W.3.5, W.3.8, L.3.5.b, L.3.6

Objectives: Students will be able to:
- Ask and answer questions about a piece of literature to identify characteristics of urban, suburban, and rural communities, referring explicitly to the text and illustrations.
- Identify and write about the type of community surrounding their school, recalling details from the text and using content-area vocabulary.

Activities:
- Review the three types of communities: rural, urban, and suburban.
- Read-aloud: *The Little House*, by Virginia Lee
  - Set purpose: *Listen to discover some of the different characteristics that make up each of the three community types.*
  - During: Students write observations on individual charts with the following headings: Urban, Suburban, and Rural. Students will need to use the information and illustrations to determine what kind of community the house is surrounded by at each point in the story. Stop at the points where the community changes to discuss and chart what the students notice about the community around the house and update an enlarged version of this chart.
  - After: Discuss the three types of communities, describing how each new story event builds on earlier parts. Then have students identify the type of community they live in. Students should give reasons to support their answers and refer to the story and class chart.
- Provide a graphic organizer with the following sections: School Name, My Community's Name, Community Type: Urban, Suburban, or Rural, and Characteristics of My Community. Students will use this as a planning sheet for an informational paragraph about their school and the community in which it is located. Students will need to introduce the topic by stating what type of community their school is located in, include facts and details, connect their ideas, and provide a concluding statement.

Lesson Assessment: Writing will serve as student work sample and will be assessed for social studies content and grade 3 writing standards using a rubric.

LESSON 4: EXPLORING PERSONAL PREFERENCES OF COMMUNITY TYPES WITH LITERATURE

CCSS in English Language Arts: RL.3.4, RL.3.6, RL.3.10, RF.3.4, W.3.1, SL.3.3, L.3.4

Objectives: Students will be able to:
- Review and identify terms specific to communities.
- Write an opinion piece that describes and supports which community they feel is best suited for them based on their interests, abilities, needs, and resources.

Activities:
- Review key terms specifically related to communities. Allow the students to determine the meaning of each word. Have students create a flipbook with the vocabulary on the top of the flap and the definition underneath to define the following words:
  o *Community*—a place where people live, work, or have fun together.
  o *Neighborhood*—an area in a community where people live near one another.
  o *Rural*—a community with open land, few buildings and businesses, and few people.
  o *Urban*—a city community with a lot of tall buildings; a community in which people live that is larger or more crowded than a town.
  o *Suburban*—a community outside of the city where people live in neighborhoods with individual houses or small apartment houses.
- Read-aloud: *Town Mouse, Country Mouse*, by Jan Brett
  o Set purpose: *Listen to find out how the two mice feel about their own communities and the reasons for their opinion.*
  o During: Model fluent reading.
  o After: Discuss how the mice feel about their own communities and the reasons for their opinion. Discuss why people choose to live in different areas/communities. Have students distinguish their own point of view about whether they think town mouse or country mouse lives in a better community. Lead the students to understand that one type of community is not better than another, it is just different. Explain that people choose where to live based on their interests, abilities, needs, and resources.
- Explain that the students will be writing an opinion piece based on which community they feel is best suited for them based on their interests, abilities, needs, and resources. Students need to support their point of view with reasons.
- Students share their writing with a partner as they finish. After listening to each other's writing, students should ask and answer questions about their partner's information provided.

Lesson Assessment: Writing will serve as student work sample and will be assessed for social studies content and grade 3 writing standards using a rubric.

LESSON 5: MAKING WORDS LESSON: COMMUNITY

CCSS in English Language Arts: RL.3.3, L.3.2.F

Objectives: Students will be able to:
- Spell words using known patterns, roots, and affixes.

Activities:

- Give the students the following letters on slips of paper: *i*, *o*, *u*, *y*, *c*, *m*, *m*, *n*, and *t*.
- Have them follow the directions below to make the words with the letters. Keep the lesson moving by selecting students to spell the words in a pocket chart at the front of the room without waiting for each student to have the word spelled.
  - o Use two letters to spell *in*: "We are *in* Miss Kramer's class."
  - o Add one letter to spell *tin*. "This is a *tin* can."
  - o Add one letter to spell *tiny*. "The little house seemed *tiny* next to the tall city buildings."
  - o Take out the *n* and replace it with two of the same letter to spell *Timmy*. "*Timmy* is a good friend."
  - o Replace the vowel to spell *Tommy*. "*Tommy* lives on a farm."
  - o Replace the vowel to spell *tummy*. "His *tummy* felt sick."
  - o Take away the middle three letters to spell the nick name *Ty*. "*Ty* is short for Tyler."
  - o Add two letters to spell *city*. "New York is a *city*."
  - o Replace the beginning letter with two different letters to spell *unity*. "We have *unity* when we all work together."
  - o Remove one letter to spell *unit*. "The class is one *unit* working together."
  - o Use four letters to spell *mint*. "I need a *mint* after eating tacos!"
  - o Add a letter to spell *minty*. "Now my breath is fresh and *minty*."
  - o Use six letters to spell *commit*. "When you sign up for volunteering, you truly have to *commit* to doing it because people are depending on you."
  - o I have just one word left. It is the secret word you can make with all your letters. See if you can figure it out. *Community*
- Place a set of cards with the words in the pocket chart to read and spell the words chorally.
- Sort the related words that share a root. Use those words in a sentence to show how they are related.
  - o *mint, minty*
  - o *unit, unity*
- Sort the rhyming words and note the spelling pattern.
  - o *city, unity, community*
  - o *unit, commit*
- On a sheet numbered 1–6, have the students spell more words using the related words and rhyming words.
  - o Use *mint, minty* to spell *frost, frosty*.
  - o Use *city, unity, community* to spell *pity, cavity*.
  - o Use *unit, commit* to spell *limit, tidbit*.

(Cunningham, 2009)

Lesson Assessment: Anecdotal notes can be taken to note students with particular difficulty.

LESSON 6: LITERACY CENTER ACTIVITY: COMPUTER CENTER

CCSS in English Language Arts: RI.3.7, SL.3.2

Objectives: Students will be able to:

- Identify characteristics of urban, suburban, and rural communities and classify communities using those labels.

Activities:

- Students watch Brain Pop Jr. video, available at *www.brainpopjr.com/socialstudies/communities/ruralsuburbanandurban/preview.weml*.

- Students write down one fact about each type of community as a checkpoint to ensure they completed the activity.

Lesson Assessment: Sheet will be checked.

LESSON 7: EXPLORING COMMUNITIES

CCSS in English Language Arts: RI.3.2, RI.3.5, RI.3.7, W.3.7, SL.3.1, SL.3.2, SL.3.4, L.3.6

Objectives: Students will be able to:

- Engage effectively in a collaborative discussion and group project with their classmates.

- Identify and use the main points and key details gained from an informational video to illustrate the features of rural, urban, and suburban communities.

- Speak clearly and at an appropriate pace when reporting findings.

- Use nonfiction text features and information presented orally to identify different characteristics within rural, urban, and suburban communities.

Activities:

- Divide the class into three groups. Assign each group a specific community to become the "experts" on: urban, suburban, or rural.

- Students view the informational videos below and then work collaboratively to create illustrations of their assigned community on a poster board. Each group should include as many characteristics as possible and label each one clearly.
  - Urban communities:
    www.youtube.com/watch?v=gGUkjzPS9sU
    www.youtube.com/watch?v=GuF2o7SaRWU
  - Suburban communities:
    www.youtube.com/watch?v=GuF2o7SaRWU
  - Rural communities:
    www.youtube.com/watch?v=gGUkjzPS9sU
    www.youtube.com/watch?v=GuF2o7SaRWU

- Before working on their display, each group engages in a collaborative discussion about what should be included on their poster. It is important that students (1) reference elements discussed in the informational videos watched and (2) share their ideas about the topic, listen to others when they are speaking, ask questions to build understanding, and explain their ideas of what should be included on their group's display.

- Students use nonfiction text features to add details and information on their posters. They should be encouraged to include captions, headings, labels, diagrams, and cut-aways.

- Each group of "experts" presents to their classmates. Each student should contribute to the oral presentation, speaking clearly and making sure to include all information presented on the poster.

- Have the other groups (those not presenting) fill out a graphic organizer for note-taking while attending to the presentation. Instruct them to listen carefully to identify the main idea and key details and use the text features to locate information on the poster.

Lesson Assessment: Posters will be checked for content, neatness, and variety of text features.

LESSON 8: LITERACY CENTER ACTIVITY: COMPUTER CENTER

CCSS in English Language Arts: W.3.2, W.3.6, W.3.8, SL.3.1.c, SL.3.5, SL.3.6, L.3.3, L.3.6

Objectives: Students will be able to:
- Comment on VoiceThread about the different features that make up a rural community.
- Write a paragraph about the features identified in the pictures on VoiceThread and record it as a voice comment for others to hear and read.
- Continue an online conversation, linking their own comments to those left by others.

Activities:
- Have students visit *voicethread.com/?#u1691797.b2433642.i12881581*. This VoiceThread contains three images of different rural communities. Students are to comment on one of the pictures by writing in the different features that they recognize.
- Next, have students write a paragraph using the features they saw in the VoiceThread images. They can also share their ideas about the important roles of those who work in rural communities. They then record their voice, reading aloud the passage they wrote. It is important that students use knowledge of language and its conventions when writing, speaking, reading, and listening to posts on VoiceThread.
- Students view each other's VoiceThread posts and use comments to continue the conversation.

Lesson Assessment: Assess VoiceThread comments for clarity and ability to link to others' comments, and determine whether students are able to identify the different features in rural communities.

LESSON 9: LITERACY CENTER ACTIVITY: RESEARCH CENTER

CCSS in English Language Arts: RI.3.5, RI.3.7, W 3.8, W.3.10, L.3.6

Objectives: Students will be able to:
- Use search tools to locate relevant information.
- Use information gained from illustrations to describe features of an urban community.
- Create a Venn diagram identifying the similarities and differences of two well-known cities in the United States.

Activities:

- Guiding research questions: *What cities have you been to? What features do you recall seeing? What different things did you do there?* During a whole-group discussion, students recall experiences and create a chart together.

- In centers students explore two well-known U.S. cities (e.g., New York City, Boston, Baltimore, Chicago, Los Angeles) using Google Earth (*www.google.com/earth/index.html*).

- Students compare and contrast the two cities, writing down the different features and landmarks recognized in each city in a Venn diagram. All similarities should be noted in the intersection.

Lesson Assessment: Papers will be checked.

LESSON 10: LITERACY CENTER ACTIVITY: WRITING CENTER

CCSS in English Language Arts: W.3.3, W.3.4, W.3.5, W 3.10, L.3.1, L.3.2, L.3.3, L.3.6

Objectives: Students will be able to:

- Use the writing process to write a narrative, applying knowledge of the characteristics of suburban communities.

- Revise and edit their work for understanding and accuracy.

Activities:

- Write a short story.
  - Prompt: *Your family decides to move from an urban community to a suburban community. Explain why they wanted to move and how life was different living in a suburban community.*
  - Plan: Brainstorm using the story elements graphic organizer.
  - Expectations: Each story should incorporate dialogue, different events, temporal words, and some type of closure. Stories should include examples and features of both urban and suburban communities.
  - Revise/edit: Check off each of the expectations as you reread and revise.
  - Conferencing: Schedule a conference with your teacher. Together, you will edit using the standards for conventions in grammar, usage, capitalization, punctuation, and spelling for third grade, and revise as needed.

- Read the story during an author share time.

Lesson Assessment: Use a rubric based on grade 3 writing standards.

LESSON 11: AN IN-DEPTH NARRATIVE TEXT STUDY

CCSS in English Language Arts: RL.3.1, RL.3.3, RL.3.4, RL.3.7, RF.3.3, RF.3.4, W.3.8, W.3.10, SL.3.1, L.3.4, L.3.6

Objectives: Students will be able to:

- Ask and answer questions about the characters, characteristics of the setting, and challenging words to demonstrate understanding of the text.

- Describe the characters in the story and explain how their actions contribute to the sequence of events.

- Read aloud *On the Town: A Community Adventure* with sufficient accuracy and fluency to support comprehension.

- Compare and contrast different communities.

Activities:

- Part A: Independent Reading: *On the Town: A Community Adventure*, by Judith Caseley
  - Set purpose: *As you read this story, write notes on your trifold bookmark for discussion after the story. When you fill out the* Setting *portion, be sure to include the clues you used to figure it out. In the* Characters *section, list the characters and include at least one characteristic to describe them. In the* Words *section, write down the words that you used problem-solving strategies to figure out, along with their meaning, and/or words you still do not know.*
  - During: Students work at their own pace to read this story and fill out trifold bookmark. If necessary, scaffold the reading for struggling readers by choral reading this story together.
  - After: In small groups, students use their notes from the trifold bookmark and discussion question cards to answer the following questions:
    - *Where do you think the story took place? What makes you think that?*
    - *What type of community was portrayed in this book? What were some of the characteristics of the community?*
    - *How is this similar/different from the community you live in?*
    - *Who were the characters and how would you describe them?*
    - *How did the characters' actions contribute to the sequence of events?*
    - *What were some words you problem-solved? Describe what you did in your mind to figure out the word and its meaning.*
    - *What were some words you still do not know/understand?*
- Part B: Paired Reading
  - With your students, create a list of what fluent readers do. Example: *Use expression to show feelings. Use punctuation to determine phrasing and pausing. Read at a good pace—not too quickly and not too slowly. Read at a good volume—not too quietly and not too loudly.*
  - Students practice rereading the story with a peer.
  - Each pair of students should offer feedback and praise to their partner in the form of "I like the way you . . . " and "Maybe next time try it . . . " using specific comments from the list.
- Part C: Comparing/Contrasting
  - In class or as a homework assignment, students independently create a Venn diagram comparing the community in the story with the one in which they live. They must include describing words and features that make each community unique.
  - Whole-group discussion: Students share the similarities and differences noted on their Venn diagrams.

Lesson Assessment: Trifold bookmarks and Venn diagrams will be checked. Teacher will circulate during discussions.

LESSON 12: ANALYZING AND CLASSIFYING IMAGES AND PRESENTING KNOWLEDGE

CCSS in English Language Arts: W.3.4, W.3.8, W.3.10, SL 3.1, SL 3.4, SL 3.6

Objectives: Students will be able to:
- Classify photographs and postcards into three categories: urban, suburban, and rural.
- Describe the factors that impact the community that develops.
- Speak clearly and in complete sentences.

Activities:
- Divide the students into small groups. Give each group a photograph or postcard of a community. Use as many different community settings as possible so the students will be focusing on different areas of the world.
- Have each group make a list of characteristics of the community and note features of the land represented in the photograph or postcard they were assigned.
- Each group presents their photograph or postcard, along with the list they created, with the rest of the class.
- After each group has shared, it is important to emphasize specific points about communities.
  o Communities are in different places and contain different landforms (e.g., near rivers, lakes, oceans, mountains, deserts).
  o Communities are known for different features (e.g., growing foods or developing products important to society).
- On the board or chart paper, create three columns with the following headings: Rural, Urban, and Suburban. Have the class identify what type of community each photograph or postcard is. Decisions should be based on the characteristics described in each picture.
- Have the students complete an exit slip, describing what they learned in the lesson. What they write about is up to them as long as they talk about three things they learned from today's lesson.

Lesson Assessment: Participation and exit slips will be checked.

LESSON 13: INFORMATIONAL AND NARRATIVE TEXT COMPARISON TO DEVELOP IDEAS OF CHANGING COMMUNITIES

CCSS in English Language Arts: RI.3.3, RI.3.4, RI.3.8, RI.3.9, RI.3.10, RF.3.3, RF.3.4.c, SL.3.2, L.3.4, L.3.6

Objectives: Students will be able to:
- Use context and phonetic word analysis to problem-solve and determine the meaning of social studies vocabulary.
- Make connections and identify relationships between ideas in the text to describe the factors that impact the community that develops.

Activities:
- Read-aloud: *Communities Change*, by Liz Sonneborn
  o Before: Review the vocabulary words using the cloze procedure.
    ▪ Write the sentences containing the targeted vocabulary words on sentence strips.
    ▪ Cover the selected word with a sticky note.

- ■ Allow students to write their guesses for the missing word on the sticky note, using the context clues of the sentence to guide their guesses.
- ■ Uncover and discuss vocabulary. If appropriate, identify known chunks in the word that will help students decode the word.
- ○ Set purpose: *As we read, pay attention to what factors contributed to the growth of the three real communities in this text.*
- ○ During: Model making connections and identifying relationships between ideas in the text. When they are comfortable, have students take over identifying the factors that contributed to the changes in each community.
- ○ After: *How did the community surrounding the little house change in Virginia Lee Burton's story? What factors caused that change?*

Lesson Assessment: Participation will be checked.

LESSON 14: INTEGRATING IDEAS TO EXPLAIN HOW LANDFORMS AFFECT THE DEVELOPMENT OF COMMUNITIES

CCSS in English Language Arts: RI.3.1, RI.3.3, RI.3.7, RI.3.8, RI.3.10, W.3.7, W.3.8, W.3.10, SL.3.1, SL.3.3, SL.3.4

Objectives: Students will be able to:
- Participate in collaborative conversations where students ask and answer questions, make connections, and identify relationships between ideas in the text to describe the factors that impact the community that develops.
- Identify landforms and natural resources.
- Ask and answer questions to further understanding of information presented orally.

Activities:
- Review how landforms can affect the development of communities.
- Divide the class into four groups, and provide each with a text to explore:
  - ○ *Life on the Plains*, by Catherine Bradley
  - ○ *Life in the Mountains*, by Catherine Bradley
  - ○ *Life in the Woodlands*, by Rosanne Hooper
  - ○ *Life on the Coastlines*, by Rosanne Hooper
- Have students split up the work by selecting jobs, such as reader(s), note-taker(s), writer, presenter.
- Offer guiding research questions: *What ways can this type of land be used? What resources are available in this type of land? What type of communities (urban, suburban, or rural) might develop on this type of land and why?*
- Each group works together using the research questions to guide the reading. Students will pause to record relevant facts on notecards and discuss how the type of land could affect the community that develops.
- Each group works together to sort facts into piles and write a response to the research questions.
- Each group shares the information they discussed.
- The teacher, presenters, and class ask and answer questions to further their understanding and clarify points the group has presented.

Lesson Assessment: Teacher will circulate during group work and can take anecdotal notes throughout the lesson.

LESSON 15: REINFORCING AND DEEPENING KNOWLEDGE OF COMMUNITIES AND RESOURCES THROUGH GUIDED READING

CCSS in English Language Arts: RI.3.10, RF.3.3, RF.3.4

Objectives: Students will be able to:
- Identify landforms and natural resources.
- Identify goods that are created from resources.
- Describe the factors that impact the community that develops.
- Read and comprehend informational texts at their reading level.
- Apply grade-level phonics and word analysis skills in decoding.
- Read with sufficient accuracy and fluency.

Activities:
- Specific literacy skills practiced in guided reading should be based on the students' needs and the text selected. Keep a balanced focus on learning the social studies content (vocabulary/comprehension) and literacy skills (decoding/fluency).
- Suggestions: repeating K-W-L activity, questioning, identifying the main topic of the text/paragraphs, making connections, using text features, and describing how reasons support specific points.
- Suggested texts:
  - Developmental Reading Assessment (DRA) DRA 34–40, guided reading O–R: Read to Learn: Social Studies—Regions and Resources series (16 titles), Newbridge.
  - DRA 30, guided reading N: *Apple Country*, by Densie Willi
  - DRA 40, guided reading Q: *Hometowns*, by George McNeill

Lesson Assessment: Running records and anecdotal notes can be taken.

LESSON 16: IDENTIFYING LOCAL LANDFORMS, NATURAL RESOURCES, AND GOODS THROUGH INTERVIEW

CCSS in English Language Arts: SL.3.1, SL.3.2, SL.3.3

Objectives: Students will be able to:
- Identify landforms and natural resources.
- Identify goods that are created from resources.
- Describe the factors that impact the community that develops.
- Ask questions to further knowledge and understanding of their community.

Activities:

- Invite a panel of local experts for an interview session. Select people with diverse knowledge of the land, resources, and local businesses. Suggestions include a member of the town's historical society, a local park ranger, long-time residents, and a member of the town's chamber of commerce.
- Students work in pairs to create interview questions. Their focus is to determine what factors helped shape their community into what it is today.
- Record the interview session and upload it onto a class website.

Lesson Assessment: Participation will be checked. Student contributions for the performance task will reflect the knowledge they have learned in this lesson as well as throughout the unit.

(Wiggins & McTighe, 2005)

REFERENCES

Cunningham, P. M. (2009). *Phonics they use: Words for reading and writing.* Boston: Pearson.

Morrow, L. M. (2012). *Literacy development in the early years: Helping children read and write.* Boston: Pearson.

N.J. Department of Education. (2010). New Jersey core curriculum content standards for social studies. Retrieved from *www.state.nj.us/education/cccs/standards/6/index.html.*

Wiggins, G. P., & McTighe, J. (2005). *Understanding by design.* Alexandria, VA: Association for Supervision and Curriculum Development.

THE SOLAR SYSTEM—GRADE 4

Desired results: Literacy	Desired results: Science
Established Goals • Common Core State Standards for English language arts grade 4 (articulated in the learning plan that follows).	**Established Goals** • Formulate a general description of the daily motion of the sun across the sky based on shadow observations. Explain how shadows can be used to tell the time of day. • Identify patterns of the moon's appearance and make predictions about its future appearance based on observational data. • Analyze and evaluate evidence in the form of data tables and photographs to categorize and relate solar system objects (e.g., planets, dwarf planets, moons, asteroids, comets). (N.J. State Department of Education, 2010)
Enduring Understandings • Cultural, literary, and content-area knowledge is transmitted through oral, print, and digital texts. • Effective communicators follow standard conventions when writing and speaking, and carefully select language, style, and structure to fit their purpose.	**Enduring Understandings** • Observable, predictable patterns in the solar system occur because of gravitational interactions and energy from the sun. (N.J. State Department of Education, 2010)

Essential Questions	Essential Questions
• How can oral, print, and digital texts be used to learn new information? • How can I effectively communicate my thoughts, knowledge, and understandings?	• To what extent are the properties in our solar system predictable? • What causes these patterns? (N.J. State Department of Education, 2010)
Knowledge Students will know: • Folktales and myths are unique forms of literature that are used to teach a lesson or explain something in nature. • Figurative language enhances writing and sets a tone. • Common nonfiction text structures include description, sequence, comparison–contrast, cause–effect, and problem–solution. • Written and oral presentation of ideas to a group of peers requires the use of formal English.	**Knowledge** Students will know: • Objects in the sky have patterns of movement. • The sun and the moon appear to move across the sky on a daily basis. • The shadows of an object on Earth change over the course of a day, indicating the changing position of the sun during the day. • The observable shape of the moon changes from day to day in a cycle that lasts 29.5 days. • Earth is the third planet from the sun in our solar system, which includes seven other planets. (N.J. State Department of Education, 2010)
Skills Students will be able to: • Identify the theme of a folktale or myth. • Compare and contrast traditional literature from different cultures. • Write folktales or myths. • Conduct research and gather relevant information from print and digital sources. • Write informational texts. • Conduct an oral presentation of information gathered through research. • Identify common text structures and use them to aid in comprehension of a text. • Explain and use simple similes.	**Skills** Students will be able to: • Observe and record the movements of shadows of objects on Earth during the course of a day. • Observe and explore the phases of the moon and arrange them in order. • Observe the stars in the night's sky. • Arrange the planets according to their distance from the sun. • Classify objects as stars, planets, dwarf planets, moons, asteroids, and comets.

Assessment Evidence

Performance Tasks
- **Solar System Objects Report**
  - Goal and Role: As a *TIME for Kids* reporter, you will research, write an article, and present information on a solar system object of your choice.
  - Audience: Children your own age
  - Situation: The challenge involves efficient organization of research and effective written and oral communication in order to transmit knowledge to peers.
  - Product: (1) A written informational article that uses formatting, illustrations, and multimedia and (2) an oral presentation of the article.

o Standards: Clearly introduce topic; use headings to create sections of related information; include illustrations and multimedia to enhance readers' comprehension; develop the topic with facts, details, and examples; use transition words and solar system vocabulary; and provide a concluding section. Speak clearly, using formal English to present main ideas from your article and include a few relevant, descriptive details.

• **Write Your Own Folktale or Myth**

o Goal and Role: As a storyteller, create your own folktale or myth to explain something in nature.

o Audience: Children

o Situation: The challenge involves establishing an appropriate theme that becomes evident to the reader by the end of the story.

o Product: A written narrative

o Standards: Create a beginning that establishes a situation and characters, use dialogue and description, use transitions and figurative language, and provide a conclusion that makes the theme apparent.

Other Evidence

• Solar system unit test

LEARNING PLAN

Routines and Morning Meeting

CCSS in English Language Arts: W.4.7, SL.4.4, L.4.6

Objectives: Students will be able to:

• Observe and report on the phases of the moon.

• Name planets in order based on distance from the sun.

• Use solar system vocabulary.

• Speak clearly and in turn.

Activities:

• Create a moon phase calendar and update daily based on student observation from the night before.

• Share: Students bring in current events dealing with space.

• Share: *My favorite time of day is . . .*

• Activity: Eight Planets Zoom—In this game of speed and memory, students sit in a circle with their heads facing straight forward. A student starts the activity by quickly turning his or her head to the student on their right and saying "Mercury." This student then quickly turns to the next, and says "Venus." Students take quick turns around the circle naming the planets in order. The ninth student begins the cycle again with Mercury, and the list is repeated until the planets zoom back to the first student. Once the first round is over, students can try it again and see if they can beat their time.

• Activity: Pneumonic devices for remembering the planets can be written on chart paper and shared. Students are encouraged to write and share their own.

- Activity: Guess Who—Pick a student to provide clues about a solar system object (e.g., "You can only see me at night. I give off light. Who am I?"). The student then picks someone to guess what is being described ("*A star*").
- Science Word Wall: Keep a running list of science vocabulary words throughout the unit.

Lesson Assessment: The moon phase chart will be student work sample. Anecdotal notes can be taken to record students' mastery of naming the planets.

LESSON 1: INTRODUCTION TO UNIT USING MYTH

CCSS in English Language Arts: RL.4.2, RL.4.9, W.4.7, W.4.8, SL.4.2

Objectives: Students will be able to:
- Identify the theme of a myth.
- Compare and contrast traditional literature from different cultures.
- Understand that the sun has patterns of movement and appears to move across the sky on a daily basis.
- Create guiding questions for experimentation and research.

Activities:
- Review the origins of folktales—stories that are passed down through the generations—and their purpose—to teach a lesson or to explain something from nature.
- Read-Aloud: "The Division of Day and Night" from *Tales of the Shimmering Sky*, by Susan Milord
  - Set purpose: *Listen to see if you can figure out if this story teaches a lesson or explains something from nature.*
  - During: Model fluent reading.
  - After: Allow students to suggest what this story tries to explain from nature (i.e., why there is a pattern of day and night). Begin a K-W-L chart to guide the creation of questions that will be used for exploration and research. Example:
    - What We Know (K): *The sun can be seen during the day. There is a definite day/night pattern.*
    - What We Want to Find Out (W): *Why do we see the sun only during the day? Is it really equal time of day and night—how many hours can we see the sun each day, and is it always the same?*
- Read the next section, "All Day Long," to emphasize that there are many folktales that explain similar concepts. Briefly compare and contrast the two stories. After hearing about Maui's tale, add to the K-W-L chart: K—*The sun takes many hours to get across the sky.* W—*Why is a day 24 hours?*

Lesson Assessment: Participation will be checked.

LESSON 2: MAKING A MODEL AND USING INFORMATIONAL TEXTS TO EXPLORE EARTH'S ROTATION

CCSS in English Language Arts: RI.4.1, RI.4.3, RI.4.9, W.4.7, W.4.8, SL.4.4

Objectives: Students will be able to:

- Understand that the sun has patterns of movement and appears to move across the sky on a daily basis.
- Conduct research and gather relevant information from multiple print and digital sources; take notes and provide a list of sources.
- Conduct an oral presentation of information, explaining concepts from scientific texts and referring to details and examples in a text.

Activities:

- Part A: Making a Model to Explore Earth's Rotation
  - Review K-W-L chart from Lesson 1.
  - Make a model of the sun and Earth to help find evidence to support what you know. Have the students make suggestions, but ultimately lead them to the following:
    - *The sun is in the center and it provides light—we can use a person holding a flashlight to represent the sun.*
    - *Earth is round and it rotates—we can use a ball on a string or a globe to represent Earth, and it should spin.*
    - *We can mark a person's location on Earth with a marker or sticker.*
    - *We can look for the parts on Earth where the sun's light is shining and where it is not.*
  - Make connections between the model and what they already know and want to find out.
    - *Where the sun is shining on Earth is day. We can only see the sun during the day because that's when we're facing the sun.*
    - *Where the sun isn't shining on Earth is night. We cannot see the sun at night because we are facing away from the sun.*
    - *One full day is 24 hours, so it must take our planet 24 hours to complete one full rotation.*
  - Add What We've Learned (L) to the K-W-L chart. As new questions arise, add them to the chart.
- Part B: Reading Informational Texts to Reinforce Learning and Answer Research Questions
  - Model using a question from the K-W-L chart to focus research by going to *www.weather.com* to determine the amount of sunlight in a given day using sunrise and sunset data. Look across the data available to determine whether the amount of sunlight each day is the same or different. Add to the K-W-L chart.
  - Form research groups. Groups will divide up the questions from the K-W-L chart to focus their reading. Students will write relevant facts and their source on index cards. Some suggested texts for research include:
    - *The Sun*, by Seymour Simon
    - *1000 Facts about Space*, by Pam Beasant
    - *The Solar System*, by Rosalind Mist
    - *What's Out There? A Book About Space*, by Lynn Wilson
    - *Amazing Space Facts*, by Dinah L. Moché
  - Students discuss and categorize facts in their groups, and select relevant facts to present.
  - Groups present their facts and update the K-W-L chart.
  - Closing discussion: Contrast information learned from the nonfiction texts and scientific model to the myths' explanations of the sun's path.

Lesson Assessment: Participation and research cards will be checked.

LESSON 3: OBSERVING SHADOWS AND INTRODUCTION TO WRITING A MAGAZINE ARTICLE

CCSS in English Language Arts: RI.4.2, RI.4.5, RI.4.7, W.4.2, W.4.4, W.4.6, W.4.8

Objectives: Students will be able to:

- Understand that the shadows of an object on Earth change over the course of a day, indicating the changing position of the sun during the day.
- Observe and record the movements of shadows of objects on Earth during the course of a day.
- Identify the main idea/details, discuss nonfiction text structure, and interpret/explain the contribution of visual/quantitative data of an informational article.
- Write informational texts.

Activities:

- Part A: Observing Shadows
  - Take students outside early in the morning. Have them each select a spot to stand, and mark it with chalk so that they can return to the exact spot later.
  - Have students observe their shadows, noting color, size, and location, and note the location of the sun in the sky. Students record all their observations.
  - Take students out at least two more times, preferably in the middle of the day and again at the end to repeat their observations from the same spot.

- Part B: Analyzing an Informational Article
  - Discuss the Solar System Objects Report Performance Task. Select and share an article from *TIME for Kids* with a cause–effect structure and explain how this format would be a good example for an article about the sun's path across the sky and its effect on shadows.
  - Select students to identify the main idea and its supporting details.
  - Review common nonfiction text structures: description, sequence, compare–contrast, cause–effect, and problem–solution. Provide the following sentence stems to help students determine the structure of this nonfiction article:
    - Description: A(n) _____ is a kind of _____ that _____.
    - Compare–Contrast: *X* and *Y* are similar in that they both _____, but *X*, whereas *Y*.
    - Sequence: _____ begins with _____ continues with _____ and ends with _____.
    - Problem–Solution: _____ wanted _____ but _____ so _____.
    - Cause–Effect: _____ happens because _____.

                                                                    (Morrow, 2012)

  - Explore the visual or quantitative information and select students to explain what it adds to the article.

- Part C: Shared Writing of an Informational Article
  - Model creating a *TIME for Kids* article about shadows using a computer program such as The Print Shop, Microsoft Word, or Pages.
  - Think aloud as you select a newsletter template that roughly gives the look you want for your magazine article.
  - Model the steps and have students make suggestions for formatting, images, text, and multimedia elements.
  - Emphasize the importance of clearly introducing the topic; using headings to create sections of related information; including illustrations and multimedia to enhance readers' comprehension; developing the topic with facts, details, and examples; using transition words and solar system vocabulary; and providing a concluding section.

Lesson Assessment: Observation record and participation will be checked. Performance task will be used to assess writing objectives.

LESSON 4: MODEL FOR THE MOON PHASES

CCSS in English Language Arts: W.4.7, W.4.8, W.4.10, SL.4.1.c, SL.4.1.d, L.4.6

Objectives: Students will be able to:

- Understand that the observable shape of the moon changes from day to day in a cycle that lasts 29.5 days.
- Observe and explore the phases of the moon and arrange them in order.
- Build knowledge through investigation, and recall relevant information from the experience to discuss, record, and report.

Activities:

- Introduce the moon calendar, which students are to complete each night throughout the month to track the phases of the moon. Keep an enlarged copy of this calendar in the classroom for students to update each day as a part of Morning Meeting.
- Prior knowledge: Make a web about the moon. Have students share what they already know about it.
- Have the students use the information they learned from the models of the sun and Earth to create a hypothesis about why the moon seems to rise and set like the sun and why it glows even though it doesn't give off light like the sun. *Like the sun, the moon appears to rise and set due to the rotation of Earth. Like the model of day–night on Earth, the sun shines on one side of the moon. What we really see is the sun's light reflecting off of the surface.*
- Make a model of the sun, moon, and Earth to investigate the cause of illumination, the appearance of rising and setting, and ultimately the phases of the moon:
  o Remind students that the sun is in the center and that it gives off light. Use a projector as the sun.
  o Tell the students that they will represent Earth in this demonstration so that they can look at the moon like they do from Earth.
  o To illustrate how the moon goes in a path around our planet, hold a basketball and rotate around a student to represent the moon (or suspend the basketball from the ceiling).
  o Turn out the lights.
- Make connections between the model and what the students hypothesized:
  o Draw students' attention to light shining on the moon. *This shows where the illumination comes from: the sun.*
  o Have students rotate in a circle and walk slowly around them. This shows how the moon seems to rise and set even though it is really Earth rotating.
  o Put the moon in front of the projector and have the students look directly at it. Have them note that they cannot see the lit part of the moon (new moon).
  o Walk around students counterclockwise, pausing every 90 degrees, and have them focus on how the lit part of the moon looks on its way there (new moon to first quarter, first quarter to full moon, full moon to last quarter, last quarter to new moon).

(Friedl & Koontz, 2004)

- Closing discussion: Ask students to talk among themselves to try to articulate what they learned about how the moon phases are created. Have students share their discussions with the whole group and come up with one well-articulated explanation. Record this on chart paper. Example: *The moon appears to grow and shrink throughout the month. This is because the moon is spherical and gets its light from the sun. Only the half of the moon that faces the sun is lit. When we look out at it from a point on the Earth, we can only see the lit portion of the half of the moon that faces us. The size of the lit portion that we can see depends on where the moon is in its revolution around Earth.*

Lesson Assessment: Teacher can circulate and listen to students' closing discussion.

Lesson 5: Literacy Center Activity: Moon Phase Flipbook

CCSS in English Language Arts: RI.4.7

Objectives: Students will be able to:
- Interpret and utilize information presented visually to create a moon phase flipbook.

Activities:
- View and read a diagram of the moon phases, available at *www.space.com/62-earths-moon-phases-monthly-lunar-cycles-infographic.html.*
- Students use the information from the diagram to illustrate the eight moon phases (new moon, waxing crescent, first quarter, waxing gibbous, full moon, waning gibbous, last quarter, waning crescent) on rectangular pieces of paper, with the moon slightly offset from the center.
- They then put them in order with new moon on top.
- Students staple their stack on the side with the larger margin.
- They hold onto one side and flip the pages with the thumb to see the moon change phases.
- Students stack multiple flipbooks to see the moon cycle through the phases again and again.

Lesson Assessment: Flipbooks can be checked.

Lesson 6: Literature Circle Activity: Traditional Literature Comparison

CCSS in English Language Arts: RL.4.1, RL.4.2, RL.4.3, RL.4.4, RL.4.10, SL.4.1, SL.4.2

Objectives: Students will be able to:
- Identify the theme of a folktale or myth.
- Compare and contrast traditional literature from different cultures.

Activities:

- Divide students into literature circle groups, and provide several pairs of traditional stories for the students to select from. Suggestions:
  - "Anancy and the FlipFlap Bird" in *Sun, Moon, and Stars*, by Mary Hoffman, and "Anansí" in *Moon Tales*, by Rina Singh and Debbie Lush
  - "The Hare in the Moon" in *Tales of the Shimmering Sky*, by Susan Milord, and "The Greedy Man" in *Moon Tales*, by Rina Singh and Debbie Lush
  - "The Woman Who Flew to the Moon" in *Sun, Moon, and Stars*, by Mary Hoffman, and "Hina" in *Moon Tales*, by Rina Singh and Debbie Lush
  - "The Rabbit and the Moon Man" in *Moon Tales*, by Rina Singh and Debbie Lush, and "Why the Moon Waxes and Wanes" in *Moon Tales*, by Rina Singh and Debbie Lush
- Students select literature circle roles: discussion director, summarizer, character captain, word finder, creative connector, passage picker, and illustrator.
- In addition to their literature circle role, all students should write down and discuss the themes of each story.
- Compare and contrast the two stories read.

Lesson Assessment: Each student's written work can be checked. Teacher can take anecdotal notes during literature circle meeting.

LESSON 7: STAR MYTHOLOGY AND FIGURATIVE LANGUAGE

CCSS in English Language Arts: RL.4.1, RL.4.2, RL.4.3, RL.4.4, L.4.5.a

Objectives: Students will be able to:

- Understand that objects in the sky have patterns of movement.
- Understand what a simile is and the purpose of this type of figurative language.
- Retell a story and identify structure and story elements.

Activities:

- Build background: Use the Starwalk iPad application (or conduct a Google image search) to look up the Pleiades (M45). Note its location in respect to the constellations Taurus and Orion.
- Mini-lesson on figurative language: Copy the following line from *Sun, Moon, and Stars* (Hoffman, 1998, p. 64): "They were like a long drink of ice-cold water in the hot country where they lived." Identify this description as a simile and work together to understand its meaning. Discuss how figurative language enhances the visual imagery and tone of a myth.
- Read "Seven Sisters" in *Sun, Moon, and Stars*.
  - Set purpose: *We will listen to an Australian aboriginal myth explaining the Pleiades constellation. As we read, visualize the story, creating a picture in your mind. Afterward we'll map out the story elements. Listen for details about the theme, characters, setting, conflict, and resolution.*
  - During: Students follow along in their copy of the text as it is read aloud.
  - After: Create a detailed story map together using the following headings: Theme, Characters, Setting, Conflict, and Resolution. Guide students, using detailed questions if necessary: *We know the theme is to explain how the Pleiades got into the sky, but there is one more detail we found out about the Pleiades. What is it? (Two of the stars are dimmer than the rest.) Tell*

me more about the characters: What do they look like, how do they act, and how do others react to them? Why does the conflict occur? What happens after the conflict is resolved? How does it affect the characters?

- At home: Observe the stars as you mark down the phases of the moon on your calendar. Look for Taurus, Orion, and the Pleiades. Note that the stars' positions with respect to each other do not change.

Lesson Assessment: Participation will be checked, and sheets from the subsequent center activity can be checked and marked.

LESSON 8: LITERACY CENTER ACTIVITIES: MORE STAR MYTHOLOGY, STORY MAPPING, AND SIMILE PRACTICE

CCSS in English Language Arts: RL.4.1, RL.4.2, RL.4.3, RL.4.4, L.4.5.a

Objectives: Students will be able to:
- Understand that objects in the sky have patterns of movement.
- Understand what a simile is and the purpose of this type of figurative language.
- Retell a story and identify structure and story elements.

Activities:
- Activity A: Analysis of "Perseus and Andromeda"
  - Students read "Perseus and Andromeda" from *The Storytelling Star: Tales of the Sun, Moon and Stars*, by James Riordan, with their literacy center group. Prompt students to use the comprehension strategy visualize and note any figurative language.
  - Students fill out the story map together (theme, characters, setting, conflict, and resolution) as well as an additional section where they analyze the simile from this story: "The evil monster did not notice Perseus approaching from behind, hanging over it like an eagle about to dive on its prey" (Riordan, 1999, p. 48).
- Activity B: Poetry Center
  - Provide a graphic organizer with the following headings to help students gather ideas for writing their own simile: My Object, How Would You Describe It?, What Does It Do?, and *My Simile.*
  - Students complete the organizer, highlight an idea, and then turn it into a simile.
  - Provide students with an example you wrote or use the following:
    - My Object—the sun
    - How Would You Describe It?—spherical, fiery, bright, hot
    - What Does It Do?—provides light and heat, floats across the sky, sinks into the horizon
    - My Simile—The bright sun floated gracefully like a ballerina across her stage.
  - Students may wish to refer to their graphic organizers and similes when they are developing an idea for the Write Your Own Folktale or Myth Performance Task.

Lesson Assessment: Sheets can be checked and marked.

LESSON 9: MAKING WORDS LESSON: CONSTELLATION

CCSS in English Language Arts: RF.4.3, L.4.2.d

Objectives: Students will be able to:

- Spell words using known patterns, roots, and affixes.

Activities:

- Give students the following letters on slips of paper: *a, e, i, o, o, c, l, l, n, n, s, t,* and *t.*
- Have them follow the directions below to make words with letters. Keep the lesson moving by selecting students to spell the words in a pocket chart at the front of the room without waiting for each student to have the word spelled.
  - Use three letters to spell the word *ace.* "We will *ace* the test."
  - Change the last letter to spell *act.* "It was all an *act.*"
  - Add three letters to spell *action.* "When the Soviets launched the rocket that carried Sputnik, the U.S. took *action.*"
  - Add one more letter to make *actions.* "Our *actions* affect others."
  - Change the first two letters to spell *lotion.* "If you squirt *lotion* in space, it will float."
  - Change the first letter to spell *notion.* "It is hard to form a *notion* of how big space really is."
  - Change the vowel in the first syllable to spell *nation.* "The United States was the first and only *nation* to send people to the moon."
  - Start over with four letters to spell *note.* "As scientists, we can *note* differences and similarities to classify solar system objects."
  - Add a letter to spell *notes.* "She writes *notes* when doing research."
  - Use six letters to spell *notate.* "You can *notate,* or label, the illustration."
  - Change the ending to spell *notation.* "There are rules for proper *notation* of sources."
  - Change the first three letters to spell *location.* "The *location* of the sun in the sky depends on the time of day."
  - Change the ending to spell *locate.* "You can *locate* many objects in the night's sky."
  - I have just one word left. It is the secret word you can make with all your letters. See if you can figure it out. *Constellation*
- Place a set of cards with the words in the pocket chart to read and spell the words chorally.
- Sort the related words that share a root. Use those words in a sentence to show how they are related.
  - *act, action, actions*
  - *note, notes, notation, notations*
  - *locate, location*
  - Sort the rhyming words and note the spelling pattern.
  - *lotion, notion*
  - *nation, notation, location*
  - *notate, locate*
- On a sheet numbered 1–6, have the students spell more words using the related words and rhyming words.
  - Use *act, action, actions* to spell *sect, section, sections.*
  - Use *lotion* and *notion* to spell *potion.*
  - Use *nation, notation,* and *location* to spell *elation.*
  - Use *notate* and *locate* to spell *vibrate.*

(Cunningham, 2009)

Lesson Assessment: Anecdotal notes can be taken to note students with particular difficulty.

LESSON 10: USING DRAMA AND INFORMATIONAL TEXT TO INTRODUCE PLANETS AND INSPIRE WRITING

CCSS in English Language Arts: RL.4.1, RL.4.3, RL.4.5, RL.4.6, RL.4.7, RI.4.4, RI.4.8, RI.4.10, RF.4.4, W.4.1, W.4.5, W.4.9, L.4.4.a

Objectives: Students will be able to:
- Arrange the planets according to their distance from the sun.
- Classify objects as stars, planets, dwarf planets, moons, asteroids, and comets.
- Evaluate characters and read fluently staying in character.
- Explain how an author uses analogy to support points.
- Compare, contrast, and evaluate text structures.
- Write an opinion piece.

Activities:
- Part A: Reader's Theatre
- Silent read "Meet Our Solar System," available at *http://discoverynewfrontiers.nasa.gov/lib/pdf/DP_poster_back.pdf*.
   - Set purpose: *As you read, decide what the characters might sound like and what kind of personality they have. Think about how readers can use their voice to convey the character's attitudes and emotions.* Model using sticky notes to write down ideas.
   - During: Students use sticky notes to jot down ideas for the reader's portrayal of the character.
   - After: Split the class in two groups. In their groups, students share and discuss their notes, looking to the text to support or refine their suggestions.
- Students select parts and practice "Meet Our Solar System" in Reader's Theatre.
- Each group performs and then evaluates the other group's portrayal of the characters, making connections between the text and oral presentation.
- Part B: Whole- or Small-Group Informational Text Reading
- Silent read *Our Solar System*, by Seymour Simon
   - Use the cloze procedure to preview vocabulary and provide practice in using context to determine the meaning of unknown words.
   - Set purpose: *As a professional nonfiction writer, Seymour Simon does an excellent job of using compare–contrast to support facts he's relaying. As you read, identify passages where he uses this technique to help you make an analogy between a familiar idea and something that is unfamiliar.*
   - During: Students complete a graphic organizer for analogies, available at *www.teachervision.fen.com/graphic-organizers/printable/48386.html*.
   - After: In group discussion, students share what they found.
- Part C: Analyzing Texts Types and Opinion Writing
- Create a Venn diagram together to compare and contrast the two texts with an emphasis on text structure. If necessary, ask leading questions: *From which point of view is each text narrated? What major structural differences are there?*
- Have students reread the Venn diagram and consider which text they enjoyed learning from more. Have them draw on the information in the diagram to develop reasons.
- Review fourth-grade opinion writing standards (W.4.1.a–d) by providing a writing rubric.
- Students use the writing process to compose an opinion piece to tell which text they prefer.

Lesson Assessment: Teacher can take anecdotal notes on students reading performance. All written work and participation can be checked. Writing will be evaluated by rubric.

LESSON 11: LITERACY CENTER ACTIVITY: PLANET ART

CCSS in English Language Arts: RI.4.1

Objectives: Students will be able to:

- Create an artistic interpretation of a planet's surface based on factual information and images.

Activities:

- Provide planet fact sheets with pictures and descriptions of the planet's surface.
- Students select a planet (more than one if time allows) and one of the following techniques to create a painting based on the information they read:
  - Crayon Resist: Draw lines with crayons and paint over them with watercolor.
  - Salt Painting: Paint with watercolor, and then sprinkle salt on top. Rub the salt off when dry.
  - Crinkle Painting: Paint with watercolor, put plastic wrap on the wet painting and crumple it; remove when dry.
  - Splatter Painting: Dip toothbrush into watercolor and thumb over the bristles to splatter the paint.
  - Marble Painting: Tape or tack paper into the inside of a cardboard box (the lids from copy paper shipping boxes work well). Roll marbles around in tempera paint and drop them in the box. Rock the box back and forth and side to side.
  - Marbleized Painting: Make a flour paste with equal parts flour and water. Pour into a disposable aluminum pan. Drop enamel model paint onto the surface and swirl with toothpicks. Lay paper on top, lift off, and wash paste off.
  - Tissue Paper Decoupage: Glue layers of tissue paper with watered-down glue.
  - Bubble Painting: In a cup mix 2 tablespoons of tempera paint, 2 tablespoons of dish soap, and 1 tablespoon of water. Insert a straw and blow until it bubbles over. Put the paper on top to collect the bubbles. Repeat.

(Milord, 1996)

Lesson Assessment: Planets can be displayed as student work samples.

LESSON 12: MATH CONNECTION: MODEL OF THE SOLAR SYSTEM AND REPORT

CCSS in English Language Arts: W.4.2, W.4.6, W.4.8, SL.4.4, SL.4.5, SL.4.6, L.4.3, L.4.6

Objectives: Students will be able to:
  - Arrange the planets according to their distance from the sun.
  - Write the script for an oral report of a learning experience.

Activities:
  - Build a Solar System—Use NASA's iPad application or another chart of data giving the size of the planets and their distance from the sun.
  - Use a scale of 1 mm = 5,000 km to create a model of each planet. To skip the calculating, use Exploratorium's solar system model calculator at *www.exploratorium.edu/ronh/solar_system/*. Enter "276" under Body Diam (mm) to produce automatic calculations.

o Use the same scale to calculate the distance of each planet from the sun, or check the "Scaled orbit radius" column on Exploratorium's calculator.

o Take the model planets to the largest open outdoor area available; a space larger than a foot-ball field is recommended. Repeat the class's selected pneumonic device to help arrange the planets according to their distance from the sun until you run out of room. Go to the farthest planet you can fit in the space available and look back at how small the sun seems.

(Friedl & Koontz, 2004)

o Select students to photograph or video record the event. Afterward, report on the learning experience. Write a script together for student reporters to read. Emphasize reporters' need for formal English and precise language. Integrate the photographs or video clips into the final report. Several digital tools can be utilized to create the final report, including iMovie and YouTube or VoiceThread.

Lesson Assessment: Students can receive feedback through comments on their website.

LESSON 13: LITERACY CENTER ACTIVITY: NONFICTION TEXT STRUCTURE OF ONLINE NEWS

CCSS in English Language Arts:

Objectives: Students will be able to:

- Identify nonfiction text structure and use it to assist comprehension.
- Further understanding of the solar system by reading news articles on space.

Activities:

- Students use one of the following online news sources to read an article on space:
  o Weekly Reader, News for Kids, Science: *www.weeklyreader.com/subcategory/74#*
  o Science News for Kids, Earth and Sky, Space: *www.sciencenewsforkids.org/category/earthsky/space/*
  o National Geographic for Kids, News, Space & Science: *http://kids.nationalgeographic.com/kids/stories/spacescience/*
  o *TIME for Kids*, News, News Archive, Science: *www.timeforkids.com/news-archive/science*
  o Scholastic News Online, News and Features: *http://teacher.scholastic.com/activities/scholasticnews/index.html*
  o NASA, For Students, Grades K–4, Stories: *www.nasa.gov/audience/forstudents/k-4/stories/stories_archive_1.html*
- Students use the nonfiction text structure sentence stems from Lesson 3, Part B to determine the structure of the article they chose.
- Students can share the main idea and structure of the article they read with their classmates during a share time.

Lesson Assessment: Written work and oral presentation of ideas will be assessed.

LESSON 14: SOLAR SYSTEM OBJECTS REPORT PERFORMANCE TASK

CCSS in English Language Arts: RI.4.9, RI.4.10, W.4.2, W.4.4, W.4.5, W.4.6, W.4.7, W.4.8, W.4.10, SL.4.3, SL.4.4, SL.4.5, L.4.1, L.4.2, L.4.3, L.4.6

Objectives: Students will be able to:

- Classify objects as stars, planets, dwarf planets, moons, asteroids, and comets.
- Conduct research on a solar system object by reading multiple informational texts, taking/organizing notes, and creating a list of sources.
- Use the writing process to create an informational article on the computer.
- Listen and take notes, identifying reasons and evidence provided by the speaker to support classification of the solar system object.
- Report on a solar system object, speaking clearly and at an understandable pace.

Activities:

- Review the Solar System Objects Report Performance Task; provide students with a copy of the task as well as the rubric from which their project will be judged.
- Allow students to select a solar system object of their choice, but ensure that there is enough variety so that each type of object (i.e., star, planet, dwarf planet, moon, asteroid, comet) is reported on.
- Take students to the library to research their chosen object or gather a supply of books to keep on a shelf, bin, or cart in the classroom. Several websites and digital texts are also excellent research sources, including:
  - *http://solarsystem.nasa.gov/kids/solarsys_kids.cfm*
  - *www.esa.int/esaKIDSen/OurUniverse.html*
  - *www.factmonster.com/ipka/A0909527.html*
  - NASA application for iPad
  - Star Walk application for iPad
- Select a solar system object to model the process of writing an informational article. A student work session should immediately follow each of the following steps:
  - Read aloud an example informational text and think aloud to model the selection of relevant facts to write down on index cards. Review how to take notes and reference the source on index cards.
  - When most students have completed their research, model physically sorting the fact cards to develop sections and select headings.
  - Review selecting a newsletter template and model drafting the article, thinking aloud about how to create a clear introductory paragraph; focused sections with headings; text that is well developed with facts, details, transition words, and solar system vocabulary; and a closing section.
  - Demonstrate how to find appropriate images on the Internet to add to the article. You may also wish to demonstrate how to create graphs and charts to support the text.
  - After the entire draft is created, students will revise and edit their drafts independently and with a peer. Mini-lessons during the revision and editing process should be tailored to the needs of the students and their particular patterns of errors—for example, grammar, capitalization, punctuation, and spelling conventions; word choice; organization; development of ideas; writing clear introductory and closing sections; or any other lesson appropriate to the fourth-grade writing and language standards.
  - Once editing is finished, students can print their article to submit to their class issue of *TIME for Kids*. Articles can also be saved as a PDF file and a digital copy can be posted to a class website.

- Students orally present their article and may use visuals from their article to support their presentation. Peers are responsible for identifying the reasons and evidence the presenter provides in order to decide which category each solar system object belongs in—stars, planets, dwarf planets, moons, asteroids, and comets. These categories can be headings on a graphic organizer the students use to take notes as they listen to the reports.
- To close, review the completed graphic organizer together. Before binding the magazine, organize the articles into sections based on the six categories.

Lesson Assessment: Reports will be judged based on the standards provided in the performance task write-up. Graphic organizers can also be checked.

(Wiggins & McTighe, 2005)

REFERENCES

Cunningham, P. M. (2009). *Phonics they use: Words for reading and writing.* Boston: Pearson.

Friedl, A. E., & Koontz, T. Y. (2004). *Teaching science to children: An inquiry approach.* New York: McGraw-Hill.

Hoffman, M. (1998). *Sun, moon, and stars* (J. Roy, illustrator). New York: Dutton Children's Books.

Milord, S. (1996). *Tales of the shimmering sky: Ten global folktales with activities.* Charlotte, VT: Williamson.

Morrow, L. M. (2012). *Literacy development in the early years: Helping children read and write.* Boston: Pearson.

N.J. Department of Education. (2010). *New Jersey core curriculum content standards classroom applications document: Science. Earth system science (by the end of grade 4).* Retrieved from *www.state.nj.us/education/cccs/cad/5/.*

Riordan, J. (1999). *The storytelling star: Tales of the sun, moon and stars.* London: Pavilion.

Wiggins, G. P., & McTighe, J. (2005). *Understanding by design.* Alexandria, VA: Association for Supervision and Curriculum Development.

A NEW GOVERNMENT—GRADE 5

Desired results: Literacy	Desired results: Social Studies
Established Goals • Common Core State Standards for English language arts grade 5 (articulated in the learning plan that follows).	**Established Goals** • Evaluate the effectiveness of the fundamental principles of the U.S. Constitution (i.e., consent of the governed, rule of law, federalism, limited government, separation of powers, checks and balances, and individual rights) in establishing a federal government that allows for growth and change over time. • Compare and contrast the Articles of Confederation and the U.S. Constitution in terms of the decision-making powers of national government.

	• Evaluate the impact of the Constitution and Bill of Rights on current-day issues. • Evaluate the extent to which the leadership and decisions of early administrations of the national government met the goals established in the Preamble of the Constitution. (N.J. Department of Education, 2010)
Enduring Understandings • Reading, writing, speaking, and listening are effective ways of communicating information. • The ability to write and speak clearly is essential to effective communication.	**Enduring Understandings** • Past and present interactions of people, cultures, and the environment shape the American heritage. • The foundation of our government comes from the people. • Citizens have rights and responsibilities at the national, state, and local levels. (N.J. Department of Education, 2010)
Essential Questions • What do proficient readers do to make sense of what they are reading? • How can I effectively communicate through my writing and speaking?	**Essential Questions** • What is government and what can it do? • How does the government established by the Constitution embody the purposes, values, and principles of the American dream? • How can citizens and groups participate effectively in the democratic process?
Essential Knowledge Students will know: • Proficient readers use a variety of strategies in order to make sense of a text. • Authors use different text structures to communicate different types of information.	**Essential Knowledge** Students will know: • Disputes over political authority and economic issues contributed to a movement for independence in the colonies. • The fundamental principles of the U.S. Constitution serve as the foundation of the U.S. government today. (N.J. Department of Education, 2010)
Essential Skills Students will be able to: • Use glossary/dictionary to determine unknown word meanings. • Read a variety of texts to gather information. • Use text structure to help comprehend text. • Summarize a text. • Exhibit fluency when reading and speaking. • Design interview questions. • Research and synthesize information from several sources. • Participate in group discussions.	**Essential Skills** Students will be able to: • Analyze other documents (e.g., Magna Carta, Articles of Confederation, Virginia Plan, New Jersey Plan) to identify ideas in the U.S. Constitution. • Analyze the goals outlined in the Preamble. • Distinguish between the roles of legislative, executive, and judicial branches of government. • Analyze the U.S. Constitution to determine whether some of its principles (separation of powers, checks and balances, individual rights) have established a government that allows for growth and change.

Assessment Evidence

Performance Tasks
- **Constitutional Convention Reporter**
  - o Goal and Role: You are a newspaper reporter conducting an interview with one of the delegates at the Constitutional Convention.
  - o Audience: Students your age

  - o Situation: As a reporter for the *Philadelphia Enquirer* in 1787, you have been asked to interview one of the delegates at the Constitutional Convention to find out how he feels about this new plan and whether he is likely to vote in favor or against it. You must create interview questions and research to find the answers.
  - o Product: You will write the interview script for you and your partner and videotape the interview to share with the class.
  - o Standards: You must have a minimum of five questions and consult at least three sources for your answers. You must speak clearly, and your speech must be appropriately paced throughout the interview. Your script may be neatly handwritten or typed.
- **Scrapbook/Journal**
  - o Goal and Role: Collaboratively write a journal with pictures to highlight places you visited with your foreign exchange student.
  - o Audience: Children your age
  - o Situation: As a group, you have been asked to accompany students from China on their trip to the United States. The purpose of the trip is for the students to learn about democracy. You must choose five different sites that you believe will teach them about our government and democracy. Each member of your group will choose a different site, find pictures, and develop a narrative as if you were the exchange students.
  - o Product: A scrapbook with an accompanying narrative
  - o Standards: Your book must have photographs or drawings and a narrative for each site visited. Use the narrative structure to create an imagined experience at your site as told from the point of view of the exchange students.

Other Evidence
- Two quizzes
- A new government test
- Book review

LEARNING PLAN

LESSON 1: INTRODUCTION TO UNIT USING THE PREAMBLE TO THE CONSTITUTION

CCSS in English Language Arts: RI.5.1, RI.5.4, RF.5.3, RF.5.4.c, SL.5.1.a, L.5.4.a, L.5.4.c, L.5.6

Objectives: Students will be able to:
- Use context and dictionaries to determine word meanings.
- Ask and answer questions about an informational text in order to understand the goals outlined in the Preamble.

Activities:

- Without discussion, students read the words to the Preamble of the Constitution silently. Ask for volunteers to explain what they have read. (It is anticipated that most students will not be able to answer.) Explain that this is an introduction to the U.S. Constitution, which they will be studying in the next unit.

- Read-aloud: *We the Kids: The Preamble to the Constitution of the United States*, by David Catrow
  - Set purpose: *Listen to hear this document explained in children's terms.*
  - During: Stop and ask questions to help children clarify unknown words using story pictures.
  - After: *Turn to your partner and share something you now understand that you did not when you read the text alone.*

- Share the explanation of the words to the Preamble using an overhead or LCD projector.

- With a partner, students define *justice, domestic, tranquility, defense, welfare,* and *posterity* using the explanations and dictionaries when needed.

- Students share definitions orally.

- Provide the following prompt and have several students complete it orally. All students write the prompt in their notebook and completes it with either a response they heard or one of their own:

  I wanted justice when . . .

  A domestic activity that I have to do is . . .

  _____ *brings me tranquility.*

- Begin a new Social Studies Word Wall and add the words to it

- Introduce the Interview Performance Task and explain that students will be writing an interview script and videotaping their interview.

Lesson Assessment: Teacher will assess based on observation of partner work and oral responses.

LESSON 2: REVIEW OF READING COMPREHENSION STRATEGIES

CCSS in English Language Arts: RL.5.10, RI. 5.2, SL.5.1, SL.5.2

Objectives: Students will be able to:

- Build background for the study of the U.S. Constitution.

- Review and apply previously taught comprehension strategies (recognizing text features, questioning, making inferences, and analyzing text structure).

- Make inferences as they hear a story.

- Give reasons for their opinions.

Activities:

- Discussion
  - After reviewing comprehension strategies (recognizing text features, questioning, analyzing text structure, making inferences, and visualizing) using wall chart, explain that students will be applying them during independent reading.
  - Suggested historical fiction texts:
    - *The Winter of Red Snow: The Revolutionary War Diary of Abigail Jane Stewart, Valley Forge, PA 1777*, by Kristiana Gregory
    - *Ben and Me: An Astonishing Life of Benjamin Franklin as Written by His Good Mouse, Amos*, by Robert Lawson

- *My Brother Sam Is Dead*, by James Lincoln Collier
- *Johnny Tremain*, by Esther Forbes
- *War Comes to Willy Freeman*, by James Lincoln Collier
- Read-aloud: Chapter 1 of *Shh! We're Writing the Constitution*, by Jean Fritz
  - Set Purpose: *As you listen to the first chapter of this narrative nonfiction book, see if you can make inferences.*
  - During: Stop at predetermined points and ask questions like "What have you learned so far?" or "What is happening in the text?"
  - After: *Think about what you learned from this book so far. Was it something stated directly in the text or indirectly? Use the prompt "The reason I think this is" and share it with your partner.* Have several students share what their partner said.
- Explain that during independent reading time students will be thinking about the reading strategies they are using and marking places where they use them with a sticky note.
- Following independent reading, students share what they found out or learned from their reading with their partner.

Lesson Assessment: Teacher observation and notation of students using strategies independently.

LESSON 3: DETERMINING WHAT IS IMPORTANT IN A TEXT

CCSS in English Language Arts: RL.5.10, RL.5.4, RI.5.1, RF.5.4.a, RF.5.4.c, SL.5.1.c, SL.5.2

Objectives: Students will be able to:
- Make inferences as they hear a text.
- Think about what is important in the text.
- Use Think–Pair–Write.
- Apply strategy to independent reading.

Activities:
- Ask students what they remember about *Shh! We're Writing the Constitution*. Take several responses, reminding students to use the prompt "In addition to what _____ said . . . "
- Explain that students will practice thinking about what is important to remember.
- Model strategy:
  - Reread a portion of text from yesterday, stopping once to model your thinking and write down a note about what you just said.
  - Repeat with another section of the text and have students do it with you.
  - Finally, reread another section, and have students pair up to discuss what they thought was most important and write down one statement they agree on.
  - Call on several students to share.
- Students will read a self-selected historical fiction book and apply the strategy to their reading. They will write their notes in their reading log and share with their partner.
- Meet with individuals or small groups to assess how they are applying the strategy.

Lesson Assessment: Responses will be noted in small-group or individual conferences.

LESSON 4: APPLICATION OF STRATEGY TO SOCIAL STUDIES TEXT

CCSS in English Language Arts: RI.5.1, RI.5.2, RI.5.3, RI.5.4, RF.5.3, SL.5.1, SL.5.2, L.5.5

Objectives: Students will be able to:

- Determine meaning of unknown words using context or glossary.
- Read text or selection about the Constitutional Convention and decide what is important to remember.
- Use Think–Pair–Write in social studies notebook.
- Write a summary.
- Make and sort words from *constitution*.
- Apply strategy to independent reading of a historical fiction novel.

Activities:

- Introduce new vocabulary: *federal, compromise, republic, bill*
  o Ask what students know about the word *federal*.
  o If understanding is minimal, give them time to look in social studies text or glossary.
  o Discuss as a whole class and create definition for all to copy.
  o Provide prompt to be completed by each student (i.e., *I had to compromise when . . .*).
  o Add the word to the Word Wall.
  o Repeat with remaining words.

- Remind students of the process for figuring out what is the most important thing to remember while you are reading. In groups of four to five, have students read a text or selection about the Constitutional Convention. Assign them stopping points to discuss with their group; everyone agrees to one to two statements they can write about the section. Continue to the end of the selection. Meet with each group to check on progress. Have one student from each group share one of their statements.

- Suggested texts:
  o *We the People: The Story of Our Constitution*, by Lynne Cheney
  o *A More Perfect Union: The Story of Our Constitution*, available at *www.usconstitution.net/constkids4.html*
  o District-approved social studies textbook

- Students write summary paragraph using statements from each section.

- Students receive a set of letters that spell *constitution*. They use the letters to create as many words as they can, write them in a word study notebook, and share them with a partner.

  (Cunningham, 2009)

- Students read novels (self-selected historical fiction) independently. At the end of the reading time, students record the pages they have read, write a two- to three-sentence summary and a personal response in their reading log, and share with partners what they have read.

Lesson Assessment: Anecdotal notes can be taken during small-group meetings. Summary of text, word study notebooks, and reading logs will be checked.

LESSON 5: EVALUATION OF VIDEO

CCSS in English Language Arts: RL.5.1, RL.5.7, RI.5.2, RI.5.3, RI.5.4, SL.5.1, SL.5.2, L.5.5

Objectives: Students will be able to:
- Build background knowledge about the branches of government.
- Make inferences as they hear a text.
- Distinguish between main and supporting ideas.
- Use Think–Pair–Write.
- Apply strategy to independent reading of a historical fiction novel.
- View a video and compare with what they have learned from reading.

Activities:
- Read-aloud: *The U.S. Constitution and You*, by Syl Sobel
  - Set Purpose: *Listen to the text and determine what is most important to remember.*
  - During: Stop at predetermined points and ask, "What is the most important thing you have heard so far?"
  - After: *Turn to your partner and discuss what you think was most important. Write one or two sentences that you agree on.* Each pair shares using prompts: "We agree/disagree with because . . . " or "In addition to what _____ said, I think . . . "
- List sentences on board and help students determine whether the statement is about a main idea or a supporting idea (details, examples, descriptions).
- Students read independently (historical fiction) and apply strategy. They write down important information in reading log and share with a partner.
- Video *Liberty's Kids: #40 We the People* (1/2), available at *www.youtube.com/ watch?v=CNTNueTl904*
  - Set purpose: *This is the first of two videos about the creation of the U.S. Constitution. Look for similarities and differences between what you have already read and heard and what you see in the film.*
  - During: Give students a T-chart to take notes. One column is for what they already know and the other is for new information.
  - After: Small groups compare their T-charts and make a list of new information on chart paper. Each group will present their findings.

Lesson Assessment: Response noted, observation of independent reading, T-chart presentation

LESSON 6: APPLICATION OF READING STRATEGY TO SOCIAL STUDIES TEXT

CCSS in English Language Arts: RI.5.1, RI.5.2, RI.5.3, RI.5.4, RF.5.3, SL.5.1, SL.5.2, L.5.5

Objectives: Students will be able to:
- Determine meaning of unknown words using context or glossary.
- Read text about the three branches of government.
- Distinguish between important ideas and supporting ideas.
- Use Think–Pair–Write in social studies notebook.

- Write a summary.
- Make and sort words from *federalist*.
- Apply strategy to independent reading of a historical fiction novel.

Activities:

- Introduce new vocabulary: *veto, impeach, amendment*.
  - Ask what students know about the word *veto*.
  - If understanding is minimal, give students time to look in social studies text or glossary.
  - Discuss as a class and create definition for all to copy.
  - Provide prompt to be filled in by each student (i.e., "A person might veto something because . . . ").
  - Add the word to the Word Wall.
  - Repeat with remaining words.
- Remind students of the process for figuring out what is the most important thing to remember while you are reading. In groups of four to five, have them read a text or a selection about the three branches of government. Assign them stopping points to discuss with their group; everyone agrees to one to two statements they can write about the section. Continue to the end of the selection. Meet with each group to check on progress. Have one student from each group share one of their statements.
- Suggested texts:
  - *How the U.S. Government Works*, by Syl Sobel
  - *http://bensguide.gpo.gov/3-5/government/branches.html*
  - District-approved social studies textbook
- Students write summary paragraph, using statements from each section.
- Students receive a set of letters that spell *federalist*. They use the letters to create as many words as they can, write them in a word study notebook, and share them with a partner.

(Cunningham, 2009)

- Students read novels (self-selected historical fiction) independently. At the end of the reading time, students record the pages they have read, write a two- to three-sentence summary and a personal response in their reading log, and share with partners what they have read.

Lesson Assessment: Anecdotal notes can be taken during small-group meetings. Summary of text, word study notebooks, and reading logs will be checked.

LESSON 7: EXPLANATION OF INTERVIEW PERFORMANCE TASK

CCSS in English Language Arts: W.5.4, SL.5.1

Objectives: Students will be able to:
- Determine who the delegates to the Constitutional Convention were.
- Formulate appropriate interview questions.
- Work collaboratively with a partner.

Activities:

- Remind students of the interview they will be preparing to record in 2 weeks.
- Provide several examples of appropriate interview questions for students to analyze.

- After assigning partners and reviewing interview question rubric, students work together to create a list of 7–10 interview questions.
- Students are randomly assigned a delegate (students pick names from hat).
- On interactive white board, show painting of Constitutional Convention from *http://teachingamericanhistory.org/convention/christy/*. Students can find and identify their delegate.

Lesson Assessment: Collection of interview questions.

LESSON 8: RESEARCH TO FIND ANSWERS TO INTERVIEW QUESTIONS
(LIKELY TO TAKE SEVERAL CLASS PERIODS TO COMPLETE)

CCSS in English Language Arts: RI.5.6, RI.5.7, RI.5.9, W.5.7

Objectives: Students will be able to:
- Locate information in the library and on the Internet.
- Gather information from at least three sources.
- Determine the most important information in each source.

Activities:
- Review how to determine the most important information in a text.
- Take students to the library/computer lab to look up information on their delegate. (If this is not possible, gather sources ahead of time.)
  o Show them how to use online database to find print sources.
  o Remind them how to determine whether an Internet source is credible.
  o Have students take notes on their delegate and copy down the source information.

Lesson Assessment: Observation of note-taking and note cards.

LESSON 9: BEGIN DRAFTING SCRIPT

CCSS in English Language Arts: W.5.1.c, W.5.1.d, W.5.2.a, W.5.2.b, W.5.2.d, W.5.2.e, W.5.4, W.5.5, L.5.3

Objectives: Students will be able to:
- Synthesize gathered information.
- Write a draft of interview script.

Activities:
- Have students sort their note cards based on the interview questions they created.
- Hand out a sample script so students can see how to format their writing.
- Go over together, pointing out roles, actions, and so on.
- Students write first draft of script.

Lesson Assessment: Conferences while students write.

LESSON 10: APPLICATION OF READING STRATEGY TO SOCIAL STUDIES TEXT

CCSS in English Language Arts: RI.5.1, RI.5.2, RI.5.3, RI.5.4, RF.5.3, SL.5.1, SL.5.2, L.5.5

Objectives: Students will be able to:

- Determine meaning of unknown words using context or glossary.
- Read text of the Bill of Rights and decide what is important to remember.
- Use Think–Pair–Write in social studies notebook.
- Write summary.
- Make and sort words from *legislative*.
- Apply strategy to independent reading of a historical fiction novel.

Activities:

- Introduce new vocabulary: *ratify, due process, political party*
  o Ask what students know about the word *ratify*.
  o If understanding is minimal, give students time to look in social studies text or glossary.
  o Discuss as a whole class and create definition for all to copy.
  o Provide prompt to be filled in by each student (i.e., *To ratify a bill, Congress must . . .*).
  o Add the word to the Word Wall.
  o Repeat with remaining words.
- Remind students of the process for figuring out what is the most important thing to remember while reading. In groups of four to five, have them read a text or a selection about the Bill of Rights. Assign them stopping points to discuss with their group where they agree to one to two statements they can write about the section. Continue to the end of the selection. Meet with each group to check on progress. Have one student from each group share one of their statements.
- Suggested texts:
  o *The Bill of Rights* (True Books series), by Christine Taylor Butler
  o *A Kids' Guide to America's Bill of Rights: Curfews, Censorship, and the 100-Pound Giant*, by Kathleen Krull
  o *www.historyforkids.org/learn/northamerica/after1500/government/billofrights.htm*
  o *www.socialstudiesforkids.com/wwww/us/billofrightsdef.htm*
  o District-approved social studies textbook
- Students write summary paragraph using statements from each section.
- Students receive a set of letters that spell *legislative* and use the letters to create as many words as they can, write them in a word study notebook, and share with a partner.

  (Cunningham, 2009)

- Students read novels (self-selected historical fiction) independently. At the end of the reading time, students record the pages they have read, write a two- to three-sentence summary and a personal response in their reading log, and share with partners what they have read.

Lesson Assessment: Anecdotal notes can be taken during small-group meetings. Summary of text, word study notebooks, and reading logs will be checked.

LESSON 11: APPLICATION OF READING STRATEGY TO SOCIAL STUDIES TEXT AND EVALUATION OF VIDEO

CCSS in English Language Arts: RL.5.7, RI.5.1, RI.5.2, RI.5.3, RI.5.4, RF.5.3, SL.5.1, SL.5.2, L.5.5

Objectives: Students will be able to:

- Determine meaning of unknown words using context or glossary.
- Read about the principles of democracy and decide what is important to remember.
- Use Think–Pair–Write in social studies notebook.
- Write summary.
- View and evaluate video.

Activities:

- Introduce new vocabulary: *union, democracy, civic virtue, naturalization.*
  - Ask what students know about the word *union.*
  - If understanding is minimal, give students time to consult social studies text or glossary.
  - Discuss as a whole class and create definition for all to copy.
  - Provide prompt to be completed in by each student (e.g., *A union is formed when . . .*).
  - Add the word to the Word Wall.
  - Repeat with remaining words.
- Remind students of the process for determining what is the most important thing to remember while reading. In groups of four to five, have students read a text or a selection about the principles of democracy. Assign them stopping points to discuss with their group where they agree to one to two statements they can write about the section. Continue to the end of the selection. Meet with each group to check on progress. Have one student from each group share one of their statements.
- Suggested texts:
  - *Democracy,* by Alex Woolf
  - District-approved social studies textbook
- Students write summary paragraph using statements from each section.
- Students read novels (self-selected historical fiction) independently. At the end of the reading time, students record the pages they have read, write a two- to three-sentence summary and a personal response in their reading log, and share with partners what they have read.
- Video *Liberty's Kids: #40 We the People (2/2),* available at *www.youtube.com/watch?v=1ZoC uXJZcsg&feature=related*
  - Set purpose: *This is the second of two videos about the creation of the U.S. Constitution. Look for similarities and differences between what you have already read and heard and what you see in the film.*
  - During: Give students a T-chart to take notes. One column is for what they already know and the other is for new information.
  - After: Small groups compare their T-charts and make a list of new information on chart paper. Each group will present their findings.

Lesson Assessment: Anecdotal notes can be taken during small-group meetings. Summary of text, T-chart presentation, and reading logs will be checked.

LESSON 12: WORD STUDY LITERACY CENTER ACTIVITY

CCSS in English Language Arts: RF.5.3, L.5.6

Objectives: Students will be able to:
- Create a variety of words from a group of letters.
- Sort the words into various categories.

Activities:
- Students take an envelope of letters that spell a multisyllabic word related to the study of the U.S. Constitution (*judicial, executive, naturalization, government, responsibilities*).
- Using any combination of letters, students create two-letter, three-letter, four-letter words and so on, with the goal being to create the largest word they can. Challenge them to figure out the word that uses all the letters.

(Cunningham, 2009)

- Once the list is created, students look for patterns in the words and list them in columns.

Lesson Assessment: Word lists will be checked.

LESSON 13: WRITING LITERACY CENTER ACTIVITY

CCSS in English Language Arts: RL.5.2, RL.5.3, RL.5.6, W.5.1.a, W.5.1.b, W.5.4, W.5.5, W.5.9, W.5.10, L.5.1, L.5.2

Objectives: Students will be able to:
- Analyze book review.
- Summarize what they have read.
- Add personal opinion.
- Revise, edit, and publish script.

Activities:
- Students work in pairs to research the structure of content of book reviews. Give each pair a book review, found on any bookseller's website (e.g., Amazon, Barnes & Noble).
- Students analyze the review and make a list of elements they see in the review.
- Teacher lists elements on chart as students share.
- As a class, go through the list and circle the most important things about the review. The list will serve as guidance as students write their own book review of the historical fiction book they have been reading independently.
- After peer and teacher conferencing, students revise, edit, and write the final draft of their book review.

Lesson Assessment: Completed book review will be graded with a rubric and kept as student work samples.

LESSON 14: FLUENCY LITERACY CENTER ACTIVITY

CCSS in English Language Arts: RL.5.5, RF.5.3, RF.5.4.a, RF.5.4.b, RF.5.4.c

Objectives: Students will be able to:
- Listen to recitation of poem.
- Chorally read poem.
- Practice reading poem.
- Fluently recite poem after repeated readings.

Activities:
- Provide students a copy of a patriotic-themed poem, and prompt a discussion of its meaning and ideas with regard to democracy.
- Read the poem aloud once.
- Have students read chorally several times.
- In the fluency center, students choose one of several patriotic poems on display to recite.
- Students voice-record their first reading.
- After listening to their recording of the poem several times, students practice reading it aloud with the whisper phones.
- When comfortable, students re-record their recitation.

Lesson Assessment: Recording will be assessed with a rubric.

LESSON 15: RECORDING LITERACY CENTER ACTIVITY

CCSS in English Language Arts: SL.5.4, SL.5.5, SL.5.6

Objectives: Students will be able to:
- Rehearse script with a partner.
- Record video of interview.

Activities:
- Once students complete the final version of their script, they begin practicing the interview with a partner. The partner is the interviewer and the student plays the role of the delegate.
- After adequate practice, students record their interviews in the recording center. If possible, have a parent volunteer or a paraprofessional to help with this activity.
- Once everyone has recorded an interview, watch them as a whole class.

Lesson Assessment: Recorded interview will be student work sample.

LESSON 16: DISCUSSION LITERACY CENTER

CCSS in English Language Arts: RL.5.9, SL.5.1, SL.5.2, SL.5.4

Objectives: Students will be able to:
- Compare and contrast the characters, setting, and events of two historical fiction books.
- Work collaboratively with a partner.

Activities:
- Remind students how to use a Venn diagram to compare and contrast things.
- Using *Goldilocks and the Three Bears* and *Little Red Riding Hood*, students compare characters, setting, and events. Any version of these stories will work.
- Display on large Venn diagram.
- In center, random pairs of students compare their historical fiction books that were read independently. Use a Venn diagram as a prewriting step.
- Students write an essay about the comparison using the rubric as a guide.

Lesson Assessment: Essay graded with rubric and kept as student work sample.

LESSON 17: SCRAPBOOK/JOURNAL

CCSS in English Language Arts: RI.5.7, RI.5.9, W.5.1.a, W.5.1.b, W.5.3, W.5.4, W.5.5, W.5.8, W.5.9, W.5.10, L.5.1, L.5.2, L.5.3

Objectives: Students will be able to:
- Work collaboratively with a group.
- Decide what sights or landmarks in the United States best depict democracy or illustrate our government.
- Research the location and activities available.
- Create a journal entry.
- Find or draw pictures of sights.
- Take a piece of writing through the writing process.

Activities:
- Explain to the students about foreign exchange programs. Students pretend that they have been asked to be a tour guide for a student from China. The goal of the student's visit is to learn about democracy and the U.S. government.
- In groups of four to five, students come up with a list of possible sights to visit and begin researching where they are, what things there are to do at the sight.
- As a group, decide how the chosen sights represent democracy and/or the U.S. government.
- Each individual in the group chooses one sight, creates a narrative journal entry about their visit to the sight, and finds pictures or draws pictures of the place they visited. They must write from the point of view of the exchange student.

- Members of each group will conference with one another during the revision and editing stages of the writing process.
- The entries will be combined to create a scrapbook of the foreign exchange student's trip to America.

Lesson Assessment: Teacher with grade completed scrapbook with rubric.

(Wiggins & McTighe, 2005)

REFERENCES

Cunningham, P. (2009). *Phonics they use, words for reading and writing.* New York: Pearson.

N.J. Department of Education. (2010). New Jersey core curriculum content standards for social studies. Retrieved from *www.state.nj.us/education/cccs/standards/6/index.html.*

Wiggins, G. P., & McTighe, J. (2005). *Understanding by design.* Alexandria, VA: Association for Supervision and Curriculum Development.

BIBLIOGRAPHY

iCivics. (n.d.). Learn about civics: Citizenship and participation. Retrieved from *www.icivics.org/subject/citizenship-and-participation.*

Kids in the House. (n.d.). What is congress? Retrieved from *http://kids.clerk.house.gov/grade-school/lesson.html?intID=1.*

U.S. Senate. (n.d.). Children's books and websites about the U.S. government. Retrieved from *www.senate.gov/reference/bibliography/kids/kids.htm.*

Index

Page numbers followed by *f* indicate figure, *t* indicate table